Implementing Psychologically Informed Environments and Trauma Informed Care

T0384961

This book gathers together the experiences of leaders across sectors, organisations and client groups to help readers introduce, develop, and maintain psychologically informed environments (PIEs) and trauma informed care (TIC) within their workspaces.

Featuring the voices of providers, commissioners, consultants, and trainers from the NHS, local authorities, and the voluntary sector, this unique text includes chapters on implementing PIE across a range of overlapping fields, including young people's, homelessness, mental health, and women's services. Each chapter describes the contributors' experiences of which factors and processes enable or disable successful implementation of PIE/TIC; the unique challenges of leadership within this process; and how to understand the different dynamics at play in an organisation that determine effectiveness. With an emphasis on practical examples underpinned by theory, and recommendations drawn from the emergent themes, the book acts as an invitation for leaders to explore how they can influence the growth and evolving shape of PIE and trauma informed approaches across health and social care and support settings, and beyond.

This book will be an invaluable resource for aspiring and new, as well as experienced, leaders who are interested in implementing and enabling PIE and TIC in their organisations.

Dr Peter Cockersell is a Psychoanalytic Psychotherapist and CEO of Community Housing and Therapy (CHT). He is a founding member of the Faculty of Homeless and Inclusion Health, and a co-author of the UK national guidance on psychologically informed environments (PIEs). He has published widely on homelessness, mental health, intercultural therapy, and related issues.

Dr Sione Marshall is an Independent Clinical Psychologist and organisational consultant who has worked across NHS, third sector and private settings for the past 30 years. Her current portfolio includes work with Pathway: Healthcare for homeless people and Canterbury Rough Sleeping Initiative.

Implementing Psychologically Informed Environments and Trauma Informed Care

Leadership Perspectives

Edited by Peter Cockersell and Sione Marshall

LONDON AND NEW YORK

Designed cover image: Human face line drawing background, abstract pattern illustration | Rawpixel ID: 8938359

First published 2025
by Routledge
4 Park Square, Milton Park, Abingdon, Oxon OX14 4RN

and by Routledge
605 Third Avenue, New York, NY 10158

Routledge is an imprint of the Taylor & Francis Group, an informa business

British Library Cataloguing-in-Publication Data
A catalogue record for this book is available from the British Library

ISBN: 978-1-032-54079-5 (hbk)
ISBN: 978-1-032-54078-8 (pbk)
ISBN: 978-1-003-41505-3 (ebk)

DOI: 10.4324/9781003415053

Typeset in Times New Roman
by KnowledgeWorks Global Ltd.

Contents

Figures and Tables

Figures

Tables

Contributors

Victoria Aseervatham has worked in homelessness for 25 years for voluntary and statutory organisations in London. Starting with five years in frontline services she moved into service development, system change, and commissioning roles. She now works as a Project Manager at Westminster City Council.

Natasha Berthollier is a Consultant Counselling Psychologist who has worked in the NHS for over 20 years. Natasha has set up and run numerous psychological therapies programmes, whilst developing innovative ways of embedding co-production and asset-based relational approaches. She is a senior lead for co-production and inclusion.

Iain Boag has worked in the field of complex trauma, problematic substance use, and residential care for 20 years and is Head of Care at St Martins, a homeless charity in Norwich. He is the author of *Psychologically Informed Environment Principles in Adult Residential Care* (2020), a book exploring the impact of living in care on people who have a history of trauma using the psychologically informed environment (PIE) framework.

Dr Jennifer Cirone is currently Director of Services at Solace Women's Aid, a large provider of services in the violence against women and girls' sector in London, UK. Experience includes working with women who are furthest from support, homelessness, and prior careers in law and neuroscience.

Dr Peter Cockersell is a Psychoanalytic Psychotherapist and CEO of CHT. He has over 30 years of experience working in the voluntary sector in homelessness, substance use, health, and mental health and over 20 years as a Psychotherapist in the NHS, private and third sectors. He is a founding member of the Faculty of Homeless and Inclusion Health, and a co-author of the UK national guidance on PIEs. He has published widely on homelessness, mental health, intercultural therapy and related issues, including editing a book (*Social Exclusion, Compound Trauma and Recovery,* 2018) on psychological approaches to working with homeless people.

Dr Andreas Constandinos is a UKCP-registered Psychoanalytic Psychotherapist having trained at the Philadelphia Association. In addition to working in private practice, Andreas is also the Co-Chair of the Philadelphia Association. Since 2020, Andreas has been employed by Community Housing and Therapy (CHT) where he works as Head of Psychotherapy.

Ali Curran is a PIE trainer and facilitator based in Dublin. As an organisational consultant her work with teams and wider systems is focused on using process, reflective practice, and Balint group methodologies. Her research interests are in the impact of group and individual psychological supports on workplace well-being.

Geoff Dennis is a Psychotherapist and retired Head of Slough NHS & Local Authority Adult Mental Health Services. Geoff has decades of experience developing services in the statutory/voluntary sector based on co-production and has a private practice/consultancy. He has been implementing innovative creative ideas through conception, design, and commissioning of services.

Dr Rex Haigh is a retired NHS consultant in medical psychotherapy who has been involved in democratic therapeutic communities since being a medical student. His path has included greencare, co-production, advisory work with the Department of Health and Royal College of Psychiatrists on 'personality disorder', 'enabling environments', and promoting a 'relational practice manifesto'.

Anthony Jones has worked in CHT's therapeutic communities for over 10 years. Starting as a student social worker in 2012, he was a service manager during the organisation's transition to PIE and joined the Senior Management Team in 2020. Anthony is now CHT's Head of Social Work. He is a Systemic Practitioner with interests including links between mental health, politics and the environment, evidence based practice and the role of group and community work across differences in race, class and gender.

Jalil Kane currently is Chief Operating Officer for Community Housing and Therapy, a leading provider of PIEs for adults with severe and enduring difficulties with their mental health. He has a background in Therapeutic Communities, Psychology, and Neuroscience. He has a particular interest in discovering intersections between psychoanalysis and neuroscience, compassionate leadership, philosophy, and in how a person's milieu interacts with their inner world. Jalil is a member of the International Neuropsychoanalysis Society, a Psychoanalytic Psychotherapist in training with the Philadelphia Association and a member and former trustee of the UK branch of the International Society for Psychological and Social Approaches to Psychosis, and regularly presents at conferences for the Therapeutic Consortium for Therapeutic Communities.

Helen Keats MBE was the National Rough Sleeping Coordinator for England, working firstly with the Rough Sleepers Unit and then with the Homeless Directorate in Department of Communities and Local Government (DCLG). She edited the 2010 and 2012 papers offering non-statutory guidance on understanding the needs of chronically homeless people with complex trauma.

Dr Sione Marshall is an Independent Clinical Psychologist and organisational consultant who has worked across NHS, third sector and private settings for the past 30 years. She is especially interested in the unconscious processes that can enable as well as inhibit the effective application of psychologically informed approaches and environments across organisations. Her current portfolio includes work with Pathway: Healthcare for homeless people and Canterbury Rough Sleeping Initiative.

Dr Helen Miles is a Consultant Clinical & Forensic Psychologist and has been Head of Psychologically Informed Environments (PIEs) at the National Youth Homeless Charity: Centrepoint since 2019. Prior to that she had over 20 years of experience of working in the UK National Health Service and Criminal Justice Services.

Iwona Munia MA studied Special Education and Clinical Psychology in Warsaw, Poland. She moved to the UK in 2005 and worked with vulnerable adults and children in variety of settings including secure units, day centres, and schools. She has worked with CHT since 2011 and is now a Head of Services. She is interested in group work and group dynamics and is currently completing a Diploma in Groupwork Practice.

Joanna Prestidge started working in frontline service delivery in 2006 and has worked in a range of settings including mental health, substance misuse, and homelessness services. Since 2015 she has worked nationally to develop and promote improved practices in homelessness. This includes introducing trauma informed care and supporting the development of Housing First.

Claire Ritchie has a track record of creative and innovative practice, thriving on the complexity and challenges of transforming organisations and improving systems. The first commissioner to embed clinical psychologists in a homeless hostel team, and author of the PIE Toolkit, commissioned by Westminster City Council, her passion is understanding how trauma informed practice, strength-based approaches and psychologically informed environments impact on the behaviour of staff, and outcomes for clients. She currently leads on a system transformation project for North Somerset Council as part of a wider trauma informed systems change programme across Bristol, North Somerset and South Gloucestershire Integrated Care Board.

Dr Amanda Skeate is an HPCP registered Consultant Clinical Psychologist with Birmingham Women's & Children's NHS Foundation Trust. She has worked with St Basils' on the PIEs programmes since 2011. Working in the NHS for 27 years, Amanda has specialised in youth mental health, early intervention and prevention, trauma, and complex needs.

Jean Templeton has been Chief Executive of St Basils' since 2000 and before that worked in public sector housing. St Basils' is a registered Housing Association and Charity providing a range of accommodation and support for young people aged 16–25 who are homeless or at risk in Birmingham and West Midlands.

Foreword

Helen Keats MBE

I was seconded to the Rough Sleepers Unit (RSU) from Portsmouth County Council Housing Service in 2000, two years after the Unit had been set up following the Social Exclusion Unit (SEU) report 'Coming in from the Cold' (SEU, 2001).

The successful good practice developed through the RSU included assertive outreach, reconnections, tenancy sustainment teams, capital funding for hostels, development of rolling shelters for hot spot areas, night centres, development of CHAIN, an information-sharing database to help track people through the hostel system nationally, and Home Office funding to provide swift access for rough sleepers to detox and rehab with accommodation available once completed. Led by Louise Casey and with Cabinet level support and scrutiny, the Unit achieved its task of reducing rough sleeping in England by two-thirds by 2002, through a combination of funding, support, and advice to frontline homelessness staff.

Despite the success of the RSU and the many aspects of good practice it encouraged, it was becoming clear that there were a group of people for whom none of these interventions worked and who could be described as entrenched or chronically homeless. Any accommodation they could access was generally short term. They tended to move between rough sleeping, night shelters, custody and squats – and sometimes the criminal justice system, drug and alcohol treatment services and/or psychiatric hospitals – with no successful outcomes and at huge cost to statutory services and to themselves.

While at the RSU, I became aware of the work developed on 'Enabling Environments' by Robin Johnson and Dr Rex Haigh (Johnson and Haigh, 2010) for the Royal College of Psychiatrists, based on Robin's background in the therapeutic approach as a social worker in community mental health and Rex's as a psychiatrist in therapeutic communities (Haigh, 2013). I began to work with Dr Nick Maguire, a Psychologist from Southampton University with a special interest in homelessness, to explore what this approach might mean for long-term, or so-called 'entrenched', rough sleepers.

This group typically describes a set of adverse experiences, often in early childhood, which underpins emotional, cognitive, and behavioural patterns in adulthood. These patterns can cause and perpetuate homelessness and lead to further mental health problems and drug and alcohol misuse, all of which present challenges to service providers. Dr Maguire led a review of the literature on the link between trauma and homelessness in 2009 (Maguire et al, 2009). It was clear that compound trauma (Cockersell, 2018) lay behind chronic homelessness and determined many of what were seen as the characteristic behaviours of the chronically homeless.

Nick and I began to work out how such a psychologically based approach might help clients and housing staff recognise and address the issues which often led to exclusion and eviction. CLG funded a pilot CBT/housing scheme in Derby Rd, Southampton for excluded rough sleepers, the outcomes of which, both positive and negative, eventually informed the May 2010 non-statutory guidance Meeting the Emotional and Psychological Needs of Homeless People, published by the National Mental Health Development Unit and DCLG (Keats et al, 2010).

Following this, alongside Robin and Nick, I brought in Peter Cockersell, a Psychoanalytic Psychotherapist and then Director of Health and Recovery at St Mungo's, which was one of Britain's leading homelessness agencies; Peter had been implementing psychotherapy services and residential services with psychotherapists embedded in the staff team, for rough sleepers and other homeless people in St Mungo's since a pilot funded by the SEU in 2007. This group together developed the Good Practice Guide on Psychologically Informed Services for Homeless People (Keats et al, 2012), often known as 'the PIE Guidance'. This set out the five basic principles of PIE – psychological framework, physical environment and social spaces, staff training and support, managing relationships, and evaluation. The guidance also offered case studies from services that were beginning to adopt or implement the PIE approach, including St Basils' (see Chapter 4 in this book) and others such as Two Saints HA, Brighter Futures, Bristol Well-being Service, St Mungos and the then embryonic Stamford St 'Complex Needs Unit' hostel developed by LB Lambeth, Thames Reach and the South London and Maudsley NHS Trust which became something of a PIE flagship (Williamson, 2018).

While it was encouraging that such a diverse range of PIE-influenced homelessness services were being developed, joining psychologically informed services in mental health through Enabling Environments and in criminal justice services through Psychologically Informed Planned Environments (PIPEs: cf Turley et al, 2013), it became clear that senior management teams and board members were often less invested than their front line staff, who could see the benefits both for clients and for themselves in addressing underlying issues leading to repeat exclusion and homelessness. There was a danger of the PIE approach being seen as an add-on to a service, rather than being a central element of them and of an organisation's core values.

I would like to say it very bluntly: the PIE approach won't work effectively, or as effectively as it can, unless it becomes an integral part of the way organisations work with people who are chronically homeless or excluded, or who have mental health problems, or drug and alcohol problems, or any other of the range of complex needs that arise from histories of trauma. It is central to that work. In order to make tackling distress and disadvantage amongst their clients as effective as possible, Senior Management Teams and Trustees/Board members should receive training in the PIE approach so that it can be embedded in the organisation's approach to everything they do.

As a current and previous Board member for a range of organisations I can attest to the difficulties frontline staff have sustaining a psychologically aware approach without corporate support. If the top part of the organisation is looking one way, and the client-facing part is looking another, the organisation will end up at best falling over itself and at worst fighting itself!

Experience shows that having organisational leadership support and encouragement to understand the emotional and psychological needs of people who use their services and of those who deliver them improves outcomes both for clients and for staff. It makes for a better run organisation which can deliver psychologically and trauma informed services more efficiently and more effectively.

We are currently seeing a significant rise in homelessness, both statutory and non-statutory, and a major increase in mental health problems, alongside big reductions in public sector funding and the capacity of public sector and charitable organisations to respond. In times like this it is even more important that PIE is integrated into the values of organisations delivering these crucial services to those most in need in our society and that middle and senior managers and Boards fully embrace the approach.

We need to create the best outcomes possible for people who may well have been let down by services in the past and PIE has been demonstrated in a very wide range of sectors to be an effective way of organising trauma informed care and support and of informing beneficial and effective leadership of those organisations. There are many ways to deliver PIE: the guidance is actually a set of principles and values, a framework for enabling organisations to effectively support staff to deliver trauma informed and person-centred care.

This book has a wide range of examples from leaders in different fields of how that can be achieved. I commend it to all senior managers and Board members trying to support their organisations in the development of psychologically informed and trauma informed services.

Helen Keats,
Isle of Wight, February 2024

Helen Keats, MBE
Former National Rough Sleeping Adviser DCLG

References

Cockersell, P. (2018) Compound Trauma and Complex Needs. In Cockersell, P. (Ed) *Social Exclusion, Compound Trauma and Recovery: Applying Psychology, Psychotherapy and PIE to Homelessness and Complex Needs*. London: Jessica Kingsley Publishers.

Haigh, R. (2013) The quintessence of a therapeutic environment. *The International Journal of Therapeutic Communities*. Vol. 34:1, pp. 6–15. https://doi.org/10.1108/09641861311330464.

Johnson, R. and Haigh, R. (2010) Social psychiatry and social policy for the 21st century – new concepts for new needs: the 'psychologically-informed environment'. *Mental Health and Social Inclusion*. Vol. 14:4, pp. 30–35. https://doi.org/10.5042/mhsi.2010.0620.

Keats, H., Maguire, N., Johnson, R. and Vostanis, P. (2010) *Meeting the Psychological and Emotional Needs of Homeless People*. Accessed at https://lx.iriss.org.uk/sites/default/files/resources/meeting-the-psychological-and-emotional-needs-of-people-who-are-homeless.pdf on 13 February 2024.

Keats, H., Maguire, N., Johnson, R. and Cockersell, P. (2012) *Psychologically informed services for homeless people*. Accessed at https://www.researchgate.net/publication/313365226_Psychologically_informed_services_for_homeless_people on 13 February 2024.

Maguire, N., Johnson, R., Vostanis, P., Keats, H. and Remington, R. (2009) *Homelessness and Complex Trauma: A Review of the Literature*. Southampton University. Accessed at https://eprints.soton.ac.uk/69749/ on 13 February 2024.

Social Exclusion Unit (2001) *Coming in from the Cold*. Accessed at http://www.communities.gov.uk/documents/housing/pdf/roughsleepersstrategy.pdf on 13 February 2024.

Turley, C., Payne, C. and Webster, S. (2013) *Enabling Features of Psychologically Informed Planned Environments*. Accessed at ded915d36e95f0525/enabling-pipe-research-report.pdf on Accessed 2 August 2024.

Williamson, E. (2018) Pie-oneering Psychological Integration in Homelessness Hostels. In Cockersell, P. (Ed) *Social Exclusion, Compound Trauma and Recovery: Applying Psychology, Psychotherapy and PIE to Homelessness and Complex Needs*. London: Jessica Kingsley Publishers.

Part I

Introduction

Chapter 1

Psychologically Informed Environments and Services from an Organisational and Leadership Perspective

Sione Marshall

Introduction

Psychologically informed environments (PIE) and trauma informed approaches seek to understand why as humans working in health and social care services, we behave, think and feel the way we do, within the context of the fundamental drivers for any change: our relationships. Key principles (Keats et al., 2012) enable this understanding and aim to guide the development and design of inclusive services for those who are often excluded due to the psychological and social consequences of compound trauma (Cockersell, 2018a; Johnson, 2017; Maguire et al., 2009), thereby enabling them to make positive changes to their lives through the reparative quality of positive relationships.

There is a growing practice-based literature demonstrating the effectiveness of PIEs in delivering trauma informed care (TIC) (Cockersell, 2016; National Lottery Community Fund 2020; Revolving Doors Agency, 2019; Williamson, 2018; Cockersell, 2018b). So, what is it that enables organisations to create PIEs that thrive and achieve longevity and what are the challenges that prevent this process? Which factors either enable or disable leaders' and organisations' ability to introduce and embed effective trauma informed PIEs? To reach beneath the surface of what is seen in the here and now and begin to understand the conscious and often unconscious processes that inform the experience of leaders and organisations, this chapter will consider common themes in relation to the key principles of PIE within the context of organisational change.

This exploration is designed as an introduction and invitation to begin to think about how leaders and organisations affect the shape and journey of PIEs. Informing this invitation are two ideas. Firstly, that relationships drive change for all of us: they are as central to successful and sustainable change in health and social care services as they are in life. Secondly, using the key areas of PIE as guiding principles for leadership approach and organisational development can drive the use of psychologically and trauma informed approaches and thereby support the creation and delivery of effective PIEs and TIC.

DOI: 10.4324/9781003415053-2

The Context

The development of a PIE doesn't happen in isolation: it occurs within the context of an existing organisation, which sits within the societal norms and values of the wider system. The introduction of a PIE represents change for an organisation. This can vary depending on the degree to which existing policy and practices are informed by psychological approaches and ways of working. At minimum, it might mean a review of existing practices, and at most, it could represent a significant shift in the way services are run and in an organisation's culture.

The Nature of Change

Change is about a future not yet conceived: moving towards it can require working with limited knowledge and control (Krantz and Trainor, 2019). Our response to inhabiting these liminal spaces as individuals and systems is often characterised by anxiety and can be understood as a defence against the ambiguity, ambivalence and uncertainty they represent (Kupers, 2011). A sense of loss and a grieving for what has once been often sits alongside a palpable sense of foreboding about what the future might hold (Grace, 2016). When introducing a PIE, organisations will, to varying extents, lose one way of being and sit within a liminal space before arriving at another way of being. Part of a leader's and organisation's ability to hold and contain therefore lies in the capacity to sit with and tolerate this ambiguity and uncertainty, to manage anxieties and, in doing so, to model this to other parts of the system. This in turn relies on the ability to reflect on experience before acting (Krantz and Trainor, 2019), to sit with uncomfortable exchanges rather than rush to know the answer or find a solution.

Negative Capability

In this sense, leaders' and organisations' 'negative capability' – the ability to hold and contain these anxieties (Bion, 1961) and to tolerate the discomfort of not knowing (Harris Williams, 2010; Krantz and Trainor, 2019) – informs the extent to which positive change can be realised within the context of developing a PIE, just as it is when working with clients who are moving away from past and present experience and towards a new way of being. This is arguably more of a challenge now as our organisational experience is increasingly characterised by unstable institutions and organisational relationships (Cooper and Dartington, 2004; Cooper and Lees, 2015). If you can't be sure what your organisation will be doing in a year's time or what its structure will be, it's difficult to experience your organisation as one that can hold and contain your anxiety (Stokes, 2019). In this sense, the short-term funding patterns often characterising commissioning of PIE or TIC can potentially hamper the capability of an organisation, whether leadership or staff, to contain anxiety, the co-traveller of change (and trauma).

So, how can leaders enable the organisation in holding and containing the anxiety that might relate to introducing PIE or TIC?

Planned Organisational Change

In thinking about effective change as planned organisational development, Neumann (1997) argues that throughout all stages, understanding and inquiry involving all members of a given social system are crucial. The process needs to support participative solutions so that people can work with uncertainty (Falcone, 2020) and it starts before any intervention, even before identifying what needs to change. It starts in thinking about existing practices, in the context of the existing culture, how the system currently thinks, feels, behaves in response to the primary task, the task that the organisation needs to perform if it is to survive (Miller and Rice, 1967) and its willingness to change (Cockersell, 2018b). Just as for client work, models of change such as Prochaska and DiClemente's (1982) can help leaders assess where any part of an organisation is in the cycle of change, thereby enabling them to model what is needed and where for the development of a PIE.

However, this pre-intervention assessment can feel like slow work and will often mean sitting with uncomfortable material and having difficult conversations (as PIE or TIC work does for frontline staff). What might this look and sound like for leaders in practice?

Defending against Anxiety

Despite the intention to create more psychologically and trauma informed services, policies are often designed to meet the needs of the system rather than the people they serve (Boag, 2020). Effective assessment of the existing culture therefore needs to think about how these policies might fit with a PIE and whether there is a willingness to change these in all parts of the system. Considering the function of these policies is a fundamental aspect of this work. PIEs seek to promote change through the development of positive relationships, thereby enabling secure attachments. Using this relational lens, policies that meet the needs of the organisation rather than the service user don't seem to make sense. However, in considering how these might serve the wider system, they make more sense.

In other words, we can understand these organisations as existing within a culture sustained by virtue of society's defence against the anxiety it experiences in response to certain populations such as those whose experience of compound trauma leads to their exclusion from mainstream services. This societal anxiety is passed on through the organisation to the specialist services tasked with serving these populations so that they become conduits for the anxiety evoked in the wider system. To manage this anxiety, organisations housing these services often develop structures and cultures that defend against this, but in doing so, focus on meeting the needs of the organisation rather than those it serves (Long, 2019; Obholzer and Roberts, 2019; Rizq, 2012). Scarce resources can often be a justification for these practices, but, in reality, they can be anti-supportive to staff (Menzies Lyth, 1960; 1979) leaving both staff and clients disabled (Scanlon and Adlam, 2019). These processes disable the organisation's effective execution of its primary task, an ability which is compromised as the system fails to consider the emotional response to the work and fails to support staff in achieving the primary task, the organisation's 'mission' of delivering PIE or TIC (Miller and Rice, 1967; see also Cockersell in the following chapter). Chapter 9 in this book also considers how this process can lead to organisations becoming both traumatised and traumatising.

Layers of Change

Working with the emotional response to the work, as required by PIE or TIC, means moving towards a more relational way of working which may, for some organisations, represent a significant cultural change in terms of the values, beliefs and assumptions of the organisation. This cultural change can be understood as fundamental in either enabling or disabling the longevity of effective PIEs and TIC (Fallot and Harris, 2009) as without it both technical (policies and practices) and behavioural (people's response to the technical) layers of organisational change are likely to revert to original ways of being (Clark, 2020). Without adopting a relational approach throughout, policy and related practices may not change and despite the intention to create a more psychologically informed service will continue, as outlined above, to be designed to meet the needs of the system rather than the people it serves. In operationalising these changes, a shared understanding of what being psychologically informed might look and sound like when working with different individuals in frontline services, in the management of these services, in the senior management team and in the board room is therefore also needed.

A Shared Understanding

So in effectively developing a PIE, all layers of the organisation from senior management to frontline staff need to have a shared understanding of how and why current culture, practices and behaviours exist. The organisation, as a whole, needs to foster a shared willingness and commitment to change and understanding of why it is introducing this change before beginning to think about how it's going to do it. This assessment and pre-intervention work, based on communication and the effective development and management of relationships, not only informs but can model smoother, progressive work later in the cycle of change, just as it does when working with clients in frontline services (Conolly, 2017).

The preparatory work for the conception and introduction of PIE or TIC can therefore be understood as a way of containing and holding the organisation through a process of change. In this way, it informs the extent to which a PIE is successfully introduced and embedded within a system and models psychologically and trauma informed leadership. For example, if staff see and hear senior management working in a psychologically informed way, placing the importance of relationships at the centre of their work, they are more likely to apply these ways of working and thereby develop a more PIE approach themselves. Equally, the development of any PIE is reliant on the extent to which this is collectively supported. Effective leaders act as change agents (Senior and Fleming, 2006) so any fractures in shared commitment caused by changes in leadership or difference in leaders' views can rupture relationships and in turn hamper its growth.

Managing Relationships

As humans, we are relational beings. We all grow and develop within the context of relationships and are shaped by the extent to which they hold and contain us (Winnicott, 1960). Throughout our lives, our physical and emotional well-being is dependent on the relationships, the type of attachments, we have with others (Holt-Lunstad, 2021; Mate, 2019; Siegel, 2020; Van der Kolk, 2014). We therefore make sense of the world through our relationships. Those relationships sit in the context of our individual life experience starting in our mothers' wombs, as well as the different systems we are both included within and excluded from along the way. So, thinking systemically, an organisation's well-being as a whole is dependent on the quality of relationships within it. In this way, the relationships between service users, frontline staff, service managers, senior managers and board members inform both the well-being of those individuals and of the system as a whole. Sitting alongside this knowledge, an expansive body of leadership literature offers up many different perspectives on what makes an effective leader but limited evidence about which approach is most effective: it does however agree, regardless of approach, that effective leadership involves relationships (Monaghan and Thorley, 2022).

Managing relationships is at the heart of what makes a PIE distinct from other approaches. In this sense, relationships are seen as the fundamental driver for change, with every interaction between staff and clients being an opportunity for learning (Keats et al., 2012), for developing and managing repair, and they are, or should be, prioritised above the organisational pressures of the economic system. So, what might enable or disable leaders and organisations in managing relationships?

Moving from 'Us and Them' to 'We'

To learn about how and why those we work with think, feel and behave, we also need to understand why we as individuals, groups and organisations in health and social care services, think, feel and behave the way we do. In other words, working relationally is about shifting from an 'us and them' to a 'we' perspective; to knowing that as humans we all need the same things to have healthy relationships and lives. Working relationally means proactively attending to what we each bring to relationships and what these engender in us, in seeking to understand our experience of those we work with, whether that be our colleagues, clients, other services or organisations: for example, being able to notice how past familial experiences inform the way we relate to others, whether that be in the board room (Schumacker and Cheak, 2022; Urnova, 2018), in a management team (Whittle and Izod, 2014) or with a client. Similarly, being able to ask and notice how our behaviour is perceived by others can enable learning that fosters relational practice and in turn promotes psychologically safe spaces (Clark, 2020).

In applying this understanding and awareness to policies and procedures, leaders can promote relational practice across all parts of organisational life, but also model a position of 'we' that acts to include rather than exclude and which develops responsibility and autonomy in others, just as frontline staff aim to foster responsibility and autonomy in their clients. This interdependent, inclusive, 'doing with' approach in turn enables client participation and co-production across service development, design and evaluation and invites a shared approach towards individual and collective well-being. It challenges the notion that an organisation can only have a few leaders (Zenger and Folkman, 2020) and enables organisations to reach a new understanding of the boundaries between power and authority in relation to organisational roles (Green and Molenkamp, 2005; Izod, 2014). In other words, if those without the word "manager" or "director" in their job title are given the appropriate power and authority, they can be empowered to lead within their roles. An example of this might be staff members who develop a particular expertise in an aspect of PIE and can act as a 'go-to' person within the organisation and wider community (Cockersell, 2018b) or an individual who has 'stepped up' to 'lead' on a particular project or task (Miles, 2020).

So what does this approach mean for the notion of leadership within a PIE? It leans towards a less hierarchical view of leadership, recognising that all individuals and parts of the system come with something to offer in working towards change. Using attachment theory to understand organisational change, Braun (2011) argues that organisations who can involve staff in strategic planning are more likely to enable secure attachments to the organisation's future and therefore to its present work and systems.

Communication: Curiosity, Connection and Creativity

Working relationally relies on benign enquiry (Stokoe, 2021), our ability to notice ourselves and others in our communications. In turn, noticing allows curiosity and a curious stance enables us to notice more. Curiosity can be defined as the desire to know and learn within the context of not consciously making assumptions. In other words, it's difficult to be simultaneously curious and make assumptions. In this sense curiosity is crucial to developing person-centred services and organisations that are relationally driven: it enables us, whatever our role, to engage, connect with the other, whether that be a client, a colleague, another team, another service or another organisation – it allows the possibility of change through dialogue (Monaghan and Thorley, 2022). In turn, it can help us to better attend to difference, whether that be of culture, race, religion, age, sex and gender, sexual orientation or ability (Marshall et al., 2022; Sweeney and Bothwick, 2016), or check our assumptions about difference, whether cultural (Cockersell, 2019) or about some-one's ability in relation to their role (Clark, 2020). Curiosity therefore helps us to cultivate sensitivity and to connect uniquely with another, rather than cutting and pasting our assumptions about them into that relational space.

It also allows for exploration and creativity and can afford an ability to hold often uncomfortable material lightly or with humour (Wilson, 2020) whilst sitting with, rather than avoiding, the complexities of our work. Leaders who use this way of communicating across all interactions can model curiosity and in turn promote spaces that are psychologically safe enough for people to show up as themselves, however much difference their self represents. In using curiosity and exercising sensitivity, these spaces enable creativity in developing and managing relationships and can in turn work to develop an organisation as a system of care for those that it serves and employs. It becomes person-centred, psychologically informed and trauma informed.

Developing a Psychological Framework

Keats et al. (2012, p. 8) define a psychological framework as "any particular school of thought on human development and personal change". The selection of a framework is not a prescriptive process: this might use one or more ap-proaches (Keats et al., 2012) depending on the service setting and client needs (Johnson and Haigh, 2011). Although frameworks vary, they are typically under-pinned by a relational approach to practice which is evidenced and underpinned by a neuropsychological understanding and physiological explanation of how trauma affects emotional regulation and social connection (Dana, 2018; Porges and Porges, 2023).

Putting the Theory into Practice

The effectiveness of a PIE relies on the extent to which any given psychological framework is used by all parts of an organisation. The successful application of a framework is in turn dependent on a shared understanding of how to apply theory to practice. So which factors might enable or disable the extent to which leaders and organisations can successfully inform this application to practice?

Creating an explicit understanding that is shared throughout an organisation takes time and relies on a shared willingness and commitment to move towards a psychologically informed approach. The first part of this chapter considered the process for creating organisational 'buy-in' to the change process, and why a psy-chologically informed relational model is key to PIE or TIC. However, in addition to this, all parts of the organisation need to be able to understand what practice looks and sounds like when the theory is applied. As discussed below, the role of ongoing staff training and support, formal and informal, is key to this process as it affords everyone, regardless of role, repeated and regular opportunities to develop their ability in applying theory to practice.

Consistency across the Organisation

Whatever the framework, effective application depends upon the consistency with which it is introduced and developed across an organisation. This may mean thinking about how training delivers the theory whilst attending to the nuances of application across settings. In other words, teaching the theory is great but for this to enable change, training needs to consider how application to practice might look and sound differently in client services, as compared to the senior management team, as compared to human resources. Ensuring that the same concepts and language are used across all training and reflective spaces can further enable learning: it's easier to learn how to apply theoretical principles to practice if the same terms are introduced and used in both training and reflective spaces.

Effective development of a psychological framework is also reliant on aligning this with policy, procedure and service design so that a PIE or TIC is understood as another way of working across the organisation rather than just another thing to do. In this sense, an organisation that embraces a chosen framework across all parts of the system will not only endeavour to develop its use in client services but in all departments whether that be Building Management, Human Resources or Accounting and Finance. In this way, policy and procedure related to processes such as recruitment, induction, continuing professional development or exit interviews for staff leaving, will be informed by the same framework so that any member of staff in any part of the organisation can explain what they are doing, why and how in terms of a PIE and TIC.

Staff Involvement

Keats et al. (2012, p. 8) suggest that staff "should be free to question how suitable, coherent or consistently applied any particular framework may be". Research has shown that staff involvement enables both organisational success and staff well-being (Hodson and Roscigno, 2004). Enabling staff involvement in the introduction, development and review of a psychological framework can promote autonomy, influence and ownership in the shape and growth of a PIE, just as it does for client participation. The extent to which leaders can promote staff involvement is reliant on their ability to adopt and model a relationally informed approach to service development, which focuses on the skills and resources that staff bring to the process, just as working relationally with clients means discovering which skills and resources they bring to the work. In this way a compassionate and collective leadership style promotes responsibility and accountability at both individual and collective levels (West, 2021). So, the more shared the ownership, the more likely that a consistent approach based on a psychological framework will be embedded in the service ethos (Cockersell, 2018b).

Leaders and organisations that create safe containing spaces are more likely to offer opportunities for difficult conversations that can attend to what might be preventing the application of a chosen framework. Obstacles to application may relate to staff's lack of understanding of the principles and concepts sitting within a psychological framework. This might indicate a review regarding the delivery of training and provision of reflective spaces but may represent an unconscious communication. Human beings often communicate through making other people feel their own frightening or overwhelming feelings (Trainor, 2019). This process, projective identification, can therefore often lead staff and organisations working with people who are living with the psychological and social consequences of compound trauma to experience this trauma vicariously. In this sense, the extent to which leaders and organisations can attend to the unconscious as well as conscious processes that may disable the development of a psychological or trauma informed framework will inform its effective application.

Working with the Wider System

Effective development of a psychological framework not only relies on communicating this to all internal stakeholders but to external ones too. For example, as Keats et al (2012) suggest, corporate commitment to this process will see an organisation's chosen framework become part of its business or commissioning plan: in this sense it can then disseminate this to key external stakeholders. This is especially pertinent in understanding how competing priorities can be addressed. For instance, if external stakeholders such as commissioners have a better understanding of how a framework is applied in client services, and staff are supported to understand how services sit within the wider system, collaborative ways of attending to these challenges are more likely to be used.

The Physical Environment and Social Spaces

Research shows that aspects of our physical environment affect our mental and physical wellbeing (Codinhoto et al., 2008; Ellaway, 2014; Evans, 2003; Guite et al., 2006). Key domains impacting this relationship include control over the environment and social participation (Chu et al., 2004). PIEs therefore seek to include both client and staff involvement in the constantly evolving process of designing and managing the environment that services physically sit within. So how can leaders enable the organisation in developing this type of environment and what might disable this process?

The Physical Environment as a Container

To enable change through a relational approach, an effective PIE will promote the development and use of social spaces in which connections can be made and developed. In this sense, just as relationships are seen as drivers for change, the spaces in which these occur, both in the immediate environment and wider community (Cockersell, 2018b), can be understood as a tool for change (Boag, 2020) and a container for relational work that is psychologically and trauma informed.

The process of using the physical environment as a vehicle for creating opportunities to connect with others and build positive relationships goes beyond attending to the physical buildings and spaces that organisations inhabit and will include thinking about what staff wear, how food is served and eaten and the language used for signs and notices (Boag, 2020). In this way the physical environment and its use of social spaces can promote a shared organisational understanding of and commitment to the values that underpin an effective PIE. As with every other aspect of an effective PIE, the involvement of staff and clients in the design and creation of physical spaces represents a core element in creating the opportunity for the development of positive relationships. This co-production can also embrace the local community by partnering with other organisations such as colleges, businesses and universities (Cockersell, 2018b).

Understanding the Primary Task

However, the extent to which the physical environment can effectively act as a container and tool for change depends on how consistently the organisation's primary task is translated into ways of working. The primary task of an organisation is usually defined by its mission statement, which identifies the formally agreed normative primary task. This contrasts with the existential primary task, that which staff believe they need to attain given their role, and the phenomenological primary task which relates to actual ways of working (Lawrence, 1977). The extent to which leaders can identify and address discrepancies between these can provide useful organisational data (Mignerey et al., 1995) and will inform how effectively physical spaces are used in developing a PIE. In other words, physical spaces can be designed to promote relational ways of working as dictated by the normative primary task. However, if the existential primary task indicates that staff believe their roles require them to focus on administrative work, the phenomenological primary task will determine actual ways of working, often not within conscious awareness, that may not promote or enable relational ways of working. The ability to notice and reflect on these discrepancies can therefore enable leaders and organisations to attend to how the actual use of physical and emotional spaces are aligned to the normatively agreed primary task of PIE, which is providing person-centred TIC.

Data from the Physical Environment

A PIE recognises that our physical environment shapes our experience and relationships. In this way, the physical environment can be used as a source of data to understand the often unconscious processes that might either enable or disable leaders and organisations in developing effective PIEs. For example, Chapter 6 of this book discusses defences from staff members against difficult projections and dynamics in the community evidenced by the physical environment. Understanding the interconnectedness between events and the environment in which they take place (Lewin, 1952) can promote the use of the environment and ourselves as data - Abu-Lughod, 2000, pp 8-24.) by decoding the processes that can disable the introduction and development of PIE. These processes often relate to a lack of clarity regarding the primary task and are characterised by anti-task ways of working that represent engagement in survival tasks which serve the survival of the relevant group or system (Green and Molenkamp, 2005). For example, if staff are unclear about prioritising the opportunity to connect and develop relationships with clients by using, for example, a shared dining area to eat together, or shared common room to sit together, splitting (Klein, 1959, cited in Klein, 1997) between staff and clients or between either group is more likely. The extent to which leaders can use this data to inform understanding of what enables or disables the delivery of a PIE and TIC relies, in part, on their ability to create space where members of the relevant group can reflect on the meaning of both individual and group behaviours (Green and Molenkamp, 2005).

Staff Training and Support

Training and support for staff is key to implementing a PIE (Keats et al., 2012). So which factors might enable or disable the extent to which leaders and organisations can successfully develop this aspect of a PIE?

As discussed earlier, staff as well as client participation is understood to be an integral part of building a successful PIE. Staff participation in the design and delivery of services acts to communicate key principles of the approach, to model co-production, to support staff within their roles and to make changes to ways of working. Training is in turn a fundamental component of enabling staff involvement in this process.

Developing Skills

For the consistent and continual development of new or existing skills, the design, delivery and evaluation of training needs to be included in an organisation's strategic plan. Working relationally, any plan needs to cultivate sensitivity in recognising and valuing the skills and knowledge that staff already bring to their work as well as attending to potential obstacles to learning and change. An organisational approach to training will ideally include all layers of the system from board members to staff working in client services.

Delivery of an organisation wide training programme takes time and proactive planning. Introducing new theory and practice isn't a one stop shop or a single tick in the box exercise: it takes time for new approaches and ways of working to develop across an organisation. An established literature suggests that despite different styles (Pashler et al., 2009), we learn in cycles rather than linear patterns (Bruner, 1960; Kolb and Fry, 1975). Training programmes therefore need to accommodate these patterns and differences by using mechanisms that evaluate how effective they are in enabling changes to ways of working. In using a proactive, relational approach which contrasts to the often reactive nature of work with people who have been excluded from mainstream care, leaders can model a psychologically informed approach to training and in doing so, attend to the relationship between individual development and organisational learning (Easterby-Smith et al., 2002; Gould, 2000; Woodcock and Gill, 2014).

In enabling the application of theory to practice, an effective PIE will plan for the provision of formal and informal reflective spaces that sit alongside and reinforce training. The webinar "Psychologically Informed Management" at Homeless Link's Knowledge Hub (2023) is a good example of what this theory looks like when put into practice by line managers for frontline staff.

A Reflective Culture

A reflective culture promotes the use of both formal and informal spaces that enable evaluation of what drives effective application of theory to practice and what might sit in the way of this. Reflective practice (RP) includes reflection on and in action (Schon, 1983) and will occur across formalised spaces such as reflective practice groups, supervisory spaces, debriefing sessions, as well as whilst working. An existing reflective culture is more likely to provide spaces in which staff can use the context of established and trusted relationships (Kurtz and Levene, 2022) to reflect on their experience. Practice evidence has shown that the extent to which reflective practices are used and embedded across an organisation will inform how successfully PIE develops and achieves longevity (Boobis, 2016; Woodcock and Gill, 2014).

Reflection requires curiosity about our own and others' experience. This self-awareness is one of the core competencies of working reflectively (Bassot, 2016) and is in essence the process of bringing what is often unconscious to the conscious (Marshall et al., 2022). It helps to keep check of the assumptions that we might have about others and in this sense it is inextricably linked to the relational approach that successful PIEs are built upon. So, to develop this type of culture, reflection needs to be a practice shared by everyone: it's not exclusive to client facing services. Leaders' capacity to adopt and model reflective ways of working is fundamental to this process as well as being linked more generally to improved organisational performance (Castelli, 2016). Creating time and a physical place for this reflective thinking is a fundamental part of staff support and training and is key to addressing the vicarious trauma often experienced by staff as well as the way in which the organisation is traumatised and/or traumatising.

Containing the Work

To work towards any self-awareness is messy and inevitably invokes anxiety as vulnerabilities surface. This learning requires a good enough holding environment (Winnicott, 1965) to contain the work. RP groups (RPG) can act as these containers providing 'temporary learning communities' (Adlam, 2014) and insights into the organisational experience if understood as fractals of the wider system (Clarkson, 1997). For example, the overwhelm noticed by a team within an RPG might be understood as a replication and representation of the organisation's overwhelm. In doing so, they can provide valuable understanding about the conscious and unconscious processes that either enable or disable effective practice across individuals, services, teams and organisations (Bassot, 2016). Understanding unconscious processes might, for instance, help in understanding how people are often drawn to a particular type of work and role as it represents an opportunity to work through their own unresolved issues (Roberts, 2019), a valency (Bion, 1961) which means that there is little coincidence in who is unconsciously recruited by a system into a role (Menon, 2019): this may help manage a situation where, for example, a particular role always seems to become problematical even though the incumbent has changed. Reflection allows these often unconscious processes to become conscious, in turn developing an understanding of how past and present experience informs our experience of the work and what we bring to it.

The extent to which reflective spaces are containing depends on a number of factors such as how robustly boundaries related to the agreed brief, time and physical location of spaces are protected. For example, RP spaces need a clear brief; designated rooms; dates and times booked out in all group members' calendars, etc. It also depends on how well a strategic plan identifies what a particular organisation's reflective culture will look and sound like, for example whether external or internal facilitators will be used across RPGs. There are funding and timetabling implications related to these decisions, but, as Scanlon and Adlam (2016) note, unless the organisation harnesses a shared commitment to this aspect of a PIE, then it's unlikely to enable positive change. In essence, the reflective space is central to positively managed change and the containment required for psychologically informed or trauma informed work across all organisational layers.

Access to Psychological Therapy

As mentioned earlier, in working with clients who experience the consequences of compound trauma, staff are often exposed to vicarious trauma. Whilst understanding a client's past experiences can inform relational work within a PIE, mechanisms for referral to dedicated specialist services providing psychological therapy for clients act to moderate the amount of vicarious trauma to which staff are exposed. In this sense services designed to support staff within a PIE will reach beyond the provision of services for staff and link with client-centred services. Although the inclusion of these services in a PIE is reliant on adequate funding (Cockersell, 2018b), the development of systemic interventions designed to increase awareness of PIE approaches and introduce these into organisations and the community (Centre for Homelessness Research and Practice, 2023) can enable leaders in delivering these services.

Evaluation of Outcomes

As outlined at the beginning of this chapter, the introduction of a PIE represents change for an organisation. Evaluating the impact of that change is essential in identifying whether the intended changes for clients, staff, teams, services, the organisation as a whole and the wider system have been realised; how they have been enabled and how they can inform future directions. So which factors inform the extent to which leaders can enable an evaluative process across the organisation?

A Relational Approach

The Good Practice Guide (Keats et al., 2012) identifies the application of three levels of evaluation: policy level, service level and individual measures. A relational approach in applying evaluation across these layers promotes the use of qualitative as well as quantitate data and can enable organisations to attend to the continual cycle of learning and development and therefore the integral role of ongoing evaluation in relation to policy, service provision and service use. Using existing outcome frameworks, as well as outcomes informed by service users' own goals (Green and Latchford, 2012), the creation of a body of practice-based evidence is central to this process and has been used to demonstrate the effectiveness of PIEs in enabling positive outcomes across a range of indicators (Cockersell, 2016; Williamson, 2018).

The flexibility in design and data collection that practice-based evidence affords can lead to better outcomes (Miller et al., 2006) and facilitates a co-participatory approach to evaluation of outcomes that can involve all parts of the system and ultimately informs organisational development (Neumann, 1997). In adopting a collective approach, evidence can also be presented with staff rather than on them (Breckon and Taylor-Collins, 2020) and with, rather than on, clients. In this way outcomes can be reviewed and shared by everyone acting as working notes (Miller, 1995) for the organisation that inform its continual learning, adaptation and growth. Positive change can also be understood in relational terms if all parts of the system understand relationships as drivers for change. For example, in Chapter 12 the impact of a relational lens on defining outcomes for PIEs from a commissioning perspective is discussed.

Despite a collective approach, the evaluative process can be challenged by the realities of everyday service provision, as competing priorities result in conflicting demands. For instance, the time taken to record and report evidence needed to secure funding often conflicts with time needed with clients. A leader's ability to acknowledge these contradictions and contain the anxiety they may cause will inform how effectively the organisation can manage these differing demands and in turn evaluate outcomes.

Relationships beyond the Organisation

Developing and establishing relationships in the wider community can lead to partnerships that further enable the process of evaluation. This might be related to the execution of evaluative work. For example, collaborations with universities in the wider community can provide opportunities for independent surveys that contribute to the overall evaluation of outcomes. Sharing positive outcomes within the framework of relational practice can also act as a mechanism for developing trusting relationships with external key decision-makers who can support future developments for PIE services.

An Ongoing Cycle

As Neumann (1997) observes, there are few interventions of organisational development that can be achieved in one cycle and most require multiple, repeating cycles. Outcomes measures enable learning at policy, service and individual levels, which will then inform assessment of what might need to change to further develop a PIE. In the following chapters, leaders' ability to attend to this ongoing cycle of organisational growth is recognised as fundamental to the successful development of a PIE and trauma informed services.

Conclusion

In exploring how leaders and organisations affect the shape and journey of PIEs and trauma informed approaches, this chapter has hopefully acted as an invitation to begin to think about what enables and disables this process at both a conscious and unconscious level.

Discussion has highlighted how as humans our relationships are central to successful change both individually and organisationally. This understanding promotes a relational approach to organisational development. Given this, it is argued that the principles of a PIE framework can be used as guidance for leadership approaches and organisational development, driving the use of psychologically and trauma informed approaches and the processes behind effective service delivery in both PIEs and TIC.

In the next chapter, Peter considers the relationship between PIEs and TIC and thinks more about the primary task and leadership, and some of the styles of leadership that fit well with trauma informed approaches and PIEs. Subsequent chapters chart the experience of leaders developing these approaches across a wide range of service settings and offer an opportunity to further explore the emergent themes identified here and in the next chapter.

References

Abu-Lughod, L. (2000 *Veiled Sentiments Honor and Poetry in a Bedouin Society*. Second Edition. California: University California Press.

Adlam, J. (2014) Going spiral? Phenomena of 'half-knowledge' in the experiential large group as temporary learning community. *Pedagogy, Culture and Society*. vol. 22 no. 10 pp 157–168.

Bassot, B. (2016) *The Reflective Practice Guide. An Interdisciplinary Approach to Critical Reflection*. London: Routledge.

Bion, W. (1961) *Experiences in Groups*. New York: Basic Books.

Boag, I. (2020) *Psychologically Informed Environment Principles in Adult Residential Care*. London: Routledge.

Boobis, S. (2016) *Evaluating a Dialogical Psychologically Informed Environment (PIE) Pilot*. Newcastle, Gateshead: Fulfilling Lives.

Braun, G. (2011) Organisations today: What happens to attachment? *Psychodynamic Practice*. vol. 17 no. 2 pp 123–139.

Breckon, J. and Taylor-Collins, E. (2020) Why Evidence Matters. In Teixeira, L. and Cartwright, J. (Eds) *Using Evidence to End Homelessness*. Bristol: Policy Press.

Bruner, J. (1960) *The Process of Education*. Boston, MA: Harvard University Press.

Castelli, P. A. (2016) Reflective leadership review: A framework for improving organisational performance. *Journal of Management Development*. vol. 35 no. 2 pp 217–236.

Centre for Homelessness Research and Practice (2023) *About Us*. Available at https://chrphomeless.co.uk/about-us/ (Accessed 8 June 2023).

Chu, A., Thorne, A. and Guite, H. (2004) The impact on mental well-being of the urban and physical environment: An assessment of the evidence. *Journal of Public Mental Health*. vol. 3 no. 2 pp 17–32.

Clark, T. (2020) *The 4 Stages of Psychological Safety: Defining the Path to Inclusion and Innovation*. Oakland, CA: Berrett-Koehler Publications.

Clarkson, P. (1997) Consulting in Rapidly Changing Conditions of Uncertainty. In Neumann, J., Kellner, K. and Dawson-Shepherd, A. (Eds) *Developing Organisational Consultancy*. London: Routledge.

Cockersell, P. (2016) PIEs five years on. *Mental Health and Social Inclusion*. vol. 20 no. 4 pp 221–230.

Cockersell, P. (2018a) Social Exclusion, Complex Needs and Homelessness. In Cockersell, P. (Ed) *Social Exclusion, Compound Trauma and Recovery. Applying Psychology, Psychotherapy and PIE to Homelessness and Complex Needs*. London: Jessica Kingsley Publishers.

Cockersell, P. (2018b) Applying Psychology as a response to the Impact of Social Exclusion: PIE and Psychotherapy in Homelessness Services. In Cockersell, P. (Ed) *Social Exclusion, Compound Trauma and Recovery. Applying Psychology, Psychotherapy and PIE to Homelessness and Complex Needs*. London: Jessica Kingsley Publishers.

Cockersell, P. (2019) Intercultural Psychotherapy, Intracultural Psychotherapy, or Just Good Psychotherapy. In Ababio, B. and Littlewood, R. (Eds) *Intercultural Therapy: Challenges, Insights and Development*. London: Routledge.

Codinhoto, R., Tzortzopoulos, P., Kagioglou, M., Aouad, G. and Cooper, R. (2008) *The Effects of the Built Environment on Health Outcomes*. Salford: University of Salford.

Conolly, J. (2017) Pre-Treatment Therapy: A Central London Counselling Service's Enhanced Response to Complex Needs Homelessness. In Levy, J. S. and Johnson, R. (Eds) *Cross Cultural Dialogues on Homelessness: From Pretreatment Strategies to Psychologically Informed Environments*. Ann Arbor, MI: Loving Healing Press.

Cooper, A. and Dartington, T. (2004) The Vanishing Organisation: Organisational Containment in a Networked World. In Huffington, C., Armstrong, D., Halton, W., Hoyle, L. and Pooley, J. (Eds) *Working below the Surface: The Emotional Life of Contemporary Organisations*. London: Karnac Books.

Cooper, A. and Lees, A. (2015) Spotlit: Defenses against Anxiety in Contemporary Human Service Organisations. In Armstrong, D. and Rustin, M. (Eds) *Social Defences against Anxiety: Explanations in a Paradigm*. London: Karnac.

Dana, D. (2018) *The Polyvagal Theory in Therapy: Engaging the Rhythm of Regulation*. London: Norton.

Easterby-Smith, M., Crosson, M. and Davide, N. (2002) Organizational learning: Debates past, present and future. *Journal of Management Studies*. vol. 37 no. 6 pp 783–796.

Ellaway, A. (2014) The Impact of the Local Social and Physical Local Environment on Well-being: A Complete Reference Guide. Volume 2. Wellbeing and the Environment Part 1. Wellbeing and the Neighborhood. Wiley Online Library. First published: 11 February 2014 (Accessed 25 May 2023). https://doi.org/10.1002/9781118539415.wbwell057.

Evans, G. (2003) The built and environment and mental health. *Journal of Urban Health: Bulletin of the New York Academy of Medicine*. vol. 80 no. 4 pp 536–555.

Falcone, F. (2020). Neumann, Jean E.: The Consultant's Consultant, Working through Complexity in Organizational Development and Change. In Szabla, D. B. (Ed) *The Palgrave Handbook of Organizational Change Thinkers*. Cham: Palgrave Macmillan. https://doi.org/10.1007/978-3-319-49820-1_51-3.

Fallot, R. D. M. and Harris, M. (2009) *Creating Cultures of Trauma-Informed Care: A Self-Assessment and Planning Protocol*. Washington, DC: Community Connections.

Gould (2000) Becoming a learning organisation: A social work example. *Social Work Education*. vol. 19 no. 6 pp 585–596.

Grace, C. (2016) Endings and loss in mergers and acquisitions: An exploration of group analytic theory. *Group Analysis*. vol. 49 no. 2 pp 134–148.

Green, D. and Latchford, G. (2012) *Maximising the Benefits of Psychotherapy: A Practice-Based Evidence Approach*. Hoboken, NJ: Wiley-Blackwell.

Green, Z. G. and Molenkamp, R. J. (2005) *The BART System of Group and Organisational Analysis. Boundary, Role and Task*. Available at: https://www.researchgate.net/publication/277890284_Boundary_Authority_Role_and_Task (Accessed 5 July 2024).

Guite, H. F., Clark, C. and Ackrill, G. (2006) The impact of the physical and urban environment on mental well-being. *Public Health*. vol. 120 no. 12 pp 1117–1126.

Harris Williams, M. (2010) *The Aesthetic Development: The Poetic Spirit of Psychoanalysis: Essays on Bion, Meltzer, Keats*. London: Karnac Books.

Hodson, R. and Roscigno, V. (2004) Organizational success and worker dignity: Complementary or contradictory? *American Journal of Sociology*. vol. 110 no. 3 pp. 672–708.

Holt-Lunstad, J. (2021) The major health implications of social connection. *Current Directions in Psychological Science*. vol. 30 no. 3 pp 251–259.

Homeless Link (2023) *Psychologically Informed Management*. Available at https://homeless.org.uk/knowledge-hub/psychologically-informed-management/ (Accessed 1 March 2024).

Izod, K. (2014) Role Space. In Izod, K. and Whittle, S. R. (Eds) *Resource-Ful Consulting: Working with Your Presence and Identity in Consulting to Change*. London: Karnac Books.

Johnson, R. (2017) Principles and Practice in Psychology and Homelessness: Core Skills in Pretreatment, Trauma Informed Care and Psychologically Informed Environments. In Levy, J. S. and Johnson, R. (Eds) *Cross Cultural Dialogues on Homelessness: From Pretreatment Strategies to Psychologically Informed Environments*. Milton Keynes: Loving Healing Press.

Johnson, R. and Haigh, R. (2011) Social psychiatry and social policy for the 21st century: new concepts for new needs- the 'Enabling Environments' initiative. *Mental Health and Social Inclusion*. vol. 15 no. 1 pp 17–23.

Keats, H., Maguire, N., Johnson, R. and Cockersell, P. (2012) *Psychologically Informed Services for Homeless People*. (Good Practice Guide) Southampton: GB. Communities and Local Government.

Klein, M. (1997) *Envy and Gratitude and Other Works. 1946–1963*. London: Vintage.

Kolb, D. A. and Fry, R. E. (1975) Toward an Applied Theory of Experiential Learning. In Cooper, C. (Ed) *Theories of Group Processes*. New York: John Wiley and Sons.

Krantz, J. and Trainor, K. (2019) Why Change Efforts So Often Fail. In Obholzer, A. and Roberts, V. Z. (Eds) *The Unconscious at Work: A Tavistock Approach to Making Sense of Organisational Life*. Second Edition. London: Routledge.

Kupers, W. (2011) Dancing on the limen- embodied and creative inter-places as thresholds of be(com)ing: Phenomenological perspectives on liminality and transitional spaces in organisational and leadership. *Journal of Critical Organisational Inquiry.* vol. 9 no. 3–4 pp 45–59.

Kurtz, A. and Levene, J. (2022) The Heads and Hearts Model of Reflective Practice. In Conniff, H. (Ed) *Psychological Staff Support in Healthcare: Thinking and Practice.* Keighley: Sequoia Books.

Lawrence, G. (1977) Management development…some ideas, images and realities. *Journal of European Industrial Training.* vol. 1 no. 2 pp 21–25.

Lewin, K. (1952) *Field Theory in Social Science.* New York: Harper and Row.

Long, S. (2019) The unconscious won't go away – especially in organisations. *Organisational & Social Dynamics.* vol. 19. no. 2 pp 218–229.

Maguire, N. J., Johnson, R., Vostanis, P., Keats, H. and Remington, R. E. (2009) *Homelessness and Complex Trauma: A Review of the Literature.* Southampton: University of Southampton.

Marshall, S., Robson, T., Servini, N. and Wells, B. (2022) Using Curiosity: A Psychologically Informed Approach to Adult Safeguarding and Rough Sleeping. In Cooper, A. and Preston-Shoot, M. (Eds) *Adult Safeguarding and Homelessness: Understanding Good Practice.* London: Jessica Kingsley Publishers.

Mate, G. (2019) *When the Body Says No: The Cost of Hidden Stress.* London: Vermillion.

Menon, A. (2019) Beyond the Individual: Reframing Blame and Responsibility for 'rogue' Behaviour in the Financial Services Industry. In Obholzer, A. and Roberts, V. Z. (Eds) *The Unconscious at Work: A Tavistock Approach to Making Sense of Organisational Life.* Second Edition. London: Routledge.

Menzies Lyth, I. (1960) Social systems as a defense against anxiety. An empirical study of the nursing service of a general hospital. *Human Relations.* vol. 13 pp 95–121.

Menzies Lyth, I. (1979). I *Containing Anxiety in Institutions: Selected Essays Volume 1.* London: Free Association Books.

Mignerey, J. T., Rubin, R. B. and Gorden, W. I. (1995). Organizational entry: An investigation of newcomer communication behavior and uncertainty. *Communication Research.* vol. 22. no. 1 pp 54–85.

Miles, H. (2020) Psychologically Informed Leadership in a post COVID-19 world. (Blog) *Dr Helen Miles.* Available at https://drhelenmiles.medium.com/ (Accessed 12 June 23).

Miller, E. (1995) Dialogue with the client system: Use of the "working note" in organisational consultancy. *Journal of Managerial Psychology.* vol. 10. no. 6 pp 27–30.

Miller, S., Duncan, B. L., Brown, J., Sorrell, R. and Chalk, M. B. (2006) Using formal client feedback to improve retention and outcome: Making ongoing real-time assessment feasible. *Journal of Brief Therapy.* vol 5. no. 1 pp 5–22.

Miller, E. J. and Rice, A. K. (1967) *Systems of the Organisation: The Control of Task and Sentient Boundaries.* London: Tavistock Publications.

Monaghan, L. and Thorley, C. (2022) Open Dialogue, Dialogical Leadership, and Staff Support. In Conniff, H. (Ed) *Psychological Staff Support in Healthcare: Thinking & Practice.* Keighley: Sequoia Books.

National Lottery Community Fund (2020) *Improving access to mental health support for people with multiple disadvantage. Evaluation of Fulfilling Lives: Supporting people with multiple needs.* Available at: https://www.tnlcommunityfund.org.uk/media/insights/documents/Report-Summary-Improving-access-to-mental-health-support-for-people-experiencing-multiple-disadvantage-January-2020.pdf?mtime=20200316152718&focal=none. (Accessed: 7 July 2024).

Neumann, J. (1997) Negotiating Entry and Contracting. In Neumann, J., Kellner, K. and Dawson-Shepherd, A. (Eds) *Developing Organisational Consultancy.* London: Routledge.

Obholzer, A. and Roberts, V. Z. (2019) (Eds) *The Unconscious at Work: A Tavistock Approach to Making Sense of Organisational Life*. Second Edition. London: Routledge.

Pashler, H., McDaniel, M., Rohrer, D. and Bjork, R. (2009) Learning styles: Concepts and evidence. *Psychological Science in the Public Interest*. vol. 9 no. 3 pp 105–119.

Porges, S. W. and Porges, S. (2023) *Our Polyvagal World: How Safety and Trauma Change Us*. New York: WW Norton and Co.

Prochaska, J. O. and DiClemente, C. C. (1982) Transtheoretical therapy; Toward a more integrative model of change. *Psychotherapy: Theory, Research and Practice*. vol. 19 no. 3 pp 276–288.

Rizq, R. (2012) The perversion of care: Psychological therapies in a time of IAPT. *Psychodynamic Practice*. vol. 18 no. 1 pp 7–24.

Roberts, V. Z. (2019) Navigating Roles in Complex Systems. In Obholzer, A. and Roberts, V. Z. (Eds) *The Unconscious at Work: A Tavistock Approach to Making Sense of Organisational Life*. Second Edition. London: Routledge.

Revolving Doors Agency (2019) *Birmingham Changing Futures Together: Evaluation of the Impact of Psychologically Informed Environments*. Available at: https://revolving-doors.org. uk/wp-content/uploads/2022/02/BHM-Evaluation-of-PIE-2019-3.pdf (Accessed 5 July 2024).

Scanlon, C. and Adlam, J. (2016) "Stuck in the Middle with You": On the (dis) stressing effects of working in (dis)stressed homelessness organisations. *Housing Care and Support*. vol 15 no. 2 pp.74–82

Scanlon, C. and Adlam, J. (2019) Housing Unhoused Minds: Complex multiple exclusion and the cycle of rejection revisited. In Brown, G. (Ed) *Psychoanalytical Thinking on the Unhoused Mind*. London: Routledge Taylor & Francis.

Schon, D. (1983) *The Reflective Practitioner: How Professionals Think in Action*. New York: Basic Books.

Schumacker, M. and Cheak, A. (2022) Developing Night Vision: Applying a Psychodynamic Lens to Understanding Supervisory Board Dynamics. Available at https://www. kdvi.com/ (Accessed 2 March 2023).

Siegel, D. J. (2020). *The Developing Mind: How Relationships and the Brain Interact to Shape Who We Are*. Third Edition. New York: The Guilford Press.

Senior, B. and Fleming, J. (2006) *Organisational Change*. London: Prentice Hall.

Stokes, J. (2019) Institutional Chaos and Personal Stress In Obholzer, A. and Roberts, V. Z. (Eds) *The Unconscious at Work: A Tavistock Approach to Making Sense of Organisational Life*. Second Edition. London: Routledge.

Stokoe, P. (2021) *The Curiosity Drive: Our Need for Inquisitive Thinking*. Bicester: Phoenix Publishing House.

Sweeney, C. and Bothwick, F. (2016) *Inclusive Leadership: The Definitive Guide to Developing and Executing an Impactful Diversity and Inclusive Strategy*. Harlow: Pearson.

Trainor, K. (2019) Feelings as Data. In Obholzer, A. and Roberts, V. Z. (Eds) *The Unconscious at Work: A Tavistock Approach to Making Sense of Organisational Life*. Second Edition. London: Routledge.

Urnova, A. (2018) How early life Experiences Could Play for and against Us in the Boardroom. (Blog) *The Kets De Vries Institute*. Available at https://www.kdvi.com/research_ items/790 (Accessed 19 April 2023).

Van der Kolk, B. (2014) *The Body Keeps the Score: Mind, Brain and Body in the Transformations of Trauma*. London: Penguin Books.

West, M. A. (2021) *Compassionate Leadership: Sustaining Wisdom, Humanity and Presence in Health and Social Care*. London: The Swirling Leaf Press.

Wilson, P. (2020) The Importance of Not Being Earnest. In Brissett, L., Sher, M. and Smith, T. L. (Eds) *Dynamics at Boardroom Level: A Tavistock Primer for Leaders, Coaches and Consultants*. New York: Routledge.

Whittle, S. R. and Izod, K. (2014) In Izod, K. and Whittle, S. R. Eds) *Resource-Ful Consulting: Working with Your Presence and Identity in Consulting to Change.* London: Karnac Books.

Williamson, E. (2018) PIE-oneering Psychological Integration in Homeless Hostels. In Cockersell, P. (Ed) Social Exclusion, Compound Trauma and Recovery: *Applying Psychology, Psychotherapy and PIE to Homelessness and Complex Needs.* London: Jessica Kingsley Publishers.

Winnicott, D. W. (1960) The theory of the parent-child relationship. *International Journal of Psychoanalysis.* vol. 41. pp 585–595.

Winnicott, D. W. (1965) *Maturation Process and the Facilitating Environment.* London: Hogarth.

Woodcock, J. and Gill, J. (2014). Implementing a psychologically informed environment in a service for homeless young people. *Housing, Care and Support.* vol. 17 no. 1 pp 48–57.

Zenger, J. H. and Folkman, J. R. (2020) *The New Extraordinary Leader: Turning Good Managers into Great Leaders.* Third Edition. New York: McGraw-Hill Education.

Chapter 2

The Relationship between Psychologically Informed Environments and Trauma Informed Care, and What They Mean for Organisational Leadership

Peter Cockersell

In this chapter, I look at the relationship between Psychologically Informed Environments (PIEs) and Trauma Informed Care (TIC) and then offer a perspective on the kind of leadership that enables PIE and TIC to work with a little reference to what gets in the way of it working.

I have divided this chapter into two parts, the first looking at the relationship between PIE and TIC and the second looking at leadership within the context of enabling PIE and TIC; however, in the real world they form aspects of a single process as the leadership required to enable PIE and TIC flows from the principles of PIE and TIC. Enabling healing, recovery-oriented environments or services is not done by imposing management or leadership models taken from industrial production or finance-driven 'market forces': it is done by managing and leading in a way that is itself psychologically or trauma informed – it is fundamentally relational rather than transactional.

Part 1: The Relationship between PIE and TIC

In the Foreword Helen Keats relates something of the history of PIEs; I will describe it a little bit more here and also give some background to the development of TIC showing how both developed from an increasing understanding of the role that unresolved trauma plays in social and healthcare problems.

Both PIEs and TIC have capital letters and acronyms: they have both become 'things' in their own right, with meanings, histories, followers, and both grew out of particular cultures and cultural perspectives. Because each has achieved 'thingdom' they are often seen as distinct or different, and people have on many occasions asked me 'What has PIE got to do with TIC?' or 'What has TIC got to do with PIE?' as if they were contrasting options that mean you have to 'do' or follow one or the other.

I would like to clarify this here: PIEs and TIC, while not exactly the same, are also not completely different things – it is not a situation where you have to choose

DOI: 10.4324/9781003415053-3

one or the other. PIEs provide a framework which enhances the probability of delivering person-centred responsive services, including effective TIC, within multiple contexts. We have examples in this book of this approach from homelessness, domestic abuse, child and adolescent, mental health, third sector, NHS, and local authority services and commissioners.

The Roots of PIE and TIC

This is not a social history book so I am not going to go into detail tracing the origins of either PIE or TIC; rather I am going to make some observations about the conflicts in perspectives on social and healthcare problems that independently gave rise to both, PIE in the UK and TIC in the USA.

Zygmunt Bauman, Professor of Sociology at the University of Leeds in the UK, observed that 'Although the risks and contradictions of life go on being as socially produced as ever, the duty and necessity of coping with them has been delegated to our individual selves' (Bauman, 2007). I think that this is fundamental to understanding the conflicts in the delivery of services in both health and social care, and particularly with regard to mental healthcare, over the last 75 years or so, and it is fundamental to the understanding of where TIC and PIE are coming from.

If we look at any of the definitions of the word 'trauma', it is something that is done to someone. The original Greek word means a 'rupture' or a 'wound'; it is the breaking of an attachment or the breaking through of a boundary. A rupture is a tear in, or the end of, a relationship where the two (or more) sides are separated or torn asunder. A wound is a piercing of your personal boundary which makes you bleed, literally or metaphorically, and which can be life-threatening or soul-destroying.

> Individual trauma results from an event, series of events, or set of circumstances that is experienced by an individual as physically or emotionally harmful or life threatening and that has lasting adverse effects on the individual's functioning and mental, physical, social, emotional, or spiritual well-being.
>
> (Samsha, 2014)

'Trauma' is socially or environmentally produced: it is done by other people, as in an attack of some sort, or by the world around us, as in a fire or other natural disaster, or by both as in catastrophes induced by other people such as wars. Although it is socially or environmentally produced, coping with it, as Bauman says, is usually delegated to the individual self. Where people have suffered trauma, either through ruptures or wounds, in early childhood they are more likely than average to experience almost any or all of the social and healthcare ills that afflict our society:

> The study confirmed earlier investigations that found a highly significant relationship between adverse childhood experiences and depression, suicide attempts, alcoholism, drug abuse, sexual promiscuity, domestic violence, cigarette smoking, obesity, physical inactivity, and sexually transmitted diseases. In

addition, the more adverse childhood experiences reported, the more likely a person was to develop heart disease, cancer, stroke, diabetes, skeletal fractures, and liver disease.

(Van der Kolk, 2005)

The more trauma they experienced in childhood, the more likely they are to suffer from any of the major social or healthcare problems (Felitti et al, 1998). Where people who have experienced childhood trauma go on to experience further trauma in their adolescence and adulthood and continue not to have the supportive relationships that might enable them to process it (i.e. where 'the duty and necessity of coping...has been delegated to [their] individual selves') they experience compound trauma (Cockersell, 2018a) compounding their difficulties in coping.

And if people do not cope – if they become drug or alcohol dependent, or become violent, or develop mental or emotional problems and begin to act 'strangely' – then they are pathologised: they are seen as having something wrong with them. It is them, not the social or environmental context that produced the trauma in the first place, that is seen as damaged and in some way 'wrong'. They are then often stigmatised and ostracised, or 'dealt with' by being put in prison or by being 'treated' with hospitalisation and mind-altering psychiatric drugs, or other forms of social exclusion, coercion and restraint. This has been a fundamental philosophy of many social programmes and healthcare: the individual is pathologised and the 'disorder' is seen as distinct from and unrelated to the social, political and physical environment from which it stems.

Treatment, whether by social services or healthcare systems, then becomes something that needs to be done to the individual in order to bring them back within whatever is seen as the 'normal', 'healthy' or 'socially appropriate' sets of behaviours and roles. It is from this perspective of health and social services that homosexuals, or women who were pregnant outside of marriage or had abortions, could be criminalised or interned in psychiatric hospitals. They could then be treated or dealt with in ways that, it was hoped, would change their 'deviant' behaviours; in many, probably most, cases this approach led to the further (re)traumatisation of the individuals who had sought or been coerced into seeking help (see, for example, Littleton and Lipsedge, 1997; McCluskey and Hooper, 2000). Sadly, many health and social services continue to traumatise or retraumatise already wounded individuals who come to them needing help. This is not because the healthcare and social services' staff don't care or don't want to help, but because they are parts of systems that deny the social contexts of trauma, and their own parts in those contexts; the leaderships of those systems therefore do not enact the social processes – for example, PIE or TIC – which would meet the resultant psychological and emotional needs of either staff or clients/patients affected by trauma.

I won't go on about this. As noted earlier, this is not a history book on health and social care; the point here is to draw attention to the worldview and mindset from which social services and healthcare were and sometimes still are engaging with the individuals who came into their remit and who had difficulty with functioning effectively in society because of behavioural problems and social circumstances.

Some of the people who came into contact with these services and some of the people who were delivering these services rebelled against this approach and began to identify a different theory of what was happening: they began to see and say that the common thread was that these individuals had been exposed to significant and often prolonged trauma, often without much or any support. They began to say that it wasn't so much a story of what was *wrong* with these individuals, as the dominant philosophy and ideology of health and social services said it was, it was more a case of what had been *done* to them or what had *happened* to them.

In the USA, this was particularly the case with two cohorts of individuals: those who were admitted into the psychiatric system and found it unhelpful, the self-styled 'survivors' of psychiatric care, and some of the professionals who worked in it, a group which at least partially overlapped with the 'anti-psychiatry' movement of the 1960s and 1970s; and the veterans of the Vietnam War who found themselves unable to simply return to engaging with work, family and life as 'normal' US civilians and who frequently found themselves on the 'done to' side of either the criminal justice or psychiatric systems, or both. In the UK, it arose from (again) survivors of the mental health system and some of the professionals who did not accept the majority perspective on what was good 'treatment' (or indeed even what it was that needed treating), and from homeless people and some of the services and professionals that worked with them. The US movement led to the development of the concept of TIC and the UK one to the concept of PIEs. Both came from the desire to see the development of alternative ways of working that would be effective for individuals who had been damaged by the experience of trauma, and particularly unresolved and compound trauma, and the creation of an alternative narrative that did not blame or pathologise the traumatised individual for the difficulties in coping with life that had arisen from trying to cope with what had been done to them.

Both PIE and TIC are intended to create alternative narratives that do not blame the traumatised individual but rather understand where they are coming from and why they might have behaved/behave as they have or as they do, and so in turn enable services to work safely with the impact of trauma on the individuals who seek help from them.

The Relationship between PIE and TIC

TIC has become a mainstream concept on both sides of the Atlantic and generally agreed fundamentals of TIC have been officially adopted by the administrations in both the USA and the UK (Office for Health Improvement and Disparities, 2022; Samsha, 2014); these state that trauma informed services should focus on the areas (Samsha, 2014):

1 Safety
2 Trustworthiness and Transparency

3 Peer Support
4 Collaboration and Mutuality
5 Empowerment, Voice and Choice
6 Cultural, Historical, and Gender Issues

This of itself is heartening for the many service users and professionals who have campaigned for decades for the recognition of the role of trauma in the development of health and social problems and of the importance of health and social services being aware of their potential to retraumatise. More disappointingly, it has not, yet at least, led to the large-scale change of the dominant paradigm that the individual and their behaviours are somehow 'the problem' rather than being understandable responses to a history of trauma or compound trauma. The necessity of coping continues to be delegated to the individuals who have been the object of the trauma, and where they are unable to cope, they continue in many cases to be pathologised.

Many people, especially among the survivors of treatment systems, would add 'social justice' to the above list of fundamental principles of TIC because of the roles of poverty, inequality, patriarchy, racism, etc., but this is not in the officially adopted versions: 'cultural, historical and gender issues' seem to be the rather anodyne accepted substitute. One can only speculate as to the political reasons for that, but it is important in the context of this book as there is a political element required of leaders if they are to lead trauma informed organisations, systems or services. Sometimes being trauma informed requires taking a stand. I will say more on that when looking at leadership in PIE and TIC in the second part of this chapter; for the moment my topic is the relationship between TIC and PIEs.

PIE was developed in the UK and its concepts are less widespread than TIC as they have been held principally in the world of homelessness services (Keats et al, 2012). They do, however, have an international dimension elsewhere in Europe and in the USA (see, for example, Feantsa, 2018; Levy and Johnson, 2017). Although PIE itself originated in homelessness it is a cousin of Psychologically Informed Planned Environments in the UK Prison Service, and of Enabling Environments in health and criminal justice services (Haigh et al, 2012). The driving force behind the development of PIE was the recognition of the role of trauma in the aetiology of homelessness and especially chronic homelessness and rough sleeping (see the foreword to this book; Maguire et al, 2009), and a recognition of the need to provide support to homelessness services in working with the impacts of trauma both on their homeless clients and on their staff.

PIE was specifically developed as a framework of practice to enable effective TIC. The original version had five principles (Keats et al, 2012) which were later expanded to seven (Cockersell, 2018b, pp 96–103). If an organisation, system or service takes actions to implement service changes in all of the domains under these principles, then they will deliver effective TIC and will experience a set of positive outcomes for their staff and for their beneficiaries (Cockersell, 2016; see also examples in this book).

The principles of PIE are:

1   Psychological Framework
2   Staff Support
3   Managing Relationships
4   Social Spaces
5   Access to Psychotherapists/Psychotherapy
6   Client Involvement/Participation
7   Evaluation

PIE has been implemented in a very wide range of organisations and services. In this book alone there are examples of organisations using PIE in homelessness, registered care, mental health, women's refuges and young people's services in both statutory and voluntary sector settings; it has also been extensively implemented in the criminal justice system in the UK. Wherever PIE has been implemented, there have been a set of positive outcomes, including (Cockersell, 2016, 2018b; National Lottery/Fulfilling Lives, 2020):

- Reduction in incidents and evictions/barrings
- Increase in positive move-on
- Reduction in hospitalisations
- Increased uptake of other services
- Improvement in mental wellbeing and resilience
- Clinically measurable improvement in mental health
- Improvement in staff morale
- Reduction in staff sickness, turnover etc
- Improved manager-staff relations

PIE, then, provides an evidence-based, tested process for the implementation of TIC.

Why and How the PIE Approach Enables the Delivery of TIC

To consider why PIE enables the implementation of TIC I want to highlight some of the principles of PIE and the role they have not only in enabling staff to support individual recovery but also, crucially, in enabling organisations to change the way they work so that they do not disable recovery or act in a retraumatising way.

Firstly, I'd highlight the importance of the 'psychological framework'. This is not because we need or want everyone to be psychologists or psychotherapists, far from it, but because the understanding of trauma and its impacts, and the processes of traumatisation and of recovery, is deeply important when thinking about how to deliver trauma informed services. This is as true whether you are a frontline member of staff or the Chief Executive.

We all experience trauma – ruptures and wounds – at some stage in our lives; obviously some more dramatically or significantly than others, but still trauma is a universal human experience. We all also cope with trauma in some way or other. There are many short-term coping strategies for dealing with a traumatic event, some of which can also be used for dealing with ongoing or repeated (compound) trauma: these strategies include everything from talking it through with our family or friends or a therapist to breathing or yoga or a spiritual belief system to self-harm or drug and alcohol use. The degree to which we turn to specific coping strategies depends upon the nature and frequency of the trauma and on our own resilience. The higher our resilience, the less we are impacted by trauma experiences in the long term; resilience is the most effective defence against damage through trauma experiences. Resilience itself is created by the 'ordinary everyday magic' of family life (Masten, 2001): it is a by-product of secure attachment. If we have strong support networks provided by loving and caring friends, family or even colleagues, then the impact of any trauma experience is diminished and is more easily recovered from; if, on the contrary, we are surrounded by negligent or even hostile family, friends or associates, then the impact of a trauma experience is magnified and much harder to recover from. This is particularly acutely so for children and young people, and for those who have experienced or who are experiencing compound trauma. Most of the people in psychiatric, prison or homelessness services have histories of childhood trauma (Felitti et al, 1998; Lankelly Chase, 2015; Sweeney et al, 2016) and damaged/ruptured attachments and display the behaviours associated with insecure attachment (see, for example, Barreto and Cockersell, 2023; Mikulincer and Shaver, 2012).

For services to provide TIC to those who most need it they have to learn to work with the behaviours associated with often deeply and acutely insecure attachment styles including disorganised attachments. For this to happen the staff and leadership need to not only understand the processes of trauma itself but also the processes of attachment, and in both cases how they affect the interpersonal behaviours of their clients and their staff. For this reason, it is not enough simply to have training on trauma and its effects; staff and management also need training on attachment and its effects, and on the interplay between attachment and trauma in the development of personality and the dynamics of interpersonal relationships and organisations. If a team, service or organisation does not understand these dynamics, then they are more likely to enact processes that repeat the trauma experiences of the clients they are trying to serve and they are likely to induce trauma experiences in the staff who they expect to support those clients (creating, for example, the high levels of burn-out experienced by staff in many 'caring' organisations) (Sweeney et al, 2016). If an organisation adopts PIE principles, then it will take on a psychological framework and significantly increase its potential to deliver effective TIC and reduce the likelihood of inducing retraumatisation in its clients or trauma experiences in its staff.

Attachment is a primary biological drive or instinct and fundamental to all human relationships (Bowlby, 1990; Lahousen et al, 2019). We form our basic attachment styles in relationships with our parents and close family or whoever it is that nurtures and brings us up in our early years: from them we learn how to relate. If these early relationships are benign enough, we are more likely to be secure in our future relationships and our personalities are stable yet adaptable, exploratory yet boundaried; if these early relationships are more variable, we will have various insecurities and fallibilities, and be a bit more volatile or neurotic about some things which will matter to us seemingly (at least to others) disproportionately; if our early relationships are severely negligent, or hostile, or chaotic, we will have unstable personalities (often diagnosed as psychiatric disorders including personality disorder), volatile behaviours, difficulty in sustaining relationships, seemingly disproportionate (including to ourselves) intensity of feelings and reactions and a deep distrust of people. In recovering from trauma we are also repairing the capacity for relationships and creating what are called 'learned' secure attachment styles; these two pieces of work go hand in hand psychologically (Fonagy and Allison, 2014).

Because attachment is learned through the experience of relationship with another human, or to a lesser extent through relationship to another sentient group animal (for example, therapy dogs, equine therapy, etc.), and damaged relationships and attachments are major determinants of whether a person recovers easily from a trauma experience or not because of resilience, then relationships are central to recovery. This is something that survivors almost always highlight and that all the major modalities of psychology, psychodynamic, cognitive, behavioural or humanistic agree on. Central among the principles of PIE is 'managing relationships' and, to put it straightforwardly, an organisation that takes active steps to implement processes and training for the management of relationships will deliver better TIC than one that does not.

I draw attention to the wording '*managing* relationships'. It is not simply about having relationships: we have those whether we like it or not, and they can be good, bad or indifferent. What a PIE does is stress the need to use relationships and to invest thought and care into managing relationships so that they are more likely to deliver a positive, progressive, healing or resolving outcome. We cannot control the outcome, but we can influence the probability of the outcome, by using our relationships to positive effect as far as is possible. This means all relationships, not just between staff and client: it also means between staff and staff, staff and managers, managers and middle managers and senior managers, members of the senior team, between the senior staff, board members and commissioners, politicians, etc. and so on. The biggest tool we all have to deliver trauma informed services is through the management of relationships. It is this, to some extent regardless of role, power or authority that we as humans have the ability to influence.

Critical to the successful management of relationships are two other principles of PIE: staff support/reflective practice and client involvement. One of the key things for a staff team to be able to deliver TIC is that it should not be traumatised itself and that it should not feel 'done to', attacked, as with job or pay cuts for example, or neglected, as with lack of recognition of skill or good work.

These damage the staff's attachment to the organisation and to its work, just as hostile or negligent parenting damages children's attachments, and they reduce staff resilience. Staff support, on the other hand – good training, regular reflective supervision (not just performance supervision), reasonable conditions and reflective groups – enable staff to feel more attached and so more committed to the organisation and its work. Crucially it also makes them more resilient and so more able to deal effectively and creatively with the complex task of working with people who have experienced compound trauma and the risks of vicarious trauma that come with the work.

Similarly, an organisation implementing the PIE principle of client involvement will engage their clients more actively in the processes of the production of their services and involve them more in the decisions about their own lives. As well as being in its own right empowering and enabling, this also disrupts power hierarchies that might reinforce social injustices and trauma experiences. In following the PIE principles, client involvement is much more than an add-on as it sometimes feels in some organisations: it is integral to the process.

Similarly the inclusion of 'social spaces', the environmental element in PIEs, brings to the organisation's attention the importance of thinking about the built and furnished environments' role in either sustaining traditional power dynamics, to which people with experiences of trauma will be very sensitive, or promoting a sense of psychological and emotional safety, and the idea that something different is possible. Delivering TIC is made harder in environments where the architecture, furnishing and noticeboards reinforce power structures or pathologisation and suggest coercion and control; it is made easier by environments with differentiated spaces that can, for example, promote social interaction or enable privacy and that suggest more democratic structures and invite participation and collaboration. This does not mean that everywhere has to be rebuilt incurring major financial outlays: it means that leaders should be giving thought to the environments in which their staff and clients work together, and listening to the comments and suggestions of their staff and clients about how to improve their physical environments. A simple exercise of client involvement in which the clients have a significant say in how the service's environment is utilised, furnished, decorated and signed can have a huge impact in terms of empowerment for the clients and promoting the sense of safety so important to TIC.

Finally, I would like to mention the importance of 'evaluation', another of the PIE principles. This is not just about complying with whatever formal evaluation is required of your organisation by funders or statutory regulations; it is about evaluating the impact of the service you deliver on the clients, on the staff and on the organisation and the world within which it operates. It is an organisational reflective activity done by individuals, teams and systems, which looks at hard and soft outcomes and the relational quality of the processes that were involved in achieving them. Continuous thoughtful evaluation is a kind of psychologically informed dynamic quality assurance system that helps make sure that all the organisation's spheres of activity, and the procedures that underpin them, are directed towards and supportive of enabling the recovery of people who have been impacted by trauma experiences. This keeps the whole organisation becoming more and more trauma informed and more resilient.

In the editors' experience as practitioners, in conversations with provider organisations' staff, trainers and consultants, and in the experience of many of the contributors to this book, staff work hard to deliver services in a trauma informed way often *despite* the processes and systems of their service's commissioning, management and leadership rather than *because* of them. This is true even when the leadership publicly supports TIC or PIEs: they sometimes do not seem to realise what their role is in delivering these approaches. Many middle and senior managers, as well as commissioners, seem to think that PIE and TIC are something that their staff need to do and not something that they need to pay attention to. Good leadership in PIE and TIC enables change in the whole organisation's systems and management so that they facilitate the delivery of TIC rather than, consciously or unconsciously, throwing obstacles in its path. There are many examples of this in this book from a series of inspirational leaders.

So now I would like to turn my attention to thinking a bit about what psychologically and trauma informed leadership might mean.

Leadership in Enabling PIE and TIC

There are many manybooks on leadership and management and I am not going to produce a literature review of management or leadership theory. I also don't intend to specifically tease out differences and overlaps in 'managing' and 'leading'; that isn't my purpose here. What I would like to do is suggest some overarching themes that influence whether the leadership and management of an organisation, a service or a system can be effectively trauma informed.

When I was about to become a Chief Executive for the first time, I asked my Chief Executive at my previous employers, Charles Fraser CBE of St Mungo's, what it is that a Chief Executive does, what their key tasks are. He said just two things: 'To keep the organisation to its mission' and 'To keep it solvent' (personal communication).

The primary task of any organisation is defined by what it is set up to achieve, and for whom – its 'mission'; the secondary task is to make sure it continues to exist or even flourishes – to keep it at least 'solvent'. This applies whether you are private sector, public sector or in the not-for-profit or charitable sector. However, what is different across the different types of business is what the mission is, what the organisation is set up to achieve. That matters: the style of leadership and management suited to achieve some objectives can be, indeed should be, quite different to the style of management and leadership suited to achieve others.

In the private sector, regardless of what the company does, the 'mission' or purpose of the company is to make money for the owners, whether shareholders or a family: it doesn't matter if it sells groceries or manufactures weapons or delivers services, its primary task is to produce a surplus which goes to the owners. It is designed for the benefits (surplus) to go *upwards*, to the Board or beyond, and its success, and its leadership's and management's success, will be measured by how much it achieves that (as well as at least staving off bankruptcy). On the other hand, most public sector organisations, not-for-profits and charitable organisations, are designed for the benefits (services, help, food) to go *downwards*, to the beneficiaries, and the organisations' success, and the success of their leaderships and management should be measured by how much they achieve this (as well as at least staving off bankruptcy).

There is a fundamental difference between the leadership and management approaches required to deliver the benefits upwards or downwards: the aim of private sector leadership is to draw as much surplus out of the system as possible and funnel it upwards; the aim of public, non-profit and charitable sector leadership is to deliver as much 'good' (services, help, food, etc.) as the system permits to its beneficiaries. The private sector leaders are in the service of their Boards and shareholders; the public, not-for-profit and charitable leaders should be in the service of their beneficiaries.

This leads to a fundamental difference in approach: private sector leadership and management is by nature transactional – you engage people's need/desire to earn money to get them to work for you and you then pay them less than the value they create for your business, and you add the surplus they generate into the profits that go to the owners/shareholders. On the other hand, public/not-for-profit sector leadership has to be relational to be effective – you engage people's belief in or commitment to whatever service you provide and you pay them what you can afford to in order to generate increased good for your beneficiaries. Both models require efficiency, but the former requires efficiency in extracting wealth, and the latter requires efficiency in delivering good: that is fundamentally a different task and requires fundamentally different leadership.

So what does PIE and TIC management and leadership entail? Firstly, a recognition that leadership in a psychologically informed or trauma informed organisation is primarily in the service of the beneficiaries of the organisation, not of the Boards or even the funders: it is for the people who are clients, residents, service users, customers – whatever the term the organisation favours (though of course in practising the 'client involvement' principle they will have asked their beneficiaries what they would like to be called).

As in most cases the leadership and middle and senior managements do not work directly with the beneficiaries, then they are actually usually working with the staff and the organisation's systems to try to enable the staff to deliver the most good possible given the level of resources they have to do the job (bearing in mind their secondary task, which is not to bankrupt the organisation). The role of the leadership and management teams is therefore to enable the staff to work as efficiently as possible in delivering whatever good it is that the organisation was set up to deliver. They will do this far more successfully if the whole organisation is set up and geared up to deliver the good than if the upper half of the organisation and its central teams think they are there to make a surplus or to comply with the funders or to satisfy political pressures while the lower half of the organisation tries, despite this, to deliver good for the beneficiaries.

It follows from this that if you want to deliver PIEs or TIC, then your leadership and management have to be driven and organised by the principles of PIE and TIC just as much as your frontline client-facing services. Leaders and senior managers need to understand how TIC works, what its principles are, and what methods and techniques help to deliver it and what gets in the way to enable their organisation and their staff to deliver care or support in the most efficient and effective way.

Each organisation will be different in the way that it implements TIC according to the needs of the organisation and the style of the CEO and their leadership and management teams, as the following chapters show, but, as they also show, using psychological approaches in general, and PIE, in particular, enables a focus on all the functional areas of the organisation so that they can all become more trauma informed and more friendly to clients who have experienced severe or compound trauma and less traumatising to staff.

We are talking here about culture change, and the leadership that enables it. Sustainable and successful culture change comes about not by imposed major structural changes (see Twitter's recent history as an example of how not to do it!) but by multiple small changes in many processes (Plsek and Greenhalgh, 2001). This is more complex and can feel daunting to implement, but the PIE principles provide a framework for doing so: the process is to take some action under the headings provided by the PIE principles in every area of the organisation's operation, applying each one to each area of activity. If these actions are implemented, then the organisation *will* deliver more TIC, and the range of positive outcomes for clients, staff and management noted earlier will begin to be achieved.

Culture, like leadership, is a word that has many definitions. Here I will use one from a textbook on leadership which defines culture as 'the learned beliefs, values, rules, norms, symbols and traditions that are common to a group of people. It is these *shared* [italics in the original] qualities of a group that make them unique. Culture is dynamic and transmitted to others' (Gudykunst and Ting-Toomey, 1988, quoted in Northouse, 2007, p 302). We might want to add into the list of things common to the group of people 'meaning' as well, though of course all the things listed, plus the relationships between the individuals, go into the creation of meanings in the individual as well as the formal meanings attributed to them by the culture itself.

Northouse's definition of leadership, 'Leadership is a *process* [my italics] whereby an individual influences a group of individuals to achieve a common goal' (Northouse, 2007, p 3), also helps us to think about leadership in the context of culture change: it is a process initiated by an individual or a group of individuals to induce change in another group of individuals. Leadership as a process rather than a simple act aligns with the idea that culture change is the result of multiple actions in multiple practices. It is not sufficient for the leadership to declare 'we are going to be trauma informed' or 'we are going to adopt the PIE approach' and expect their staff to do it, however enthusiastic the staff themselves may be: leadership has to enable the process that shifts the 'learned beliefs, values, rules, norms, symbols and traditions' and meanings of the organisation to enable the effective and efficient delivery of psychologically informed or TIC or support.

There is strong evidence that for leaders or leadership groups to influence the organisation effectively they must reflect the values that they are trying to inspire in their services. People see leaders as fair, just or even wise to the extent that they represent the group's stereotypical ideal: influence is significantly associated with identity, and with the degree to which the staff identify with the organisation and with its values and aspirations (Haslam et al, 2020). Where staff find contradictions in the organisation's leadership-endorsed procedures, policies and practices with the leadership's declared values such as TIC, then it is traumatising for the staff and retraumatising for the clients (Sweeney et al, 2016). If a psychologically and trauma informed approach is not taken by the leadership and enacted by them, although the organisation may say it delivers TIC, it will not actually deliver it. As a senior nurse in an NHS psychiatric hospital that was a 'beacon of excellence' in recovery practice once said to me, 'We're supposed to do recovery here, but we haven't got time for that' (personal communication).

Leaders are also very important to the staff of an organisation, and the more the staff identify with the organisation the more important the leaders are (Haslam et al, 2020). Leaders serve a vital purpose for the organisation and its staff: 'they reduce the number of decisions [the staff member] must take, the responsibility for mistakes becomes less, the responsibility for colleagues becomes less, [the staff] can blame the leader if something does not work' (Alsted and Haslund, 2020, p 156). Leaders also 'provide space for different points of view', 'create a framework for the community', offer 'caring and stability' and 'create meaning' and 'interpret the world' (Alsted and Haslund, 2020, p 152, following Bolman and Deal, 2017). Leaders offer 'responsibility and empathy', 'equilibrium between the organisation's support for the employee and the employee's support for the organisation', the ability to 'assess and use knowledge' and 'authenticity' (Alsted and Haslund, 2020, p 153).

Leadership styles that most align with the values of PIE are quite simply most likely to lead to effective trauma informed services. One of the most obvious for PIEs are psychodynamic leadership approaches (see above and also Alsted and Haslund, 2020; Northouse, 2007, pp 237–264; Obholzer and Zagier-Roberts, 2019). They have an obvious correlation with the PIE principle of a psychological framework and easily lend themselves to holding together the core values and key practices of the organisation, as well as enabling leaders to lead by example in taking psychologically informed and trauma informed decisions and having psychologically and trauma informed interactions and relationships.

Another leadership approach whose ideas can be seen as aligning very closely with delivering PIE and TIC is Ethical Leadership which has been influential in the field of leadership in healthcare settings including psychology (Northouse, 2007, pp 341–370). It talks about leaders who 'respect others' and that 'respect includes giving credence to others' ideas and confirming them as human beings. At times it may require that leaders defer to others…leaders should nurture followers in becoming aware of their own needs, values, and purposes and assist them in integrating these with the leader's' (Northouse, 2007, p 351). Ethical leadership ideas overlap with those in the concept of 'servant leadership' (Reddy and Kamesh, 2016). Servant leadership itself was developed by Greenleaf (Greenleaf, 1977); he states that

> The Servant-Leader is servant first … It begins with the natural feeling that one wants to serve, to serve first. Then conscious choice brings one to aspire to lead…The best test, and difficult to administer is this: Do those served grow as persons? Do they, while being served, become healthier, wiser, freer, more autonomous, and more likely themselves to become servants? And, what is the effect on the least privileged in society? Will they benefit, or at least not further be harmed?
>
> (Greenleaf, 1977, p 7)

This is obviously directly relevant to the leadership in PIE and TIC: many of the leaders in this field, and all those in this book, came into the work with the idea and ideal of helping, caring for and supporting 'the least privileged in society' – the homeless, people with mental health problems, women escaping gender-based violence and so on. They took on leadership roles so as to be better able to have a greater influence on delivering good quality care and support and see empowerment of both staff and clients as a way to do this. Northouse (2007) describes this in terms of 'beneficence': 'Beneficence is derived from the Hippocratic tradition which holds that health professionals should make choices that benefit their patients…beneficence asserts that providers have a duty to help others pursue their own legitimate interests and goals' (pp 351–352). This echoes what I said earlier about the leadership in PIE and TIC being primarily in the service of the organisation's beneficiaries not in the service of its owners or funders.

Van Dierendonck (2010) writes that 'A high-quality dyadic relationship, trust, and fairness are…the most important mediating processes to encourage self-actualisation, positive job attitudes, performance, and a stronger organisational focus on sustainability and corporate social responsibility' in a servant leadership-led organisation. This trust between leadership, management and staff drives the internalisation and true adoption of the principles of PIE and TIC, so enabling the 'sustainability' and 'performance' he speaks of. It resonates with the central principle of PIE, 'managing relationships'.

Another leadership style that seems well adapted for use in leadership in PIE and TIC is Enabling Leadership; this is specifically highlighted by NHS England (NHSE, 2023) as being appropriate for creating the adaptive systems which are required for working with complex challenges. Though NHSE are really focusing on the response to Covid-19, adaptive systems are needed for the complex challenges of working with people who have experienced compound trauma and who face the added dysfunction of a complex health and care system (Cockersell, 2018c).

Uhl-Bien and Arena (2018), starting out from the perspective of Complexity Leadership, confirm the value of enabling leadership in dealing with complex systems: Complexity Leadership proposes three leadership functions, operational, entrepreneurial and enabling, but 'enabling leadership is the vehicle for operational and entrepreneurial leadership to align; this supports innovative organisational adaptability, alongside the day-to-day operational dimensions' (BERA, 2023).

Here I would also like to highlight the so-called 'Nolan Principles', the Seven Principles of Public Life drafted for the first report of the Committee on Standards in Public Life set up by the UK Government and chaired by Lord Nolan. His report identified 'selflessness, integrity, objectivity, accountability, openness, honesty and leadership' (Nolan, 1995): these are, I think, some of the qualities required in leadership and management of PIE and TIC. I also think we could add passion, and commitment to the beneficiaries. Social workers in Scotland were asked by the University of Stirling what they thought was most important in a good leader and they said: 'good leaders…demonstrate that they care' and '[show] their determination to make a difference. Good leaders…have passion and desire to take others along with them' (Scottish Social Services Council, 2016).

Leaders also need a *practical vision* because 'Vision is very important but it's not enough to have a grand vision – you need understanding of the organisation and the processes – you need to know how the vision is able to be implemented to make it work' (Scottish Social Services Council, 2016).

Ensuring that the social and healthcare services that we deliver best meet the needs of people who have experienced trauma or compound trauma is something to aspire to: it is an ideal and a vision. To make it a 'practical vision' requires good leadership and a good system of implementation: the principles of PIE offer a structured approach to put the vision and ideal of TIC into practice.

Finally, I would like to come back to the topic of social justice referred to in the first part of this chapter. Leaders in PIE and TIC need to be not just conscious of social justice issues but actively fighting for them in their domains. I don't mean that they need to be politically active in the traditional sense – that is a personal choice – but I do think that they need to be political. Many of the problems that health and social care and support services' clients have to deal with are the result of a combination of poverty, deprivation, gender oppression, racism, and domestic and child abuse compounded and exacerbated by individual experiences of hardship and trauma within damaged and damaging relationships. Many of these are chronic issues experienced over a lifetime. Politicians' promises of magic bullets, often colluded with by senior executives in the public and not-for-profit sectors, combined with short-term solutions, contracts and thinking, high throughput targets, low pay for frontline staff and poor working conditions, and cost-cutting exercises pretending to be efficiency savings – all of these are issues of social justice which leaders of PIE and TIC services need to fight against if they are to deliver good quality psychologically- and TIC. The leaders of PIE and TIC need to affirm what is required to deliver good quality TIC, not pretend that it can be done quickly or on the cheap or at the expense of staff well-being

(Iles, 2013); they need to be willing to refuse to take on contracts and endorse initiatives that they know can't work; and they need to affirm the rights of the beneficiaries to receive better treatment from the society that creates and allows such disadvantage and exclusion to occur. These are political acts with a small p, perhaps, but they are of major importance in the delivery of PIE and TIC. If the leaders of caring organisations do not fight or take risks for their staff and their beneficiaries, who will?

In the following chapters of this book, contributed by leaders in many fields of health and social support and care, you can read the richness of their experiences of leadership in implementing PIE and TIC: their struggles and the ways they have found resolution, and the challenges and successes they have found on the way. All the authors of these chapters have adopted psychologically informed approaches to working with people who have experienced significant, often compound, trauma and have achieved great outcomes for their staff and their clients. I hope you will find their experiences stimulating and encouraging in your own leadership journeys in PIE and TIC.

References

Alsted, J. and Haslund, D. (2020) *Psychodynamic Organisational Theory: Key Concepts and Case Studies*. Abingdon: Routledge.

Barreto, E. and Cockersell, P. (2023) Attachment, trauma and homelessness. *Journal of Mental Health and Social Inclusion*, **28:1** pp 30–41. https://doi.org/10.1108/MHSI-06-2023-0066.

Bauman, Z. (2007) *Liquid Times: Living in an Age of Uncertainty*. Cambridge: Polity Press.

BERA, British Educational Research Association (2023) *Leadership in a Complex World*. Accessed at www.Bera.ac.uk/blog/leading-in-a-complex-world. August 2023.

Bolman, L. and Deal, T. (2017) *Reframing Organizations: Artistry, Choice, and Leadership, 6th Edition*. Hoboken, NJ: Wiley & Sons.

Bowlby, J. (1990) *A Secure Base*. London: Basic Books.

Cockersell, P. (2016) PIE five years on. *Mental Health and Social Inclusion*. **20:4** pp 1–10.

Cockersell, P. (2018a) Compound Trauma and Complex Needs. In P. Cockersell (Ed) *Social Exclusion, Compound Trauma and Recovery: Applying Psychology, Psychotherapy and PIE to Homelessness and Complex Needs*. London: Jessica Kingsley Publishers.

Cockersell, P. (2018b) Applying Psychology as a Response to the Impact of Social Exclusion. In P. Cockersell (Ed) *Social Exclusion, Compound Trauma and Recovery: Applying Psychology, Psychotherapy and PIE to Homelessness and Complex Needs*. London: Jessica Kingsley Publishers.

Cockersell, P. (2018c) The Problem and Potential of Complexity. In P. Cockersell (Ed) *Social Exclusion, Compound Trauma and Recovery: Applying Psychology, Psychotherapy and PIE to Homelessness and Complex Needs*. London: Jessica Kingsley Publishers.

Feantsa (2018), *PIE4Shelters Guide*. Accessed at https://www.feantsa.org/download/pie4shelters-guide-en-17380554497860580950.pdf. August 2023.

Felitti, V., Anda, R., Nordenberg, D., Williamson, D., Spitz, A., Edwards, V., Koss, M. and Marks, J. (1998) Relationship of childhood abuse and household dysfunction to many of the leading causes of death in adults: The adverse childhood experiences (ACE) study. *American Journal of Preventative Medicine*. **14:4** pp 245–258.

Fonagy, P. and Allison, E. (2014). The role of mentalizing and epistemic trust in the therapeutic relationship. *Psychotherapy*. **51:3** pp 372–380. https://doi.org/10.1037/a0036505.

Greenleaf, R. (1977) *Servant Leadership: A Journey into the Nature of Legitimate Power and Greatness*. New York: Paulist Press.

Haigh, R., Harrison, T., Johnson, R., Paget, S. and William, S. (2012) Psychologically informed environments and the "Enabling Environments" initiative. *Housing Care and Support Journal*. **15**:1 pp 34–42.

Haslam, A., Reicher, S. and Platow, M. (2020) *The New Psychology of Leadership: Identity, Influence and Power, 2nd Edition*. London: Routledge.

Iles, V. (2013) *Let's Stop Believing in Magic*. Accessed at www.reallylearning.com/lets-stop-believing-in-magic/. August 2023.

Keats, H., Cockersell, P., Johnson, R. and Maguire, N. (2012). *Psychologically informed services for homeless people*. Accessed at https://eprints.soton.ac.uk. August 2023.

Lahousen, T., Unterrainer, H. and Kapfhammer, H.-P. (2019) Psychobiology of Attachment and Trauma – Some General Remarks from a Clinical Perspective. Published online. https://doi.org/10.3389/fpsyt.2019.00914.

Lankelly, Chase (2015) *Hard Edges: Mapping Severe and Multiple Disadvantage in England*. Accessed at https://lankellychase.org.uk>publication>hard-edges. August 2023.

Levy, J. and Johnson, R. (2017) *Cross-Cultural Dialogues on Homelessness: From pre-Treatment Strategies to Psychologically Informed Environments*. Ann Arbor, MI: Loving Healing Press.

Littleton, R. and Lipsedge, M. (1997) *Aliens and Alienists: Ethnic Minorities and Psychiatry*. London: Routledge.

Maguire, N., Johnson, R., Vostanis, P., Keats, H. and Remington, R. (2009) *Homelessness and Complex Trauma: A Review of the Literature*. Accessed at https://eprints.soton.ac.uk/69749/. August 2023.

Masten, A. (2001) Ordinary magic: Resilience processes in development. *American Psychologist*. **56**:3 pp 227–238.

McCluskey, U. and Hooper, C.-A. (2000) *The Psychodynamics of Abuse: The Cost of Fear*. London: Jessica Kingsley Publications.

Mikulincer, M. and Shaver, P. (2012) An attachment perspective on psychopathology. *World Psychiatry*. **11**:1 pp 11–15.

National Lottery/Fulfilling Lives (2020) *Evaluation of the Impact of Psychologically Informed Environments*. Accessed at https://www.tnlcommunityfund.org.uk › insights. August 2023. https://revolving-doors.org.uk/wp-content/uploads/2022/02/BHM-Evaluation-of-PIE-2019-3.pdf

NHSE, National Health Service England (2023) *Spread and Adoption: Enabling Leadership*. Accessed at https://www.england.nhs.uk/spread-and-adoption/seven-interconnected-principles/leadership/. August 2023.

Nolan, M. (1995) *The Principles of Public Life*. Accessed at www.gov.uk/government/publications/the-7-principles-of-public-life. August 2023.

Northouse, P. (2007) *Leadership: Theory and Practice, 4th Edition*. London: Sage.

Obholzer, A. and Zagier-Roberts, V. (2019) *The Unconscious at Work: A Tavistock Approach to Making Sense of Organisational Life, 2nd Edition*. London: Routledge

Office for Health Improvement and Disparities (2022) *Working definition of trauma-informed practice*, published online. Accessed at www.gov.uk/government/publications/working-definition-of-trauma-informed-practice. August 2023.

Plsek, P. and Greenhalgh, T. (2001) The problem of complexity for healthcare. *British Medical Journal*. **323** pp 625–628.

Reddy, A. and Kamesh, A. (2016) Integrating Servant Leadership and Ethical Leadership. In M. Chatterji, L. Zsolnai (Eds) *Ethical Leadership*. London: Palgrave Macmillan.

SAMHSA (2014) *SAMHSA's Working Concept of Trauma and Framework for a Trauma-Informed Approach, National Centre for Trauma-Informed Care (NCTIC)*. Rockville, MD: SAMHSA.

Scottish Social Services Council (2016) *Enabling Leadership: Research to identify what good leadership looks like in Scotland's social services.* Accessed at https://www.stir.ac.uk/research/hub/publication/577614 August 2023.

Sweeney, A., Clement, S., Filson, B. and Kennedy, A. (2016) Trauma-informed mental healthcare in the UK: What is it and how can we further its development? *Mental Health Review Journal.* **21**:3 pp 174–192.

Uhl-Bien, M. and Arena, M. (2018) Leadership for organizational adaptability: A theoretical synthesis and integrative framework. *The Leadership Quarterly.* **29**:1 pp 89–104.

Van der Kolk, B. A. (2005) Developmental trauma disorder: Towards a rational diagnosis for chronically traumatized children. *Psychiatric Annals.* **35**:5 pp 401–408.

Van Dierendonck, D. (2010) Servant leadership: A review and synthesis. *Journal of Management.* **37** pp 1228–1261.

Part II

PIE Leadership: Implementation in Practice

Chapter 3

Embedding PIE into Care Services

A Leadership Experience

Iain Boag

Introduction

A strength of the PIE model is its capacity to be adapted for use in many different services – from the homeless sector to schools and prisons (Levy & Johnson, 2017) and from sport sciences to heart clinics (Dekker et al., 2023; Wagstaff & Quartiroli, 2023). The concept of being 'psychologically informed', then, resonates across a diverse field of human services and, as an increasing number of case studies show, may be applied wherever there is the determination to do so.

However, this quality of being so adaptable can, in my experience, lead to a lack of clarity about how to implement the PIE model. To some extent PIE principles and methods are invisible and therefore difficult to quantify (RDA, 2019). PIE literature to date provides few tangible examples for managers to action, rather, they are provided with a set of guiding principles from which they can develop their own PIE approach. Despite the PIE ethos resonating with them, time-poor managers may find this overwhelming. As we introduced PIE into my organisation, I found the most significant challenge was developing user-friendly guidance for the person-facing team as well as a concrete proposal for the senior directors to support. This process has been healthy and explorative, but time consuming.

The process of introducing the PIE framework has led me to question my own, and my organisation's approach to supporting people with complex trauma, and how we could do better. Before being introduced to PIE in 2016, most of the team would not have recognised the term 'complex trauma' nor known there was a burgeoning knowledge base around how to improve support for people who have experienced traumatic life events. The search for a clearer definition of what a PIE could look like in practice lead me to write a book, *Psychologically Informed Environment Principles in Adult Residential Care*, published in 2020. I wrote this to help create a clearer definition of PIE, which can become lost in a reductive message of 'just be kind' – a misunderstanding of the PIE and TIC concepts which is unfortunately prevalent within caring services.

Drawing from personal experience, statistics, personal communications, and PIE literature, this chapter explores how PIE has been introduced into St Martins, a charity in Norwich serving vulnerably housed and homeless people, and more

DOI: 10.4324/9781003415053-5

specifically at Highwater House, a dual diagnosis care home that I manage, which specialises in working with complex and challenging behaviour. The description of our PIE journey will provide examples of how leaders might introduce the framework at service and organisation level; examine what a PIE might feel like; give examples of successes and honest accounts of barriers; and look beyond, towards how PIE leaders can influence other organisations and systems.

As a manager my role is to link the senior directors' strategy with the actions of the frontline team, balancing the day-to-day realities of providing a service with the broader direction of the organisation. Although middle management is renownedly busy and stressful (Brower, 2023), the role holds the unique potential to connect different strata within an organisation. This role, then, exemplifies the PIE ethos that building and sustaining relationships is key to enacting change. While managers in the middle layer of an organisation may not have the capacity to easily influence the whole organisation, it is however possible to enact change both up and down the management structure, helping to create incremental, rather than explosive, change.

To introduce PIE successfully, managers must be willing to push the boundaries of traditional service development, rethinking, and redefining their approaches to leading. With the daily stresses of running a care home ever present, challenging myself and others to create change has inevitably been daunting at times. Inevitably, when you are close to change you may lack the objectivity to see it happening, and slow-moving systems can sometimes seem to allow services to stagnate. However, finding opportunities to step back and reflect – through, writing, training, and delivering presentations – gives us a chance to collate and evidence the real change that the PIE framework can bring. This leads to an enthusiasm to continue the process despite the (sometimes frustrating) slow nature of organisational development and change.

The change, then, lies first and foremost in the manager or PIE practitioner – the interested and willing participants who might, for example, choose to read a book on developing psychologically informed approaches. If they begin the process in themselves, then their language, actions, and behaviour will influence those around them. This pro-social modelling, deliberate and reflective, can be the spark which starts the change process in a service or organisation. Certainly, on a personal level, having worked for 15 years with the complex and challenging behaviour of chronically dislocated individuals on the 'frontline', typically driven by heavy substance use and poor mental and physical health, I now recognise that I was regularly working in a very reactive space – providing good, but prosthetic care. With little time to focus on reflective practice, the service was in a holding pattern of behaviour management characterised through explosive events (fights, aggression, deaths, self-injury) that were coped with by staff, but which often led to residents receiving exclusions or 'bans' from the home for a period. High stress situations were dealt with by largely formulaic 'de-escalation' responses. This tiring and ultimately unfulfilling approach to providing support meant I was eager to learn more when the PIE framework was introduced to me – the change it offered resonated deeply both individually and professionally.

We can draw an analogy between the lives of the service users and that of the service. Having witnessed hundreds of adrenalised fight or flight responses of team members and service users, I suggest that services, systems, and procedures themselves can become locked into a high stress, reactive state, where 'good enough' becomes an acceptable norm. The PIE framework can challenge this unfortunate status quo by changing the actions of the individual staff, the service user, and eventually the systems which contain them.

Using the PIE element *psychological awareness*, I have found three psychosocial models have helped to frame how a service can be improved, and these will be reflected upon throughout this chapter. They are the trauma informed care (TIC) approach, Dan Siegel's (1999) window of tolerance, and Maslow's (1943) hierarchy of need. Together they provide an excellent explanatory framework and point of reference for managers, prompting us to ask, as we strive to meet the needs of our service users, are our team's needs being met? As we focus on alleviating our clients' stress levels, are we also ensuring our staff, and the service itself, are functioning within their window of tolerance? And, as we busily cope with our day-to-day tasks, do we take the necessary time to reflect on the impact that working with complex trauma can have upon a team and service?

PIE and the Care Sector

The process of embedding PIE in a registered care home has been a hugely satisfying journey, and yet doing so has brought with it a host of challenges. The care sector is beset by underfunding and understaffing, and while there are high levels of legislative oversight, there is little money on offer to improve staff knowledge through training and development. These sector-wide stressors are echoed across other services providing support at the 'sharp edge' of care – homelessness, severe mental illness, and problematic substance use. The care sector is renowned for being time-poor, which can sadly lead to functional, task-orientated, or generic care provision as employees struggle to meet their responsibilities (Bottery, 2019). Carers can feel discouraged by the perceived lack of professional status and feel forced to focus on targets instead of providing good care (Oung & Hemmings, 2023). If staff don't feel that they are on their own journeys towards self-actualisation, how can they be expected to support residents on their own?

As the process of embedding PIE has developed within Highwater House and St Martins, the PIE model has gained traction across the UK homeless sector and beyond – being 'psychologically informed', alongside the trauma informed movement, is becoming an accepted short-hand for services that strive for best person-led practice. Against a background of austerity and cuts to social care, the PIE model has provided the team at Highwater House with a narrative which has helped to define and grow the best of person-led support. When asked why they are proud of the care they deliver, the team, without exception, speak in terms of resident involvement and of feeling invested in the home's community. The *feel* of the home is paramount to the care they deliver. The PIE model has helped to formalise, frame, and develop this intuitive, quality-driven approach to answering the needs of each resident. The use of the PIE model, then, has helped define the service through a new lens, moving away from service specifications and diagnostic models towards one that places the residents' experiences at the heart of every decision (Johnson & Haigh, 2010) – values driven and transformational, and reflecting the core PIE premise that services should take into account thinking, emotions, personalities, and past experience of its participants in the way it operates (Keats et al., 2012). In 2019, three years into the homes PIE journey, the change to the service was so clear that it was highlighted in our CQC inspection report which says

> A healthcare professional commented that the staff at Highwater House developed strong, trusting relationships with people using the service. The service promoted a kind, caring and empathetic culture using a new initiative Psychological Informed Environment (PIE) approach. This approach aims to reduce social exclusion and improve the mental health of homeless people. It also aims to improve staff morale and encourage positive interaction. PIE puts the relationships staff develop with people at the very heart of the care process.
>
> (CQC, 2019)

There has, then, in the face of cuts to funding and wrap around services, been a Pygmalion cycle between us introducing the PIE model and improving care practices, which has impacted how the service has been monitored and framed by external agencies. This in turn further consolidates the service as a PIE.

While the process to date can largely be viewed as positive, the development of PIE within the service and across the wider organisation has not been without its challenges. From introducing and defining PIE, delivering training, and rewriting policies and procedures, to managing person-facing staff, the challenge can feel daunting, not least knowing where to start. Enacting change is never easy and made all the harder by the non-statutory nature of PIE – it may resonate, but remain an outlier or non-essential element of service delivery.

Highwater House

Highwater House is a relatively unique service. As a dual diagnosis care quality commission (CQC) registered care home supporting 22 people the home faces multiple and diverse pressures as it supports an eclectic and diverse client group. All the residents at Highwater House have experienced homelessness and have a diagnosed mental illness as well as ongoing, often chronic, substance use issues. The social dislocation, trauma, and exclusion that each person we support has experiences have deeply impacted how they negotiate their lives, falling into patterns of destructive relationships, chaotic lifestyles, and dysregulated and challenging behaviour – a common outcome from experiencing multiple and complex trauma (Herman, 1997). Most have been supported by several statutory and non-statutory services for many years and have experienced mental health wards, prison, street homelessness, and social dislocation. This is the sharp end of residential care, where the social and clinical needs of an individual vie for primacy, often creating fractured identities and a fractious environment. To live at the home, a resident will have taken part in untold numbers of assessments, interviews, referrals, and evaluations. The sheer number of helping services can be overwhelming, with many residents feeling paranoid and persecuted even as the workers try to support and guide them towards stability or recovery (Boag, 2020).

The nature of CQC registered premises means there is strong oversight and legislation around providing care and support, while at the same time the service operates on the edges of usual care home provision. The complexity of this oversight can, much like the sheer number of support workers involved with each resident, be overwhelming. So, while the service is framed through its CQC rating, remit and specification, its percentage occupancy, statistics, its monitoring by funders, and risk assessments, a resident's experience will be defined through a network of social workers, psychiatrists, probation, keyworkers, care-coordinators, and housing officers. Managing this space can feel like a fraught balancing act between meeting the systems and individual's needs.

A service that is over-stretched, risk-averse, and focused on logistics and regulations will cause further stress for the residents. Residents will be assessed, risk managed, defined through their illness, or needs, with their 'person-ness' relegated to passing notes in their daily logs. Just as individuals can be pushed outside their pocket of optimal being, so too can services. Existing in a heightened and reactive state, beyond of their window of tolerance, services can become reactive and hypervigilant spaces. Aiming to meet the demands of multiple stakeholders, they can lose equilibrium and sight of their purpose.

Redressing the balance in favour of the people using the service, then, is key to providing good person-centred support. To do so, an explanatory framework which champions connection, relationships, and the social ecology of the service is crucial: a framework which can reframe the experiences of both staff and residents by placing their stories and experiences, their emotions, and psychological needs, at the forefront, rather than, for example, any costs or convenience of running the service (Johnson & Haigh, 2010).

If you were to walk into Highwater House today, the clinical aspects of the service wouldn't be obvious. It is unlikely that anyone would speak to you about the external pressures outlined above, or that any visitor would sense any stress or see overt busy-ness or bustle. Rather, at mealtimes they would see residents and staff sitting and eating together, sharing space, with few markers to differentiate the team members from the residents. They would experience a welcoming space, where the sharper edges of the system have been filed down to curves. Ultimately, they would feel as if they've walked into a *home*.

This 'feel' permeates the service and beyond and is tangible to visitors. For example, I was pleased to recently receive an unprompted email after a visit from a social worker who works on the local mental health wards: 'I think your service at

Highwater is brilliant. I've watched staff interact with residents – the whole atmosphere is lovely – and the food is great too' (private communication, 2023).

Practical Application of PIE

In 2016, the commissioner for adult mental health services in Norfolk tasked the team at Highwater House to pilot using the PIE framework, a first in adult registered care. We were lucky that a commissioner had made this request, which gave the PIE model credence. There was an expectation that we would action their request and develop the model. Importantly, we didn't therefore have to fight to introduce the model, and this support from the top down has been invaluable, continuing to this day. The interest in PIE from that commissioner has been passed on to her successor, and together we are now developing ways for PIE to be embedded into commissioning and evaluation systems across Norfolk. In Norfolk we have been very fortunate to have people at the commissioning level who are supportive and keen for the model to develop, and to help guide policy and future commissioning decisions.

Introducing PIE into the Service

The news that we would be introducing a new model of support was initially met throughout the organisation with muted enthusiasm. Some team members showed a degree of acceptance and interest, others were clear they felt a hefty dose of cynicism (Breedvelt, 2016). Circumspect staff, working in highly charged environments, felt that their skill set was being challenged (Boag, 2020). Team members used to the traditional power dynamics of 'us and them' were reticent to share more time and space with our 'challenging' residents. Fearful that there would be a breakdown of control, the team's behaviour was incidentally replicating stressful and disempowering relationships, particularly for the people with experience of the mental health system (Herman, 1997).

The process of introducing PIE into the service and wider organisation is ongoing, however, at service level, it was during the first three years that the greatest change happened. Initially a series of team meetings followed by training on PIE laid the foundations. We explored the five key elements we had learned about in our training and looked at ways that we could enhance the service using these guiding areas. These elements are psychological framework, environment, evaluation, relationships, and staff support and training.

Service Level

Before introducing PIE, the team had already been trained in areas such as motivational interviewing, challenging behaviours, risk management, and de-escalation. To develop our *psychological framework*, we bought in training on TIC and dialectical behaviour therapy, although it was TIC which resonated most, giving the team a psychological lens to understand complex behaviour. Later, as we rolled PIE out throughout the St Martins ecosystem, we have trained all of our teams on TIC.

A key benefit of this element is supporting leaders to reframe the language they use as they make changes within the service, and to define the service to stakeholders and interested parties. The PIE framework can support a service to frame its care choices as it is inspected and monitored by external agencies such as the CQC. Managers can use psychological lenses as tools to explain the processes driving their choices – this then helps further reinforce the service as a PIE.

We explored ways to make the *environment* more welcoming, initially as a physical space, and later concentrating on the social and emotional space. Due to budget restraints, changes we made were relatively basic, and every change had to comply with care regulations – negotiating restrictive Infection Prevention and Control legislation while creating a homely space can be relatively daunting. Other PIE literature has ably suggested changes that can be made to the physical environment (see the Psychologically Informed Environment Good Practice Guide and others) which we used as a scaffolding to make our own changes.

While physical adaptions undoubtedly had a positive effect, the most impactful change to the environment, and the most challenging for the team, came through directing the team to leave the main office, and to eat meals with and to use the same lounges as the residents. To this day, this manipulation of the social ecology of the home remains the most controversial, but most effective, PIE intervention that we introduced. Embedding the team into the same space as the residents creates a greater sense of equality, of power sharing, of shared ownership. While this was not necessarily a welcome intervention by teammates who have depended on the safety of separation, it has undoubtedly been a high impact, low-cost intervention. It is unequivocally the case that social and emotional distress and challenging behaviours will be managed more successfully in the moment, before they escalate, rather than through de-escalating an already fraught situation (Bourne, 2013). The most effective way to do this is by sharing a well-regulated space – that is, one regulated by trained and mindful workers. During this period, working as a deputy and then co-manager, I would often work weekends and evenings. As a key proponent of introducing PIE, this was invaluable as I could model the behaviour I wanted from the team, filling the quieter times of the day with quality-focused, accessible support. The team needed clear direction around this process, with some struggling to understand the purpose of being in the lounge and dining room instead of the office. I am certain that many of them became tired of my repeating of the mantras that relationships are healing and that community is curative.

Care homes are places of almost continuous assessment and *evaluation*, which can often be felt as threatening (Rogers, 2004). While introducing the PIE model could not remove the requirement of a high level of assessment, it did help us to question how this evaluation was taking place and consider different ways of approaching assessment. Small language shifts helped to soften the more bureaucratic aspects of the service. For example, rather than someone being brought to the service for an assessment, the language we use now is of a service introduction; instead of discussing risk management, we try to speak of meeting needs. The extra knowledge and confidence drawn from TIC training and improved psychological awareness allows this development to take place – the confidence to humanise the system one word at a time.

Carers are traditionally viewed as unskilled workers, and yet they spend more time with the residents than any other specialist worker, with the *relationships* they build creating positive change. The PIE model gave us the chance to raise the profile of the carers' connections and attachments, lending a new sense of professionalism to their daily routines. My mantra for this area of the framework is that people are paid per hour not per task and that every interaction can be an intervention (Treisman, 2020).

Honouring the bonds that develop between the service users, carers, and the service itself led to the creation of a 'parachute period'. Funding models usually require residents to make abrupt changes to their housing and support network as they move through the system, jettisoning emotional ties as they move to new providers. Recognising that this loss can unsettle people who have only just recalibrated their lives, leading them to use old adaptions (such as excessive substance use) to cope with the unknown we have built in a slow reduction of support from the team as the resident moves on. Working with the new service's team we invite their workers into Highwater House before the move and continue to visit the resident in their new accommodation for as long as they want us to. Ideally, as they settle into their new space, they will reject our support as they move on with their lives. This intervention is 'unfunded', but an important phase of relationship development and providing stability.

Reflecting on the models of TIC, the hierarchy of need, and the window of tolerance, we can see that providing reliable, accessible leadership, supported by trustable systems, will help provide teams with the consistency needed to work closely and collaboratively with distressed people. Without these foundations in place, delivered through *staff support and training*, managers cannot expect frontline workers to take the emotional risks associated with truly good work. If they don't feel safe, how can they provide safety? If they are not supported to feel successful and professional, how can they guide others towards recovery? Providing monthly reflective practice sessions run by an external provider without managers present promotes power sharing. Deliberately flattening the hierarchy and using a transformational approach to leadership models how the team can share power with the residents.

How Does the Service Feel Like a PIE?

The changes outlined above have deeply impacted the way we approached providing care and support within the service. As we adopted the PIE approach, we could see very quickly that the number of 'time-outs' from the home reduced, as did our use of emergency services and evictions. We were able to correlate these

Table 3.1 Highwater House Statistics 2016–2019

Event	2016	2017	2018	2019
Two-hour our time-out	104	68	60	48
Twenty-four hour time-out	7	2	2	2
Police called by staff	28	14	2	3
Untoward incident	67	53	20	18
On-site activity	560	959	2293	2662

reductions with the service having a less easy to measure 'feel' of calm. Importantly, the changes we made were managed by a relatively static team, and there was no obvious change in 'type' of client – they continued to be referred into the service as high risk, complex, challenging people who had few other options, and who had been evicted from many other services. Unfortunately, we didn't have the resources to undertake a true academic study of the process – we simply didn't know that the speed and quality of change was going to happen. And so, we have some quantitative evidence, a series of statistics, which we gather as part of our annual report which suggest a definite improvement in hard outcomes. Alongside these we have qualitative reports and case studies showing an improvement – less easy to define, but collectively they support the premise that we have moved the service closer to feeling like 'home'. Certainly, it runs firmly within its window of tolerance.

Table 3.1 shows the statistics we collected between 2016 and 2019 – we started to introduce PIE towards the end of 2016. For the purposes of collecting these figures, we consider an activity to be an engaged, focused period with a resident – a meaningful connection between two or more people. This might include a shared moment watching TV and talking, playing a game, going out for coffee, or a shared walk.

The figures clearly show that as the team were supported to focus more on creating shared spaces and, using a TIC lens, understand the positives of creating a greater equality within the service, the number of 'untoward' events, such as fights, self-harm, or other harmful events, reduced dramatically. As residents were supported in the moment to regulate their nervous systems and ground their distress through a more present, consistent team, there was less need for them to increase their dysfunctional behaviour as they attempted to solve their distress through self-medication or extreme actions. The challenge to their autonomy was reduced as points of power within the building, for example, the office, were left empty, and a shared space developed. It may be that simple social interventions become 'psychologically informed' when their purpose is therapeutic (Cockersell, 2018), certainly, if trustable attachments are the best means of alleviating distress (Allen, 2013), then being physically available is surely key to developing this.

Helping to showcase the work we had undertaken the service won an award recognising the PIE-focused changes we had made. The narrative of *becoming* a PIE began to move into *sustaining* a PIE – creating a continuously developing model of best, person-centred practice.

Organisational

Introducing PIE across the organisation remains an ongoing process rather than a destination we've reached. The framework has been introduced through a series of incremental changes which have been relatively organic. Again, as a middle manager, I have not had the capacity to enforce changes to policy and procedure, nor to introduce sweeping change, so I would characterise this period as one of consistent negotiation. My line manager has been supportive of the development of PIE within the organisation as has our CEO, however, that has not equated to PIE being placed centrally to the organisation's goals, rather it has been used as one of many developmental tools as the organisation has evolved.

At the outset of introducing the PIE framework, I was working as a deputy manager and so had little influence on the senior team. However, as previously noted, there was the great fortune of having a commissioner tasking us to introduce the framework – the conversation around using PIE, then, was started externally.

Following on from our PIE training at service level, and now a cheerleader of PIE, I enthusiastically wrote an organisation-wide three-year PIE plan and asked for it to be presented to the senior team. Seen below, I created SMART goals, including a statement of purpose, aims, and timeline. Although at the time I didn't feel confident that I would be able to influence the organisation, in fact, looking back, most of the targets have been achieved over time through incremental change.

St Martins PIE framework, delivered to the senior team in 2019:

Short-Term 6–12 Months

- Run a 'Working Together' steering group to provide a forum for all voices to be heard with representatives from all areas of the organisation.
- Introduce the PIE concept to all staff (using seminars, staff meetings and newsletter).
- Create a set of golden rules or standards for the trust which reflect PIE best practice.
- To organise lines of accountability for the PIE implementation period.
- To appoint PIE 'champions' across the trust (not necessarily managers).
- To increase roots to branches awareness of PIE.
- Set out an organisational PIE strategy and make this easily available (e.g., newsletter, website).
- Begin to embed a PIE 'language' of client-led 'emotion first' work.

Medium-Term 1–2 Years

- Provide the PIE champions with additional training.
- To create accessible information packs regarding therapeutic process and put online – e.g. cycle of change, solution focused, person centred, attachment, TIC, cognitive behavioural therapy (CBT), mentalisation based therapy (MBT).

- To make and strengthen contact with other organisations such as the local university.
- Champions feedback and forum.
- A communications strategy – increase focus on PIE in presentations and media
- Collect and collate statistics and anecdotal evidence.
- Focus on a user-friendly PIE 'interface' – a source of explanations and expectations made freely available.
- Work with a therapist to assist broader understanding of trauma informed care.
- Create an organisation-wide PIE policy.
- Support the development of reflective practice in all areas of the trust.
- Introduce counselling 'drop-in' service for service users.

Long-Term 3 Years

- To have embedded St Martins PIE 'language' across the trust
- To have updated policies to reflect PIE.
- Ongoing PIE assessments of services.
- To ensure all job specs are updated to incorporate PIE.
- All advertised jobs to mention PIE and be raised in interview.
- Longer-term reflective report and statistics.
- Stay abreast of changes and best practice.
- Create a reflective loop through champions who will 'self-train' and self-govern.
- Work with other organisations to create a Norfolkwide PIE forum led by St Martins to share knowledge and information.

While this framework was not officially adopted by the organisation, it provided enough of a roadmap to continue pushing the PIE agenda. I'm pleased to note that almost all these goals have been completed after four years and, evidenced through feedback, attendance at training, and changes to policy over that period, support for the PIE approach has increased dramatically throughout all areas of the organisation.

With the aim of further consolidating PIE into the organisation, and as a push for more recognition, I began to write articles for local care and support magazines, wrote pieces for internal newsletters and social media, and made PIE a central theme of my service's annual report to trustees. A personal interest in developing PIE led to publishing a book in 2020, mentioned above. We created an information drive to share the PIE ethos, and, as our statistics at the home began to show improvement in the residents' outcomes, also wrote numerous case studies promoting the changes we had put in place to share with social services and the local mental health trust.

Over time, I created a training programme for the organisation and trained all staff, and I continue to train on PIE for new starters. We created a PIE forum where interested teammates can meet and discuss the future of PIE at the organisation. Topics have included, how to evaluate clients without impacting their mental health; whether elastic tolerance means high tolerance; and how PIE might look differently across different services.

With the aim of rooting PIE into organisational systems, the forum created a PIE statement of purpose which impacts all policy and procedures and shows an organisational direction of travel, it begins

> As a learning organisation, St Martins strives to develop and deliver the very best care and support for people experiencing homelessness or who are vulnerably housed.
>
> Using the Psychologically Informed Environment (PIE) model, existing good practice will be enhanced, with a focus on person-led and strengths-based practices.
>
> St Martins views the PIE framework as a tool to promote continuous development, and as a point of reflection.
>
> The PIE framework is designed to be an operational framework which helps team members negotiate potentially complex and challenging workspaces.
>
> There are five key areas – or elements – to the PIE framework. These are - psychological awareness; environment; evidence and evaluation; relationships; and staff support and training. As each of these areas are developed, the organisation will move further towards best practice.

Over this period, I was promoted into the senior team which provided more scope to influence the direction of travel of the organisation. We have since embedded trauma informed questions into our interviews, and ensure PIE is mentioned in job advertisements as well as being prominent on our website.

Currently, the PIE forum is exploring how to embed psychologically informed language, with a view to create guidance for the whole organisation.

Systems

PIE supports teams to create spaces which honour the thoughts, feelings, and emotions of the service users. We have seen so far in this chapter that to create the sort of enabling environment which provides the frontline team members with the confidence to build authentic relationships, managers must focus on creating internal systems that focus on safety and support for all, reducing stress and promoting connection. Both PIE and TIC place at their core the importance of community in the quest to provide truly supportive services (Coccoma & Evans, 2014). Collaborative, mutually supportive systems promote engagement and fluidity of use. As service managers this asks us to look outward from our organisations, and to search for ways to connect into other human services, creating a lattice of best practice, a filament network stretching between organisations which shares knowledge, promotes best practice and drives a culture of human-centred growth.

Looking further afield, with a view to promoting the PIE framework into other care and support services, I regularly train students on the Approved Mental Health

Professionals (AMHP) course at the local university on PIE and TIC. It is through processes like this that the purpose of PIE becomes clearer. For example, it is likely that at some point one or more of these professionals will attend the home I run to detain a resident under the Mental Health Act, and if they do this with a psychologically informed approach in mind, the resident will be served well by the entire caring community. If the AMHP can approach the situation aware of the impact of compound trauma on residents' behaviour, then as they mindfully move through the home they will reduce the distress in other residents, helping to keep everyone safely inside their window of tolerance. The wider system if then working together to serve the distressed individual.

Using training opportunities to further promote the PIE message, I have worked with the University of Essex school of nursing to introduce PIE and TIC as part of a unit on working with complex and challenging patients. Invited to speak by the Norfolk care quality improvement board, I presented alongside a CQC representative to a broad range of providers from across the county, always looking for ways to share the psychologically informed message. Training other organisations creates a feedback loop of continuous development. Upholding the PIE ideal of collaboration, it places the trainer in a state of analysis and reflection as they learn from the services they are sharing knowledge with.

Casting further afield still, the commissioner for Norfolk adult mental health services and I are currently working on a county-wide PIE/TIC framework which could impact all services in Norfolk commissioned by the local authority. Further still, working alongside PIElink, we recently organised a valuable PIE and commissioning networking meeting. Attended by a broad sample of services from across the UK, we began to explore the possibility of developing a national PIE framework, with more meetings organised over this year.

Conclusion

The process of introducing PIE has been characterised through personal and professional growth, exhilarating moments of breakthrough and periods of frustration. While the relative freedom of being a deputy manager at the beginning of the process allowed me the time and space to fully explore and formulate a PIE plan, not having the influence within the organisation to fully enact it was, at times, exasperating. Progressing in my career, I have become increasingly time-poor, but have gained a louder voice to promote the psychologically informed approach.

The PIE journey of Highwater House and St Martins suggests that evidencing interventions and outcomes is paramount. Without performance indicators there is a risk of the PIE ethos being subsumed by other interventions or being lost amongst other organisational requirements. As a person-centred framework, it is through dialogue and qualitative evidence that PIE is best consolidated, so I would urge interested parties to consistently evidence interventions through case studies, articles, reports, and presentations. As shown through Highwater House's CQC report, PIE can provide proof of quality care and support.

To infuse PIE into services, managers should personally acquaint themselves with the psychological models they expect their team to adopt, and model behaviour by changing the language and procedures used day-to-day – small shifts in language and behaviour can create a large impact. Just as we expect service users to be adept at using the different terminologies of multiple support services, so too should we be ready to shift our language between the personal and organisational, taking the best of frontline interactions and embedding them into policies and procedures.

I suggest that managers should allow time for the team to adjust to new ways of working. Enforcing change will drive people towards the edges of their window of tolerance, creating stress in the service which will be felt by the service users. Consistently reflect with the team on the successes of working in a psychologically informed way.

Undoubtably, stressed systems and services will affect the most important re-source of any organisation, the team. This chapter has shown how embedding PIE on the frontline can improve outcomes for service users and therefore also support workers to have their physical and psychological needs met. Using PIE helps to frame their drive to care through a professional lens and places the connections they build at the forefront of their days' work. In turn, PIE can influence how ser-vices are run and shape systems and governance. Closing the loop, the influence of PIE at a strategic level then filters down and helps ensure that the end user, the resident, is provided with secure supportive relationships whose emotions and life story are always kept to the fore.

Effecting change begins with the individual. Through a symbiosis, their values suffuse into the services they lead and ultimately the systems which govern them. PIE provides the scaffolding to embolden caring professionals to take risks and to ensure that systems always favour the service user.

References

Allen, J. G. (2013) *Mentalizing in the Development and Treatment of Attachment Trauma*. London: Karnac Books.

Boag, I. (2020) *Psychologically Informed Environment Principles in Adult Residential Care*. Abingdon: Routledge.

Bottery, S. (2019) What's your problem, social care? The eight key areas for reform. The Kings Fund. Available at https://www.kingsfund.org.uk/publications/whats-your-problem-social-care (accessed December 2023).

Bourne, I. (2013) *Facing Danger in the Helping Professions*. Berkshire: Open University Press.

Breedvelt, J. F. (2016). *Psychologically Informed Environments: A Literature Review*. London: Mental Health Foundation. Available at https://www.mappingthemaze.org.uk/wp-content/uploads/2017/08/PIES-literature-review.pdf (accessed December 2023).

Brower, T. (2023) Middle Managers Have It Bad: 5 Things They Need Most. Forbes. Available at https://www.forbes.com/sites/tracybrower/2023/03/26/middle-managers-have-it-bad-5-things-they-need-most/ (accessed January 2024).

Care Quality Commission (2019) 'St Martins Housing Trust Highwater House Inspection report'. Available at https://www.cqc.org.uk/location/1-119736051 (accessed December 2023)

Coccoma, P. & Evans, A. (2014) *Trauma-Informed Care*. London: Routledge.

Cockersell, P. (Ed.) (2018) *Social Exclusion, Compound Trauma and Recovery*. London: Jessica Kingsley Press.

Herman, J. (1997) *Trauma and Recovery*. New York: Basic Books.

Johnson, R. & Haigh, R. (2010) Social psychiatry and social policy for the 21st century – New concepts for new needs: The psychologically informed environment. *Journal of Mental Health & Social Inclusion*. vol. 14, no. 4. Available at https://www.emerald.com/insight/content/doi/10.5042/mhsi.2010.0620/full/html (accessed December 2023).

Keats, H., Maguire, N., Johnson, R. & Cockersell, P. (2012) Psychologically informed services for homeless people. Available at https://www.researchgate.net/publication/313365226_Psychologically_informed_services_for_homeless_people (accessed January 2024).

Levy, J. S. & Johnson, R. (2017) *Cross-Cultural Dialogues on Homelessness: From Pre-treatment Strategies to Psychologically Informed Environments*. Ann Arbor, MI: Loving Healing Press.

Maslow, A. H. (1943) A theory of human motivation. *Psychological Review*. vol. 50, no. 4, pp 430–437. https://doi.org/10.1037/h0054346.

Oung, C. & Hemmings, N. (2023) Addressing social care workforce challenges: what can England learn from Wales, Scotland and Northern Ireland? Nuffield Trust. Available at https://www.nuffieldtrust.org.uk/news-item/addressing-social-care-workforce-challenges-what-can-england-learn-from-wales-scotland-and-northern-ireland (accessed December 2023).

Private communication from a mental health social worker, 22 December 2023 (2023)

Revolving Doors Agency (RDA) (2019) Birmingham Changing Futures Together: Evaluation of the impact of Psychologically Informed Environments. Available at https://revolving-doors.org.uk/wp-content/uploads/2022/02/BHM-Evaluation-of-PIE-2019-3.pdf (accessed December 2023).

Rogers, C. R. (2004) *On Becoming a Person*. London: Constable.

Siegel, D. J. (1999) *The Developing Mind: Toward a Neurobiology of Interpersonal Experience*. New York: Guilford Press.

Treisman, K. (2020) Every interaction can be an intervention. Youtube video by Dr Karen Treisman. Available at https://www.youtube.com/watch?v=8pBkXbCP3Q4 (accessed January 2024).

Wagstaff, C. & Quartiroli, A. (2023) A systems-led approach to developing psychologically informed environments. *Journal of Sport Psychology in Action*. vol. 14, no. 4, pp 227–242. Available at https://www.tandfonline.com/doi/epdf/10.1080/21520704.2023.2215715?needAccess=true (accessed December 2023).

Chapter 4

St Basils' Psychologically Informed Environments

Amanda Skeate and Jean Templeton

Introduction

St Basils

St Basils is a Registered Provider (Housing Association), a Registered Company and Charity with 50 years track record of providing a holistic range of accommodation and support services for young people aged 16–25 who are homeless, at risk or in conflict. We operate over 45 sites in Birmingham, Solihull, Coventry, Sandwell, North Worcestershire and Warwickshire offering a range of accommodation, prevention and support services.

We recognise that homelessness is fuelled by both systemic and personal issues. Whilst our services are focused on the individual, we contribute to national policy and systemic change.

We take an outcomes-focused approach providing a range of services based on an integrated pathway model, aimed at preventing both primary and secondary homelessness and increasing planned, successful transitions.

St Basils' Core Values

St Basils' unwavering philosophy predates our Psychologically Informed Environment (PIE) model. Firstly, there is a commitment to recognising that Young People aged 16–25 are developmentally different to adults. Of those we support, 20% are aged 16 and 17 and therefore legally children.

Secondly, it is not simply about housing Young People, but delivering a holistic approach to enable them to move on to a better future and reduce the risk of repeated homelessness. Stereotypes of homelessness can all too quickly attach themselves to Young People and trap them in a deficit world, focused only on need, risks and problems. Moreover, efforts often concentrate on the crisis at hand and can neglect wider consideration about the young person's future. Simply providing a roof over a young person's head for a commissioned period is extremely unlikely to influence their long-term negative trajectory. Factors that resulted in homelessness may continue unchanged, whether that

DOI: 10.4324/9781003415053-6

is poverty, lack of employment or other meaningful activity, unmet physical or mental health needs, or limited or non-existent family and community relational support.

We want young people who come to St Basils to have the opportunity to develop a different narrative; to have the safety, security and support to visualise a brighter future and take advantage of resources, friendships and opportunities. Some Young People will not have had an environment that nurtures their dreams, so first steps include a period of stabilisation and relationship building, so the Young People can start to recognise their strengths and ambitions. By supporting a young person not only to stabilise, but to start to identify and believe in their talents and skills, their worthiness, and provide opportunities to gain practical, educational and relational skills, they are more likely to build the confidence and self-esteem that can help transform those dreams into a reality.

The History of St Basils' PIE

Despite St Basils' strong commitment to a holistic approach, systemic barriers affect outcomes for a significant proportion of our Young People. We recognised that many homeless Young People had traumatic childhood experiences that continued to impact on their mental health and well-being. However, when seeking support from mental health services, St Basils' experience was that Young People never seemed to be a priority. Often the focus was on the young person's perceived self-defeating or uncooperative behaviours, along with judgement that they needed to take responsibility for changing. Emotional distress and problematic behaviour were often viewed as either part of adolescence and thus that they would grow out of it in time or attributed to a diagnosis of personality disorder and the perception that there was little that could be done about it.

A second obstruction is professionals' expectations of help-seeking Young People in homelessness systems. Systems created for adults can quickly become exasperated by typical adolescent behaviours. The young person is perceived as the problem, "This YP needs to take responsibility…" may be heard from exasperated workers when trying to support a young person who is impulsive, fails to consider consequences or assiduously avoids problems rather than face them.

Demands made of homeless Young People to achieve their independence quickly often differ significantly from the expectations of those living within a supportive family. Additionally, many of our Young People are care experienced, have histories of childhood trauma and meet criteria for diagnoses of neurodivergence, factors that are likely to affect cognitive and functional development.

To complicate matters further, on reaching 16 years of age, Young People and their helpers must navigate a myriad of age-related criteria, with eligibility for services and resources depending not only on age but on other circumstances such as whether they are enrolled in education or not. For Young People without resourceful family or other supportive adults, it is easy to fall through nets and to fail to secure vital services.

In such circumstances, homeless Young People, already struggling with the complexities of our mainstream systems, might feel overwhelmed and frightened, or angry at the unfairness. Behaviours related to these strong emotions may result in problematic presentations such as shouting, threatening or demanding; utilising substances to cope; or psychological distress with associated risks such as self-harm or suicidal thinking. Whilst academically the behavioural impact of these systemic challenges is compassionately acknowledged, in reality such presentations are generally met with further exclusion and marginalisation. In their survey, Homeless Link found that, of all refusals and declines to accommodation projects, 79% were due to the client being assessed as too high risk as opposed to their not having any vacancies (Homeless Link, 2015).

St Basils' PIE

It was in this context, in 2009, that the Department of Health (DoH) and Department for Communities and Local Government (DCLG now DLUHC) commissioned research into the mental health needs of single people who had experienced homelessness. We were pleased Young People were included and contributed to the research led by Dr Nick Maguire from the University of Southampton. The published report felt like a light bulb moment, providing a psychological paradigm for understanding the lasting impacts of complex trauma without pathologising Young People or ignoring structural reasons for Youth Homelessness such as lack of affordable housing. This published guidance was the first step in considering PIEs (Maguire et al., 2010).

Launch of St Basils' PIE

In 2011, the benefits and risks of a whole organisation approach were considered by our Board and a decision taken to invest in becoming a PIE. Led by the Chief Executive, implications, costs and intended impacts were carefully considered and a programme developed. As the first youth organisation to take a whole organisation approach, we were initially supported by pilot funding from DCLG and later by the London Housing Foundation to monitor implementation and share learning and impacts (Figure 4.1).

We take a holistic "strategic doing" approach at St Basils and used the social pedagogy model of 3H (Head, Heart, Hands) to plan the implementation of our programme.

The Head: Strategic Implementation

With the support of Dr Maguire, along with involvement from applied psychologists and therapists from the local Youth Mental Health service, senior leaders came together to consider objectives, resources, and develop a clear action plan. In June 2011, the PIE approach was launched with a staff conference emphasising that this was a substantial programme, different from a one-off training course.

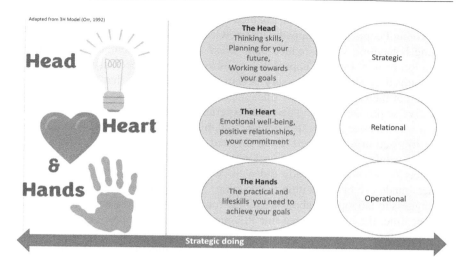

Figure 4.1 3H (Head, Heart, Hands) Model (Orr, 1992)

The training component followed, including all colleagues in what later became known as St Basils' PIE Foundation Training course. This initial phase was undertaken over four months and took considerable effort to coordinate whilst simultaneously delivering busy services. However, it was felt to be valuable, to reinforce the mission of establishing a whole organisational approach. Shortly after training, scheduled reflective practice sessions in small groups started. Different configurations of participants and formats were tested at this stage, until a suitable framework was established.

Led by Dr Nick Maguire, all training and reflective practice sessions were delivered and facilitated by applied psychologists and therapists. Advantages to this model became evident: for St Basils it removed the need to identify and train individuals internally and ensured the content and delivery was of a high standard, and it provided colleagues with regular access to professional support for situations where mental health problems factored. Reciprocity in the arrangement was perceived by the local Youth Mental Health team who committed to the partnership as a way of extending and improving targeted services for Young People most likely to have experienced complex trauma but who were unlikely to benefit from standard community mental health provision.

The Heart: Relational

Fundamentally PIE is a relational approach corresponding to our existing philosophy. PIE provided a robust platform to give further attention to understanding the potential and value of relationships at different levels. We believed Young People would benefit from building relationships with staff who helped them feel heard and validated, whilst colleagues, enabled to feel more confident in their approach with Young People and equipped with knowledge to understand confusing or challenging behaviour, would reduce their stress and avoid potential burnout. Consideration of how the PIE approach was introduced was necessary to avoid staff perceiving it as either unnecessary because "we already do that" or worse, as a criticism of their current work. Colleagues in the homelessness sector are likely to have diverse professional and personal experience and recognising this was important: it was necessary to create a context that minimised the risk of colleagues feeling patronised or undermined. From the start of training, there is a clear, explicit narrative valuing all attendees, an acknowledgement of expertise and an invitation to reflect on what they already did well. Where participants had specific skills, trainers made use of this within the training. This approach increased colleagues' willingness to talk openly about what they found difficult and wanted to improve.

Over time, the evidence that our PIE model is about people – all of us – has become compelling. Our PIE approach has developed to emphasise that all staff from senior leaders to frontline colleagues need to reflect first on their own emotions, reactions and behaviours before considering those of others. Encouraging self-reflection and providing tools to promote a better understanding of our own behaviour advances learning to understand others and reduces attitudes that artificially separate clients as different or abnormal. To sum up, PIE is not just about learning why "others" behave in the way they do, but examines the reasons why we behave in the way we do and the interactions between.

The Hands: Operational

For all St Basils' employees, PIE Foundation Training was mandatory and attendance at reflective practice sessions a priority. Training comprises one day for all at St Basils, with a further two days for frontline staff and managers spread over a few weeks. Initially, an additional session was organised for managers, to support their confidence with embedding and nurturing what had been learnt. The Senior Leadership team attended training with colleagues and over time our Board members also participated.

As the PIE programme rolled out, the psychologists quickly observed the need to reflect on the different views of this initiative, with some perceiving it as a welcome development opportunity and others a threat or even an unwelcome burden. A psychologically informed approach to this organisation-wide change was considered by leaders at different levels. Managers' positive participation in training and discussions with their teams about the application of PIE to their local setting were key to implementation.

Considering what "better" would look like within a PIE meant identifying not only outcomes for Young People but examining staff and organisational improvements too. Our impact monitoring took account of outcomes for Young People and staff within the overall context of organisational change. Staff and Young People communicating well and collaborating on goals would improve positive change such as building resilience and capability to enable Young People to move on and sustain independence in a challenging environment. Additionally, it would reduce the frequency of incidents and unplanned departures resulting in benefits at an organisational level. For colleagues, having skills, attitudes and behaviours to deliver high-quality psychologically informed services results in benefits to their own well-being and job satisfaction.

Developing a Psychological Framework

It was important that our PIE model had a clear structure, where training and reflective practice sessions are clearly linked. A PIE approach that lacks a central coherence, where training draws upon theoretical models which differ from those used in reflective practice, can result in people feeling confused. Additionally, training that focuses on psychological theory and research with little explanation about how that can be translated into practical application results in people having to interpret what is expected of them and is likely to increase disengagement with the process.

Our view is that a PIE includes an understanding of trauma but is broader as it considers other human behaviours as well. In this way, it helps us to understand the power differential that can arise between the helper and the help-seeker, and how this can be misused.

A wealth of literature informs us about how to build up relationships with other people, particularly with those perceived to require some type of help. There are models of how to engage people in collaborative conversations about their future dreams, and research evidence about supporting people to change unhelpful behaviours, overcome obstacles and build resilience. Much of this literature comes from a base of mental health therapy and counselling, but also from occupational psychology and the field of business leadership and change. This literature almost universally describes the need to build connection and trust, to find ways to work collaboratively and to provide the scaffolding to facilitate an individual to make their own changes rather than to force or coerce a person to change.

However, in spite of this consistent evidence-base, most humans across environments instinctively tend to try and achieve change in others from a position of powerful "expert", using tools such as instruction, persuasion and coercion. Furthermore, if the person we are wanting to "help" fails to follow our guidance and advice, we can end up feeling frustrated, perceiving our time and valuable knowledge is being ignored or wasted, and resorting to sanctions and exclusions, coercion in fact.

PIE for Young People Services

Incorporated into PIE Foundation Training and reiterated in reflective practice sessions is knowledge specific to this client group and the developing adolescent brain (Blakemore, 2018). Adolescence is a time of instability, even in the absence of significant trauma, and tasks of achieving adulthood, developing your identity, values and goals can be challenging. This appreciation helps to provide an environment more tailored to the needs of our Young People.

Through our PIE approach, we aspired to create a service where the workforce has this psychologically informed understanding of relationships and can actively apply the tools directly with Young People, to people management and to external partnerships. The approach augmented the pre-existing culture of strengths-based practice and empowerment and helped create better understanding of a young person's behaviour within a historical or systemic context.

The St Basils' Model

A transtheoretical model, the St Basils' PIE Pyramid, provides a structure that serves to remind us about the steps in our relational approach, whilst our C-Change values provides a framework to guide us through those steps (Figure 4.2).

The St Basils' PIE Pyramid provides a visual outline of the steps for engagement and reflective interaction. Based on the evidence-base for developing therapeutic relationships, it starts by reminding the PIE practitioner that to successfully engage another person we need to start and encounter by really hearing what is being communicated and then validating this. There is a temptation to miss out these first two steps and launch into a more directive or instructional conversation; listening can feel counter-intuitive, particularly when working with a youthful population. However, there is a wealth of evidence from motivational theory (Rollnick et al., 2008) that confirms that this strategy will lead to better rapport, as the person senses that

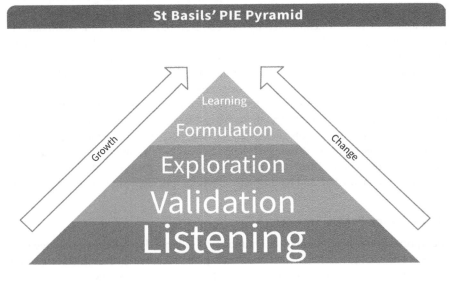

Figure 4.2 PIE Pyramid

they are being accurately heard and their experiences acknowledged and understood. Through PIE activity, colleagues learn to appreciate that, whilst they hold valuable knowledge, a Young People's expertise on their own history, experiences and feelings is as important.

Once rapport and trust are a little more established, then together the PIE practitioner and help-seeker can move up the pyramid by being curious and asking questions to explore situations in more detail. This step facilitates reflection on the situation and an opportunity to gain a deeper understanding, perhaps by considering different perspectives or linking separate elements to discover how they interlink. Through this dialogue, sense-making or formulation can develop for both the PIE practitioner and help-seeker. The process of formulation can support a more reflective understanding, providing an alternative to our natural unconscious human programming that treats first impressions, judgements and beliefs as factually correct.

The pinnacle of our PIE Pyramid is learning for both PIE practitioner and help-seeker. In our field, this might be the young person learning from their worker's advice, but equally, the PIE practitioner may learn more about an individual and how they need to be supported. Learning might be a significant insight into an unhelpful pattern or behaviour, or it may be detecting the next small step to get closer to a greater goal.

Importantly, it is recognised that all these steps contribute to processes of growth and change for both the PIE practitioner and help-seeker; listening and validation provide the bedrock of a mutually respectful relationship that supports reflection and increased self-awareness. Shared exploration and formulation can lead to critical learning for both parties. Significantly, this structure delineates the shift in the traditional paradigm of powerful "expert/professional" assuming control or responsibility and directing or teaching the help-seeker.

Intertwined with the PIE Pyramid, St Basils' C-Change Values framework defines 12 qualities that PIE practitioners are encouraged to reflect on, develop and practise. Familiar to therapists, these qualities serve as a template or guide for all types of interaction beyond the counselling room, enhancing relationships at all levels: frontline colleagues with Young People, managers with their team and the organisation with its workforce (Figure 4.3).

Starting from a position of care and compassion, we are reminded that to be able to remain in a reflective state calmness is a requirement. As described in our PIE Pyramid, our first aim is to connect or attune with the other person, to foster a collaborative relationship. After socialisation into ascribed roles of expert/help-seeker or manager/staff this may require an attitudinal shift for both parties: collaborating with others poses the never-ending challenge that as individuals what connects us to one person will not necessarily be meaningful to another. We encourage the aspiration to be creative in the way we seek to relate to others and to remain curious, as opposed to becoming frustrated or critical. Young People often tell us that systems and processes in homelessness settings can be challenging and confusing: aiming for consistency in our approach across service settings can help Young People to feel contained and reduce some of this frustration.

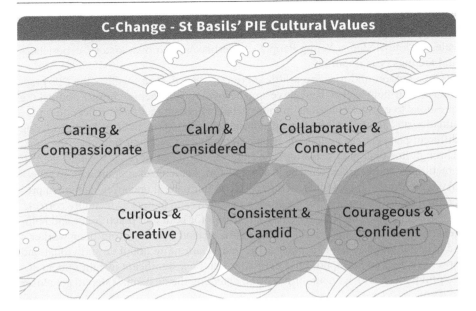

Figure 4.3 C-Change Cultural Values Famework

In our early days of becoming a PIE organisation, the approach was sometimes depicted as soft or lenient, with exclusive focus on tolerance. In our journey, we have sought to learn the art of being more candid in our conversations. This does not prohibit praise, encouragement and offers of help, but includes discussion about realistic expectations, behaviours that are unsafe, and boundaries that need to be maintained for the benefit of all. More recently, Young People have defined this need for consistency and candour in their creation of Youth Standards: "Communicate expectations, rights, responsibilities and co-develop house rules with Young People" (Standard 1) and "Be friendly, approachable, and fun but keep boundaries clear and consistent" (Standard 6).

Finally, our ambition is that all managers and colleagues have courage and confidence to perform their roles to a high standard. This can take many forms from advocating for a Young People who is experiencing a system which is not trauma informed, offering another opportunity to a Young People who may be challenging systems, or being confident to continue to reflect on ourselves about whether practices and processes are aligned with our values.

Building, Establishing and Maintaining a PIE

Working to become a PIE is the business of culture coherence and takes time, and we quickly recognised that our implementation programme would require constant attention. Initially, we focused on training, reflective practice and applied PIE learning to managing frontline situations. Our learning over a decade is that PIE training and reflective practice sessions do not automatically precipitate behaviour change without other strategies in place. Moreover, the challenge of PIE is that it is not prescriptive, but extremely complex by its very nature. Thus, we started to view all our policies, processes, systems and environments from a psychological lens. As our understanding developed, we have been better able to slow things down and review inconsistencies and incompatibilities in our approach. It is a great leveller and requires everyone to understand better why and how we behave as humans, and the impacts of those behaviours on each other.

As PIE implementation developed, utilising an iterative process helped to harness learning and make improvements. Training was advanced through attendees' feedback and ensuring it was psychologically informed not only in content but in how it was delivered. Over time, we learnt to see development and learning as continual, and our PIE approach has evolved and deepened rather than lurching into "next new thing syndrome". It is generally not an "either/or" situation but rather enhancement, focus and perspective which enriches our PIE.

As a frontline worker focuses on listening attentively to build rapport with Young People, it became clear that developing new processes needed to start by listening to different perspectives and welcoming challenge – which sounds easier than it often is in practice. It has taken many years before our staff would confidently say that they worked within a PIE and be able to describe what that meant.

Hearing Our Young People

At the heart of PIE training is learning about how childhood trauma and abuse can manifest later in young adulthood and may negatively affect relational and functional behaviours. Being able to comprehend how anti-social or self-defeating behaviours relate to adverse childhood environments promotes compassion and insight. With this knowledge, staff can listen to Young People's verbal and non-verbal communication, observe behaviours and then formulate why Young People may reject offers of assistance when in need of help, exhibit behaviours that are harmful to themselves or others or seem compelled to form unhealthy relationships. For staff, this awareness can reduce frustrations and give insights to promote validation. Furthermore, it empowers staff to be curious to learn more, and be creative in finding ways to connect and engage.

Co-design with Young People and colleagues is another critical example of listening. Young People have developed 12 Youth Standards[1] which have been adopted by our Board. These standards ensure that what is important to Young People is at the heart of how we operate. Accountability is strengthened each year, as these standards are reviewed by our Youth Advisory Board in consultation with Young People across our services. The findings are presented to our main Board and the action plan responding to the recommendations is owned by the Chair and Chief Executive.

Validation has resulted in the development of a range of services to meet the diverse needs of Young People including Live and Work schemes for working young people without the benefit of family support, and specialist provision for serially excluded Young People.

Hearing Our Colleagues

As well as being guided by the voices of Young People, paying more attention to colleagues at all levels became integral to our improvements. This meant leaders within St Basils enhancing compassionate and collaborative relationships with colleagues. By the very nature of becoming a PIE, the toll on the frontline colleagues increased in specific situations: as colleagues developed deeper connections, young people were more likely to feel safe and disclose information about their experiences of trauma and abuse. Additionally, our mission to reduce evictions in the context of extreme problematic and antisocial conduct results in staff having to countenance and creatively manage these behaviours. As Francoise Mathieu states in her book on Compassion Fatigue:

> The expectation that we can be immersed in suffering and loss daily and not be touched by it is as unrealistic as expecting to be able to walk through water without getting wet.
>
> (Mathieu, 2012, p. 7)

Contextual factors: delivering frontline services during the coronavirus lockdowns, long-term underfunding in housing, support, health and social care within a commissioning landscape of "do more for less", and, most recently, the economic downturn with the cost-of-living crisis have all impacted on colleagues. Many services in housing and care sectors have struggled with a negative cycle of poor staff retention and increased burdens on the remaining workforce, resulting in burnout and absence from work.

The PIE Pyramid model guides managers through steps of listening, validation and exploring with our colleagues, understanding their perspectives and making sense of situations through formulation. Listening in multiple forums such as our Employee Council, Performance and Development Reviews, and staff feedback surveys was integral to this process. This was not simply reminding the workforce to engage with self-care strategies: it is understood that care staff who are exhausted and traumatised are more likely to overwork (Mathieu, 2012) and neglect their own well-being. It also meant presenting evidence across the organisation that compassion and care towards the workforce ultimately engender better environments and outcomes for all, including Young People who need our services. Learning together about burnout, vicarious and secondary trauma, and the workforce perceiving C-Change values are as applicable to themselves as to Young People, have been essential. Candour around the fact that, as a Homeless charity, staff will be exposed to narratives around trauma and encounter anti-social behaviour has been balanced with a commitment to mental health through the provision of incident debriefing, counselling, well-being opportunities and recognising and celebrating achievements.

Leaders are continually challenged in this dimension in calibrating compassionate understanding of all involved, maintaining everyone's safety, and finding ways to support colleagues to manage the transference of strong emotions. However, the narrative related to self-care is consistent: compassion and care towards oneself is not a selfish act but as important in a PIE as caring for Young People and our colleagues.

Changes to Core Practice

We have learnt that our PIE framework cannot rely solely on improving understanding about how trauma affects Young People if we want to foster a change in our organisational behaviour. Equally important is to promote self-reflection in the workforce, to understand our own emotions, needs, triggers and motivations.

Without considering our own motivations for wanting a Young People or staff member to change their behaviour, we may act in ways that are controlling or unhelpful. In addition to training and reflective practice sessions, St Basils made a conscious decision by renaming frontline Support Workers to "Progression Coaches". For Young People, it felt that the concept of having a "coach" held less stigma; for workers, it helped to convey the sense that their role was to provide the resources for Young People to achieve their goals, not to take responsibility and make decisions on their behalf. Valuing engagement from Young People in service delivery and design and promoting the voices of those with lived experience of homelessness and mental health difficulties within the workforce has also been critical to change.

Secondly, to reduce eviction and maintain motivation when working with Young People who present with challenging or confusing behaviour, it was important to reflect on reasons why compassionate staff struggle to adhere to our "Calm and Considered" C-Change value when triggered by certain situations. PIE Training comprises developing self-awareness about our own emotional state and recognising situations that destabilise this. Without the ability for emotional regulation and to pause when faced with a situation that may be frightening, frustrating or upsetting, we have limited ability to effectively interact and promote calmness with others. Drawing upon Marsha Linehan's States of Mind model (2014), training advocates a process of self-reflection in order to be more effective when responding to an emotionally charged situation. Other models that convey the build-up and loss of emotional control in the presence of a perceived threat such as Professor Siegel's "Flipping your Lid" Hand model (2020) have also proven beneficial. The need for PIE tools has proven particularly pertinent in a new service for serially excluded Young People, where behaviours that challenge are frequent and often more intense than would previously have been expected.

Reflective Spaces

Without a culture established around reflection, these changes to practice would not have become widespread and would be more reliant on individuals' preference of approach. As an organisation the infrastructure to support PIE training and reflective practice sessions was crucial. Managers were key to the success, ensuring staff are released from their duties, promoting attendance and modelling the value by participating themselves. Reflective practice sessions were designed to provide opportunities for reviewing PIE models and tools and the opportunity to apply them to real-life situations.

Careful consideration of configurations of groups was important when first establishing reflective practice sessions. From having mixed groups in the initial six months, the differing needs of frontline staff and managers become evident. For colleagues in the field, the focus of the reflective group is generally on Young People and developing self-awareness. In contrast, frontline managers tend to demonstrate excellent skills and confidence in working with Young People, which was often what resulted in their recognition and promotion within the organisation, so managers utilise their peers to construct a psychologically safe place to be open and feel validated and to consider application of the PIE model to more systemic challenges.

Reflective practice sessions have become so embedded in our organisational routines that, following the first lockdown during Covid, they were quickly re-established, along with training in online formats.

It is important to recognise that this reflective culture would not have embedded if exclusively reliant on reflective practice sessions. Managers are critical in leading by example and providing opportunities for teams to reflect in everyday situations such as team meetings, 1:1 supervisions and Performance Development Reviews.

Changes at an Organisational Level

Often policies and procedures are designed to protect the organisation, sometimes at the expense of the help-seeker or others who may wish to challenge the organisation. For example, a zero-tolerance policy towards abuse, without reflection about unintended consequences, seems a positive step in providing a safe environment for those working in that setting. However, this can reinforce experiences of rejection and isolation for those people with the greatest needs. As the PIE approach influenced attitudes, judgements and perspectives of Young People at an individual level, our policies and procedures were examined to review whether they aligned with practice.

Similarly, it is acknowledged that legislation, commissioning processes and other systemic factors may produce unintended challenges for a PIE approach. Staff often struggle with contradictions in demands: Young People are the priority, but significant time is spent on recording and reporting to provide evidence to secure further funding. Managers being candid and openly acknowledging this tension between competing priorities with frontline colleagues, rather than ignoring this, are more likely to harness cooperation and collaboratively find a way forward with their teams.

Evaluating Our PIE Approach

An important domain of the original PIE model (Johnson & Haigh, 2012), drawing upon evidence-based research and evaluating outcomes to monitor performance, has been integral to our approach from the start. When embarking on our PIE journey, we developed key performance indicators (KPIs) based on information that was already collected in order to have a baseline comparison. Overtime, KPIs have changed to meet our priorities, and we have invested in effectively utilising practice-based evidence to inform our approach.

St Basils has hugely benefited from independent evaluation and rigour through collaboration with the University of Birmingham Business School and Department of Sport, Exercise and Rehabilitation.[2] After five years, in 2016, UoB psychologists undertook an independent survey with staff examining attitudes and beliefs around PIE and its impacts, reporting on job satisfaction, burnout, work engagement, and PIE knowledge and ability. As part of their work, they developed a theory of change model for PIE, to scrutinise how it works and what elements are important. UoB also provided evaluation around a specific Care Leavers' project exploring the differences between a St Basils' PIE setting and typical specialist care provision. Findings demonstrated favourable outcomes for Young People at St Basils at a significant cost saving.

Whilst listening to feedback from Young People and staff has always been critical, we have become more refined in how we design surveys and collect and analyse data. For example, Young People were supported to design the Young Person's Survey focused on what they believe was important, mapped onto ambitions related to our PIE model, such as staff creating an environment that was welcoming. More recently in 2022, an audit of St Basils' Youth Standards provides guidance about where performance was high and where there were areas for improvement. Importantly, this information is published to key stakeholders including staff and is influential in bolstering motivation through highlighting strengths in the face of contextual challenges.

Leadership in a PIE

Our learning over the past 12 years is that commitment and implementation have to be intentional and perpetual. This is not a "sheep dip" approach. It is much harder if PIE implementation is seen as an approach specifically for frontline colleagues or for certain teams, sometimes funded through short-term funding. If the motivation is not clear or may be for contract compliance purposes rather than a deeper consideration of the benefit to the organisation and its stakeholders, then impact is likely to be limited or even be counterproductive. In these circumstances, frontline colleagues have been quick to detect that the only change that is being proposed is to how they deliver a service to their clients. Questions such as "why should I think in a valuing way about my client, if the organisation does not value me?" are asked, and buy-in to the message of the PIE approach is diminished.

You don't "boss" within a PIE organisation and you can't "boss" people into being psychologically informed. In the same way as staff are unlikely to change a Young People's entrenched behaviour by instructing them, as a leader within a PIE organisation you need to commit to becoming psychologically informed in your own approach. You need to ensure that your leadership structure applies the learning to strategy, policy, procedures and relationships both internally and externally. You need to ensure that you do not live in an echo chamber and are open to challenge and different perspectives. You need to understand power differentials and the impacts of structural inequalities on systems. You need to be willing for it to become part of your organisation's DNA. Furthermore, to achieve a whole organisational approach, all of the workforce needs to have a sense of ownership and pride in the achievements, as opposed to the programme being the responsibility of a few leaders.

PIE Support for Frontline Managers

For frontline managers, particularly those colleagues engaging in practice that did not align with PIE found the application of the PIE framework transferred from Young People to working with their teams challenging: it was not an automatic process for everyone and required reflection and dialogue. It was helpful to remember that human beings are not designed to operate in a reflective way when faced with a level of physical, psychological or social threat. In fact, learning from neuroscience provides understanding how capacity to reflect, solve problems and control emotions becomes impaired when we perceive we are under attack. Providing safe and confidential spaces for managers to reflect on their own beliefs and judgements about these situations and sharing practical examples of using PIE tools to resolve difficulties enhanced our whole organisational PIE approach.

Applying a Theory of Change Model (Prochaska & DiClemente, 2005) helped managers evaluate where individual colleagues or whole teams were in terms of adopting PIE skills in their everyday practice. Appreciating that a new colleague might be "pre-contemplative" – not yet interested or perceiving change as a priority – in their PIE learning informs the required response. In such a case, there is a need to engage and utilise a motivational approach if attitudinal and behaviour change is going to occur. Similarly, reinforcing PIE principles such as engaging in self-care, and validating feelings of frustration and disappointment, can help colleagues experience and value the PIE approach.

In a PIE, the tension between the needs of Young People and rights of frontline staff require leaders to hold multiple perspectives and recognise that these may converge or conflict. Young People who have faced discrimination and abuse require a validating, compassionate environment, with an understanding of behaviours that may challenge, to avoid cycles of repeated homelessness. However, ignoring the detrimental impact on colleagues results in them perceiving an organisation as uncaring, feeling devalued, traumatised and resentful, and therefore unable to work in a PIE way. Support work is generally not a highly paid profession and a proportion of colleagues will have personal experience of discrimination, abuse or bullying. Validating staff experience in a diverse West Midlands workforce resulted in reflecting on our PIE approach in the context of structural inequalities and seeing the approach through an anti-racism, anti-homophobic and feminist lens. There is no prescriptive approach to this type of situation; instead leaders must work with colleagues and provide a platform for conversation, making the dilemma explicit and helping people to feel safe to express their concerns and work together on resolutions that are positive for all.

Conclusion

Whilst a perfect "Psychologically Informed Environment" does not exist, with enduring commitment and sustained effort, St Basils has incrementally developed our PIE approach to become part of our DNA. Training is an important element of our programme, but without reflective practice sessions and a range of other strategies, cultural change would not have been accomplished. Over the past 12 years, establishing an effective balance between improvement through iterative and reflective feedback, whilst maintaining sufficient consistency for staff to experience a coherent programme, has required continual attention. Clarity around our overarching vision and outcomes, along with engagement and coproduction with Young People and colleagues at all levels, has been integral to this process.

For us at St Basils, complacency is not an option. In order to meet young people's individual needs within a complex and changing environment, we need to ensure that our approach remains relevant, human, personalised and understanding of structural and systemic inequalities. We need to learn from the rapidly expanding evidence-base around trauma, compassionate leadership and organisational practice in order to further transform our systems and processes and also to influence the wider systemic change required within universal systems. What is certain is that to achieve these things will take a collaborative and creative effort from all: leaders, colleagues, partners and the young people who use our services.

Notes

1   St Basils' young people create 12 youth standards to "build back better" post COVID.
2   Almost £1 million of public funds saved thanks to programmes to get young residents into work (stbasils.org.uk).

References

Blakemore, S. (2018) *Inventing Ourselves: The Secret Life of the Teenage Brain*. London: Penguin Random House.

Homeless Link (2015) *Support for Single Homeless People in England: Annual Review*. London: Homeless Link.

Johnson, R. & Haigh, R. (Eds) (2012) *Complex Trauma and Its Effects: Perspectives on Creating an Environment for Recovery*. Brighton: Pavilion.

Linehan, M.M. (2014) *DBT Skills Training: Manual*. New York: The Guilford Press.

Maguire, N., Johnson, R. & Vostanis, P. (2010) *Meeting the Psychological and Emotional Needs of Homeless People*. London: DCLG.

Mathieu, F. (2012) *The Compassion Fatigue Workbook: Creative Tools for Transforming Compassion Fatigue and Vicarious Traumatization*. East Sussex: Routledge, Taylor & Francis Group.

Orr, D. (1992) *Ecological Literacy: Education for a Postmodern World*. Albany, NY: State University of New York. [Google Scholar].

Prochaska, J.O. & DiClemente, C.C. (2005) The transtheoretical approach. In Norcross, J.C. & Goldfried, M.R. (Eds) *Handbook of Psychotherapy Integration*. 2nd Edition. Oxford: Oxford University Press.

Rollnick, S., Miller, W.R. & Butler, C.C. (2008) *Motivational Interviewing in Health Care: Helping Patients Change Behavior*. New York: The Guildford Press.

Siegel, D.J. (2020) *The Developing Mind: How Relationships and the Brain Interact to Shape Who We Are*. 3rd Edition. New York: The Guildford Press.

Chapter 5

PIE and Violence Against Women and Girls Work

Jennifer Cirone

Setting the Scene – Violence Against Women and Girls Sector in the UK

There are a large number of voluntary sector organisations providing services to survivors of Violence Against Woman and Girls (VAWG) within the UK. These range from small, grassroots organisations, addressing unmet need and providing specialist support to local communities, to medium-sized enterprises and a small number of organisations with large geographical or national reach. Whilst most of these organisations consider themselves specialist women's sector organisations, some providers are larger organisations that have later developed women's specialties from a more generic service model that was originally designed to meet the needs of homeless men. Tensions can exist between these organisations not just because of ideological differences in approach but also due to competition for available resources; generic organisations traditionally have a lower cost base that can be used to subsidise specialist work than highly specialised providers. There is also competition between larger and smaller organisations. This tension is particularly felt where smaller, often "by and for" grassroots, organisations perceive that larger organisations, who have greater capacity to build and utilise infrastructure to secure funding, are applying for, and are successful in winning, a greater share of funding.

The sector is supported by some second-tier membership organisations providing campaigning and public affairs work that many organisations do not have the capacity to do on their own. Much service provision is focused on meeting crisis needs, such as safe accommodation for women and children to flee to, and community-based support, often prioritised for those assessed to be at the highest risk of harm. Provision for medium- to longer-term needs such as therapy, group work, and child and parent work can be patchy, are often funded for a year at a time and therefore only partially able to meet needs. In the UK, in contrast to many other countries, many services operate from confidential locations, with most funded on a short- to medium-term basis from local, rather than central, government.

DOI: 10.4324/9781003415053-7

Who Do We Work with?

The author's organisation works with survivors of different types of VAWG – this includes domestic and sexual abuse, so-called "honour-based" abuse, stalking and harassment, including offences facilitated by the use of technology. Other work includes working with children and young people as preventative work. We also work with a small number of men who wish to make changes to their abusive behaviour. The majority of survivors we work with are women (95% 2022/23, of which 2% have told us that they have a transgender history) which reflects the highly gendered nature of intimate partner and intra-familial abuse. Ninety-two per cent of survivors worked with have experienced abuse or violence from a man, of which most are current (28%) or former partners (62%) or male relatives (8%). Because of this, VAWG has been changed by some organisations with the addition of M (male) to give the terminology MVAWG. This is to highlight that abuse and violence is not something passively experienced by women and girls but actively caused by men and that, without addressing the root cause, women and girls will always continue to experience violence and abuse throughout their lifetime.

A striking feature is that the survivors who approach us for support have experienced abuse for a very long time with an average of 82 months – over six and a half years. Most of the survivors approach us for help with current abuse (62% 2022/23) but can also approach us when they are ready to work with how non-recent abuse has impacted them. Many survivors will access a number of different services during their journey to recovery. Most services are time limited in their capacity to support and, given the length of time that abuse has been experienced by survivors, it is unsurprising that, e.g., 12 weeks of phone-based advice is unlikely to adequately address years of abuse. Long-term impacts may persist for many years, particularly if there has been economic abuse or if there are children from that relationship, and this may drive the high repeat presentation rate to crisis services (40% for 2022/23 in the author's organisation).

Who Are Our Workforce?

As a by and for MVAWG provider, there is a genuine occupational requirement (Equality Act 2010, Schedule 9, and Part 1, Section 7(2)e of the Sex Discrimination Act, 1975) that services are provided by women. Given the prevalence of MVAWG (Office for National Statistics, 2023) it is unsurprising that a significant part of our workforce will be or have been affected by this issue. Lived experience either as a child and/or adult may be the reason that workers chose to work within the sector, and it is possible that the VAWG sector includes a higher prevalence of lived experience of the organisation's main purpose, compared to other fields such as homelessness or problematic substance use. Such experience has the potential to both positively and negatively influence how a worker carries out their work and how the work impacts them. A key consideration for any leader within the health and social care sector is to be alert to the high rate of survivorship and associated trauma which may exist, as well as to how this may present.

In my work for a number of providers, lived experience is not frequently disclosed by staff. I am unclear if these are organisation-driven factors: a survivor may feel that they are less likely to be seen as professional, or viewed as not being able to be objective, or less resilient. Another possibility is that survivors working as professionals may have absorbed widespread societal views including feelings of blame, guilt and shame in the very same way clients do and that this can be a barrier to disclosing survivorship in the workplace. The approach taken by many leaders in the VAWG sector is to make an assumption that everyone has been personally affected by VAWG at some point in their lives and that this will be carried by them to a greater or lesser extent in the present.

In common with many other voluntary sector organisations, organisational hierarchies are relatively flat with leaders often emerging from the frontline rather than obtaining leadership experience in other settings. Because of this, leaders are commonly managing former peers and, whilst having excellent understanding of frontline work, may lack formal management learning and/or breadth of leadership experience.

Where Did It Start? Our PIE Work in Refuges and Work with Survivors

Our formal work with Psychologically Informed Environment (PIE) started with six months of funding, with the desired outcome of improving outcomes for women with support needs around mental health and problematic substance use in refuges. This project was called "Refuge Access for All" and the evaluation report titled "Peace of Mind" was published in 2017 (AVA and Solace, 2017). The basis for the project was that there are very few specialist refuge spaces to meet the needs of women with these additional problems, and there is a need to upskill and increase confidence within refuge provision in order to work with them despite a huge recognition of the unmet needs of these women and a will to work with them. Staffing in most refuge services is very stretched, including lone working, and staff can express a lack of confidence in feeling able to properly meet the needs of or to contain these women.

Working with AVA (Against Violence and Abuse), the aims of the original project were:

- Establish a PIE within the refuge service to improve access to and support for women experiencing multiple disadvantages
- Provide training to upskill the workforce to establish and maintain the PIE
- Ensure that the approach to the support provided was holistic in nature
- Improve sustainment of refuge placements, and tenancy sustainment on move on, for women experiencing multiple disadvantage
- Embed reflective case discussions for staff

- Establish a service user group to input into the project and to sustain continued development
- Provision of creative therapy including concurrent therapy for mothers and children

It was acknowledged that our approach prior to this included ways of working that are recognised as being part of a formal PIE approach. It is a conversation point at conferences when, in an attempt to better understand PIE, we think about ways of working we had before which were successful and were based on the simple concepts of kindness, treating those we work with as having their own individual needs and desires, and flexing our support to best meet those individual needs: person-centred care in fact.

Awareness training for staff was provided, which included basic counselling approaches, how to listen and ask questions appropriately, the impact of trauma, and strategies used by survivors to cope with trauma and poor mental health. Additionally, many service delivery-focused policies, including House Expectations, Warnings and Ending Licenses, and Keyworking, were re-written with service users, changing both the language and approach. Outcomes from the pilot included fewer women being refused spaces due to presenting mental health needs, and an increase in staff knowledge and confidence around core PIE principles. Staff also reported an increased understanding of the support they can receive from the organisation.

Managers felt that there was a definite need for the PIE work and that there was little resistance to implementation, with staff quickly seeing the benefit of the approach. Managers felt this way of working created more solution-focused and creative approaches were being identified and implemented by teams, with the approach seen as empowering to both service users and staff. Managers using psychological approaches also felt more able to work collaboratively with staff.

Given the short funding for the pilot project, perhaps the key finding was that with strong organisational commitment to implementing PIE, it was possible to establish a PIE, and to improve outcomes for service users, even with modest financial investment.

Are PIE and Trauma Informed Care the Same Thing?

The core PIE principles from the original "Refuge Access for All" project were continued and rolled out across the whole organisation. Although there has been considerable turnover in the organisation, some staff from the original pilot remain and continue to celebrate what was achieved and ensure the work continues. More recently, many VAWG organisations, including the author's organisation, now mainly describe their approach and work as being "trauma informed" (sometimes called Trauma Informed Care – TIC) rather than using the term PIE.

The key desired outcomes of both PIE and TIC are essentially the same – to improve the psychological and emotional outcomes of both users and providers of services. Both approaches understand that for those using services their prior experience of services, as well as what has brought them to the service, will impact upon their engagement and how successful interactions will be. TIC can be thought of as an extension, rather than a different framework, to PIE where the psychological framework is explicitly informed by knowledge of how experiencing trauma impacts those in the system.

PIE was introduced in the UK after being championed in the homelessness sector. The relationship between TIC as a derivation or extension of PIE is rarely explained and more recent workers in the sector may be entirely unaware of PIE as being the wider encompassing underpinning principle of TIC. Whilst the majority of people experiencing homelessness have experienced trauma, it is perhaps more obvious that those approaching a VAWG organisation are all assumed to have experienced trauma on multiple occasions, and this is a likely factor why TIC may feel like a more relevant approach, or has a more relevant language, for those in VAWG services. I will return at the end of this chapter to consider whether TIC is in itself helpful language to use.

One key difference between PIE and TIC principles is that with PIE one of the key requirements is evaluation of the psychological inputs – how do we know that what we are doing is worthwhile? This is not part of the TIC model, and it is important to consider how to measure, monitor, evaluate and feed back the changes that have been implemented to ensure that interventions are obtaining the desired change for both staff and service users.

The Challenges for Leaders in Maintaining a PIE in an Organisation That Deals Predominantly with Crisis

Risk management is a fundamental feature of VAWG services in the UK, with most commissioned services required to identify and work with those at the greatest risk of serious harm including murder/homicide. Expected outcomes are that risks will be well managed by the service and actuarial risk scores reduced to a tolerable, or at least tolerated, level upon the survivor's exit from the service. In terms of establishing and maintaining a PIE, it is a challenge to establish the desired psychological framework with such a strong risk focus: risk naturally leans us towards a deficit approach rather than an asset- or strengths-based system.

There has been discussion within the sector of shifting commissioning and service provision from such a risk-led to more of a needs-led approach. Drivers for this include a desired shift towards asset-based approaches across care and support services, and an acknowledgement that, due to the length of time that abuse is experienced, recovery journeys are non-linear. There is also anecdotal evidence from colleagues from domestic homicide reviews that most of the women killed were not experiencing visible high risk abuse at the time of death, with many women entirely unknown to VAWG agencies. It could of course be that the focus on risk-based provision means that these services are highly effective in preventing serious harm and homicide. However, it is also apparent that there is a requirement to also ensure non-crisis provision is available.

In considering that much of our work is focused around crisis, the concept of Non-Violent Communication (NVC) has been a very helpful tool, not only in its practical application but also in helping leaders understand the nature of our work and the challenges this can cause for individuals and organisations. It could be argued that NVC is part of the psychological framework for implementing PIE in VAWG organisations.

Nonviolent Communication – The Challenge of Being an Organisation That Deals with Crisis and How That Influences Our Own Behaviour

NVC evolved from person-centered therapy during the 1960s, with Marshall Rosenberg's seminal text "Nonviolent Communication, A Language of Life" (2015), considered a cornerstone for both professionals and lay people.

Key principles and techniques involve creating empathy between individuals, and expressing needs and feelings in a way that rejects coercive discourse and tries to establish collaborative solutions for both the current and future discussions. Within the author's organisation, NVC is a key concept and the stated aim of all communication is an intention to create empathy and to collaboratively resolve conflict, difficulty or difference. Although initially introduced to improve communication between colleagues (just as PIE was originally introduced to support staff), there was a natural extension to implementing and modelling this with service users, particularly in interactions they may find challenging such as sharing facilities with others in accommodation services, or interactions with professionals where there is a perceived or actual power differential.

In the VAWG sector, we are frequently dealing with individuals who are in crisis and have engaged with us to work with this. It is common that, as well as crisis arising in the lives of those we work with, we will often be dealing with problems which are either the result of late presentation of problems or due to actual or perceived inaction on the part of other professionals. When a significant part of our workload is driven by actual crisis, or when the presentation of problems is framed in a way that without an effective resolution from us the outcome could be disastrous, as professionals our nervous systems (much like that of our clients) can and do become highly activated. In such situations effective communication can be negatively impacted. What may follow from this is that we begin to see all situations, interactions and all our work as being crisis driven, even when the matter is actually routine or where there is no significant pressure of time for a decision or resolution. In situations where one party may feel that there is no urgent or pressing need, this mismatch can cause further frustration and an assumption that there is no empathy or shared desire to work collaboratively to achieve an outcome.

It has been very helpful during periods of relative calm to remind ourselves that a lot of the work we do is in response to crisis and reflect that because of this we can become highly activated, and that during this time we are more likely to make negative assumptions about those we are interacting with.

How Do Leaders Demonstrate Shared Vision and Commitment within the PIE?

In any organisation, disconnects between front line staff and more senior colleagues will be present to some degree. Frontline staff may express views that their senior colleagues do not share the same values, do not know or understand the work they do, or indeed assume that they have never undertaken such work themselves. Senior colleagues may feel that more junior colleagues do not understand their roles and the pressures upon them and that their previous contributions are not recognised.

As leaders, there is a need for us to message the values we have agreed upon and re-state them to build more empathy and collaboration which may be stressed and limited when individuals are highly activated. Building a greater shared sense of purpose within the organisation can also contribute to working with colleagues from other agencies in a more collaborative way that respectfully acknowledges difference, but finds ways to quickly build empathy and focus on desired mutual outcomes. When staff are "always having to advocate" with external agencies, this can result in an undesirable internal communication style where requests or issues raised can be presented in a way which is received as combative, resulting in rejection or disinterest by the recipient. An important part of the NVC model is that it is important to remember that your answer may be a "No" and being prepared to receive this. Rather than responding by forcing the issue, NVC encourages us to reflect on what barriers there may be to changing that to a "Yes" response, and identifying ways to address this.

Related to this persuasive approach, and thinking about the position we occupy in different interactions, we have found that a working knowledge of Transactional Analysis (TA) theory is helpful, and this could be considered another part of the psychological framework of our PIE approach. In TA, Berne (1957) describes the ego state of the communicators as either Parent, Adult or Child. In a professional setting, it is ideal for our interactions with each other to operate within the Adult-Adult context but as leaders we may often be placed or assumed to occupy the position of Parent, with those we manage taking up the Child position, particularly at times of stress or challenge. Leaders need to be able to recognise when an unhelpful interaction is at play and to be able to adapt our personal style to change the interaction dynamic where needed.

Extending the TA theory to Thomas Harris' popular text largely based on TA "I'm OK, You're OK" (Harris, 1969) is also a helpful tool for leaders. Harris' position states that many identify with "I'm not OK, You're OK", and it is an attractive assumption that many survivors of VAWG may initially identify with this view. Psychological tactics employed by perpetrators of VAWG cause many survivors to self-report very low self-esteem and to internalise a negative view of self whereby many will identify with "I'm not OK". In contrast, professionals (or those assumed not to have ever experienced VAWG) are perceived to have all the answers and so are assumed to "be OK". The goal of our service provision is for those who use our services to be able to confidently express "I'm OK". Further along they may hopefully have had enough positive interactions with others to also come to the view that "You're OK" is a starting point in how they view the world.

Ideally, (as per Berne) we would like our professional colleagues' world view to be "I'm OK, You're OK". Where there have been difficulties or fractures in professional relationships, they may view leaders as "You're not OK". For some workers, this can extend to entire cohorts of professionals such as Police, Housing Officers, Lawyers, Judges and Social Workers. Although this is a hugely simplified model, it can be a useful tool to engage colleagues in understanding what position or world view point they occupy, to challenge views that may be unhelpful or act as a block to their effective practice, and to ask them to reflect on whether they wish to move from this position.

But Isn't the Organisation Run on Emotions?

With such an emphasis on the consideration of the emotional states of both self and others, it is important for leaders to ensure that decision-making is still evidence based. Ideally, decision-makers have sufficient time and space to make considered decisions which allow the weighing up of all available evidence whilst still acknowledging the fear that may be present in the system and which can influence our decision-making. The nature of our work has inevitably resulted in times that have been very difficult for us, when we experience, for example, death or serious harm to a service user, harm to a colleague, or a reputational crisis. We must pay attention to what we have previously learned to inform our practice but we do need to be alert to when fear is a significant driver in our decision-making, and when that may mean we may be paying less attention to other information that is available to us. A note of caution to leaders setting up and establishing PIEs is that the increased focus on emotional states will also be a strong driver for the staff team and that they may challenge decisions and policy as "not being PIE" or "trauma informed": it is critical that there is a shared understanding by all of what the organisation's PIE or TIC approach is.

The Need to Sometimes Be Directive and Authoritative as Leaders

As PIE practitioners we are aware of how experiencing trauma can impact how survivors present and this helps us understand where behaviour that challenges arises from. As leaders, we are required to monitor and arbitrate where this behaviour is negatively impacting the workforce and others. Given the importance of structure and frameworks (often visible as organisational policies) to the safe operation of a PIE, workers will often want policy to explicitly stipulate thresholds for withdrawal (whether that be providing a service or some other process such as a complaints' process) and of course policy cannot provide for every eventuality. As part of any PIE, we wish to consult and engage the views of those in the system and in these situations it has been more helpful for managers to provide a clear outcome or decision and then ask workers for their view. Where we seek views from those impacted first, this can put too much responsibility on them to continue to accept physical or psychological risk and re-traumatise those already impacted. Leaders in a PIE must be prepared to identify where an authoritative management style is appropriate and where not, and be comfortable that an occasional directive leadership style is an important requirement for helping staff feel contained within the system.

Current Status of the PIE

Physical Environment and Social Spaces

A core aim of a PIE is to create a non-institutional, safe and welcoming space for service users and others who share the space. The physical environment is often identified as an easy starting point as it is relatively quick to achieve and has a tangible outcome.

Although there has been a high focus on aesthetics (paint colours, accessorising space), designing the physical environment also involves thinking about how spaces are used, including managing the needs of different users and how safe users feel. Space in services is often limited and used to meet multiple uses – examples from our own services include refuge living rooms which have a co-use as a children's playroom and a therapy space. We have negotiated protected time for different users and expectations of how the space is left ready for the next users. Our services are often contacted by corporate organisations wanting to improve spaces as part of their community responsibility programmes: we encourage a longer-term relationship with us – rather than many volunteers coming in for a single day to painting a communal space, we have asked them to consult with users of the service and to commit to sourcing items which will have the greatest impact. Recent examples have included fold-away desks within living spaces so that older children have suitable and protected space to do homework, and dividing up space within a single room so that it meets the needs of different users. Examples of having protected time to meet the needs and engagement of different users include having women-only sessions for drug and alcohol services' in-reach within a generic homelessness service, a lesbian, bisexual and trans group within a rape crisis centre and culturally sensitive provision as an addition to generic service provision.

Staff Support

Within a crisis-led service it is especially necessary to protect time for reflective practice opportunities. Skilling up managers to facilitate reflective practice sessions (whether that is to discuss casework, incidents or specific issues) has proven to be extremely helpful in embedding PIE: managers actually quickly gained confidence with this task after initial, minimal set-up support from therapeutic colleagues.

Working with trauma is part of the job but vicarious trauma and burnout should not be seen as inevitable consequences. Clinical supervision has been a cornerstone of the early warning system within the author's organisation, as well as being crucial for maintaining well-being and resilience. In addition, "Debrief" is also available for an hour daily to allow same-day access with a therapist for immediate needs that cannot wait until supervision.

The provision of clinical supervision is highly dependent upon available funding. Some organisations have financial provision to provide this to frontline staff, a smaller number make provision through frontline staff management because they are frequently dealing with frontline issues. At the author's organisation, clinical supervision is mandatory for most staff including senior managers and (at a reduced frequency) non-service delivery staff. The rationale is that no matter what our role is, we are all working with experiences of VAWG in different ways. Even in roles where it is perceived that staff are too remote from direct trauma, such as senior managers, the right clinical supervisor can still form a highly effective supportive relationship that supports practice, including focus on more strategic mentorship or a more coaching style of conversation. Most clinical supervision is provided within a group setting and where members prioritise attendance, attend consistently and prepare material to discuss, supervisees frequently report high levels of satisfaction with the process and feel it effectively supports practice. It is acknowledged that within a group setting it can be difficult for some colleagues to raise intra-team dynamics, but it is also accepted that where the space and time is used well, colleagues have the opportunity to learn much from seeing and hearing colleagues effectively discuss difficulties and reflect upon the feelings involved.

Although clinical supervision is frequently viewed as the focus point for staff support, a high value should also be placed on other opportunities to debrief and reflect upon our work, and to consider and process the work in a way that is helpful and sustaining. Staff are more likely to pay regard to and take responsibility for their own well-being when time for these practices is scheduled into their working time and not viewed as an extra task which they need to organise themselves.

Many of the difficulties brought by staff on a daily basis to managers involve negative experiences and interactions with other agencies. Conventional approaches to more effective inter-agency working such as training delivery, training swaps and network meetings may often be limited due to staff turnover, capacity and prioritisation. An approach which has had multiple benefits is colocation of staff within key agencies including children's social care, safeguarding hubs, police, housing, sexual health and job centres. The primary aim is to improve reach and provide a seamless, integrated and responsive approach for service users but a secondary benefit is that workers have the opportunity to build sustained relationships and demonstrate a continuous, consistent, PIE approach to their work and to influence interactions with others. Because workers will be more remote from their employing organisation, ways to keep in touch are important and the selection of experienced workers who have demonstrated resilience in other services is advantageous. Another benefit is that there will undoubtedly be good practice identified in host locations and this experience and wider perspective can be very helpful for the development of the staff member individually and for both organisations collectively.

Awareness of Trauma, Its Impact and How One May Recover

Our work with service users frequently includes a psychoeducational approach whereby a survivor's experiences, feelings and reactions are explained in terms of neuroscience and physiological responses. Such information can be hugely empowering and transformative for survivors in providing important context, and explanations for experiences that may have felt irrational or that evoke feelings of guilt such as "why did I freeze rather than fight when I was under attack". As psychoeducational approaches are commonly utilised in group settings with peers, an important benefit is also gained by participating in an informal support relationship with other survivors. With the focus on acute risk and crisis in VAWG services, such opportunities for step-down support and non-crisis and non-risk-focused work with survivors are relatively rare but very much needed.

Actively Avoid and Prevent Re-Traumatisation

One of the most important themes raised by survivors is that they have presented to a number of different agencies with their experiences before finding an effective response and that this has entailed re-telling traumatic accounts of what has happened to them. Even when they feel they have reached a place where there is an effective response to their needs, they are still required to re-tell this account to different professionals to progress through the system and obtain what they need to move onto the next phase of recovery. Good multi-agency working with information sharing can alleviate a lot of this. Another approach has been for the survivor to develop her own written statement, which the survivor can write with support if she wishes to: this provides a written account for the different agencies that may require it – housing, legal purposes or children's social care for example. Many women have found the process difficult to start with but when completed have reflected that they found it helpful to process, take account of what has happened to them and observe the progress, which often had not been apparent to them before, that they have made.

Commissioning of Services and PIE: Contract Length, Outcomes and the Drive for "innovation"

In common probably with many of the contributors to this book, care and support providers will typically have a mixture of commissioned contract services, with additional funding provided by grants and foundations.

Public procurement rules require services to be re-tendered periodically. Within the VAWG sector, public contracts are typically 3 + 1 + 1 giving a total of five years (at best) prior to re-tendering. It is very difficult for providers to negotiate any increase in value for additional years, and, adding to these frustrations, public bodies will sometimes find pots of money during a contract year and request that providers quickly find use for the money and ensure that it is spent within a short period of time.

The short-term approach to funding provides significant challenges. Firstly, there is often a constant requirement to "innovate" and do something new: even for core services such as advocacy and refuge provision, innovation finds its way into contracts via the Social Value Matrix where providers are required to demonstrate and provide additional value to the local community in the course of carrying out the work. Whilst providers must always be mindful and open to how they can improve their services, this is not the same as having to often artificially stretch ways of working to meet the requirement for innovation or demonstrating additional value. Social value can also be a challenge for discrete service provision such as confidential refuge space or women-only centres which will need to balance visibility in the local community with confidentiality and safety for service users.

The requirement to do something new to retain existing or attract new funding can result in "mission drift" and distraction from the core work, and pushes organisations to become involved in the wrong type of growth. For frontline service delivery staff, with limited exposure to and understanding of the funding landscape, this can result in them feeling that there is a lack of value in the work they do and has the potential to create confusion in what direction the organisation is taking and to generate mistrust in managers. For implementing long-term, values-based approaches such as PIE or TIC, it is simply undermining.

A factor in staff turnover is not just the impact of the work, but insecure employment (coupled with relatively low salaries). Frequent turnover of staff negatively impacts those who use services and, when coupled with uncertainty over service continuance, leads to poorer outcomes for them. The women experiencing multiple disadvantage themselves can struggle to find support as there are few specialist projects available who have the capacity and skill to build relationships with this client group, and where services do exist, many are funded year on year. Using a psychologically informed or trauma informed approach takes time, because time is needed for people who have spent years experiencing abuse. Advocates in such projects typically spend many months building trust and engagement with women and when trust is established need to work at a pace that the women are comfortable with. When a short-term contract is ended, staff may be having to manage endings with service users at the very start of trying to build a relationship which is evidently and directly counter-productive to the very aim of the work. Leaders of organisations have to try to contain this tension and conflict and protect their services, staff and service users, and part of leading a PIE is trying to contain staff anxieties and to enable the organisation to take a long-term approach within a system that is geared up for short-termism.

Commissioners and providers must always be accountable for public and charitable money, but there is a pressing need for less restricted funding, and for trusting providers to manage money, how services are provided, and what outcomes are meaningful for their service users to achieve and for the organisation to report on. There is also a pressing need for more realism in how long good psychological and emotional work takes and that stability of funding to facilitate organisations to develop PIE and trauma informed approaches better.

Provider organisations should also ensure that, when we are partnering with organisations to deliver services, we approach those relationships in a psychologically informed way. This includes identification of partners at the earliest stage of funding applications so that there is real collaboration over the model including shared values and frameworks, joint development of the budget, and ensuring that both partners' actual delivery costs are included. Larger organisations need to realise that, when working with smaller, grassroots organisations, these may not have well-developed infrastructure and will have more limited capacity to attend to time-sensitive requests or may require support to fulfil due diligence requirements such as policy development and writing, structuring bid responses and developing budgets.

The Need for Investment in the Whole Organisation

PIE is not expensive to deliver of itself. However, to safely deliver services, organisations must be adequately insured, have systems in place to ensure governance and an infrastructure that supports service delivery, and these need to be funded in addition to the moderate additional costs of establishing and maintaining a PIE. Such costs can be poorly understood by those who commission services and by staff, and it is necessary to ensure there are ongoing conversations about what core costs cover and why they are essential. Most charities will incrementally grow the number of service users they support year on year, and this is usually viewed as an indicator of success. When a commercial company grows its customer base, its income also grows; when a care and support provider grows its user base, it grows its costs. For small organisations to be able to create, operate and sustain a PIE, there must be not only proper investment in services but also investment into organisational infrastructure.

Post-2020 Challenges

Year 2020 brought about significant changes to both the work needing to be carried out and how it was delivered due to the Covid-19 pandemic. During this time, many voluntary sector organisations providing services to some of the most socially vulnerable in society faced an increased demand for support, coupled with a very rapid mobilisation to agile, remote and hybrid ways of working. For a sector where a high value was placed on establishing trusted in-person relationships, the pandemic period brought opportunities to explore different ways of working and how services are delivered.

Post-pandemic, the workforce is a significant driver for hybrid ways of working, even in service types where in-person delivery was considered an absolute requirement such as counselling and supported accommodation. Many of the reasons why remote delivery worked so well during the pandemic were because there was a high focus on well-being for everyone at the time and organisations were able to put in place added practical and emotional support with the additional funding that was available. It is very possible that many workplaces became more "PIE like" during that time as the considerable focus on a well-being agenda engineered in some PIE approaches at a large scale. Going forward, pressure on spending due to the cost-of-living crisis has scaled back many of these funds.

The driver for increased remote working now provides significant challenges for organisations wanting to work in a psychologically informed way. Spending less time together in one physical space leads to less opportunity for teams to establish a healthy reflective culture, less opportunities for peer learning, or to establish informal rapport with service users, peers and seniors.

The spring of 2020 also drove significant social change in terms of prioritising inequalities, notably around race; inequalities and injustice were brought into focus in many different spaces, including the workplace and service provision. Insufficient attention has been paid to how race and ethnicity impact those providing and receiving services within a PIE or TIC framework and going forward it is important that sufficient attention is paid to the inherent power imbalances in the work we have direct influence over, and also in the wider systems and structures we operate in. This attention will lead to meaningful discussion and collaboration to design ways of working within the PIE that are genuinely anti-discriminatory for everyone within the system.

Post-pandemic, public budgets are extremely stretched and, at the time of writing, inflation and other fiscal pressures are negatively impacting upon both organisations' (of all different types) and individuals' financial health. For leaders, this presents additional management challenges, both practically in terms of sustaining services and staff but also in terms of messaging around such challenges. Leaders can be criticised for being too focused on the financial aspects of the work, with an implied association that service users are a far less important consideration. It is now even more important for leaders to ensure a prudent and realistic financial approach that enables stability and safety for those receiving and providing services within the PIE. Part of the psychological containment is protecting the staff and service users from the economic pressures on the organisation, which compound the social injustices that led many service users into the service in the first place.

In his 1984 thesis Jameton (1984) introduced the term moral distress, with the terms being further defined to explain when a worker knows the right thing to do, but institutional constraints make it impossible to pursue the right course of action. Although originally introduced as a concept applicable to nurses and healthcare staff, this is now recognised as being applicable to workers in all care and support sectors. It is very possible that fiscal pressures present in society may lead to increasing moral distress for workers as time, resources and increased demand lead to worker frustration that they are not able to perform their role to the standards they wish or work with their service users as before; it also significantly contributes to worker burnout. Leaders themselves may feel disempowered in feeling able to support staff in these situations and become frustrated themselves.

It may be helpful at these times to remember that a "good enough job" (rather than a perfect job) is still likely to have made a positive difference to a service user and that continuing to operate and understand our work within the PIE structure offers us a very good chance of being able to successfully navigate a challenging internal and external operating environment.

Is "trauma informed" Helpful Language to Use?

At the beginning of this chapter, I explained the shift from PIE to TIC in VAWG services as an underpinning concept to our work. Victim Focus (Taylor, 2022) make extensive reference to the "pathologisation" of responses to traumatic life events whereby these become medicalised into mental health diagnoses. In line with PIE principles, this author outlines that a trauma informed approach is likely to be a more helpful approach when working with survivors of any adverse life event than a pathologising one, which implies that there is something "wrong" with the individual. Working in a TIC environment naturally leads us to be highly reflective on many of our interactions and gives us a heightened awareness of the experiences of others, including trauma experiences. However, by using the word "trauma" so extensively, is there the risk of seeing everything through this lens and therefore seeing even neutral everyday interactions and events as traumatic? Is this in itself pathologising? In effect the opposite of what is apparently sought by the trauma informed approach?

The author's own observations and experience suggest that the more neutral language of "psychologically informed" may ultimately be a more helpful and sustaining language choice to underpin and inform our work going forward than the more emotionally charged language of, and heightened focus on, "trauma".

Conclusion

It is important to remember that establishing and setting up a PIE is a continual process and not a journey with a defined endpoint and that being a leader within such an organisation is a continual learning process. For many readers, it is very likely that their organisation is working in a way that that embraces many or much of the content of PIE principles and that a lot of positive changes can be made with relatively little financial investment. A key recommendation for leaders is to ensure that there is a clear shared understanding of what PIE is and looks like for *their* organisation, and to revisit this regularly. This understanding is vital to provide containment and safety for all and to facilitate thoughtful, considered and effective service delivery. A well-established and evolving PIE allows us not only to understand what is helpful for those who use our services and work in them, but also what behaviours are unhelpful and distracting for the organisation.

References

AVA and Solace (2017) Peace of Mind: An evaluation of the Refuge Access for All Project. Accessed at https://www.solacewomensaid.org/centre_of_excellence/refuge-access-for-all-project-evaluation/

Berne, E. (1957) Ego states in psychotherapy. *American Journal of Psychotherapy*, 11(2) pp 293–309.

Equality Act (2010) United Kingdom Legislation Equality Act 2010 (legislation.gov.uk). Accessed 29 August 2023.

Harris, T.A. (1969) *I'm OK, You're OK. A Practical Guide to Transactional Analysis*. New York: Harper and Row.

Jameton, A. (1984) *Nursing Practice: The Ethical Issues*. Englewood Cliffs, NJ: Prentice-Hall. Vol. 6.

Office of National Statistics November (2023) *Domestic Abuse, Prevalence and Victim Characteristics*. ONS. November. Available at https://www.ons.gov.uk/peoplepopulatio nandcommunity/crimeandjustice/bulletins/domesticabuseinenglandandwalesoverview/november2023 Accessed 29 August 2023.

Rosenberg, M.B. (2015) *Nonviolent Communication – A Language of Life*. 3rd Edition. Encinitas: Puddle Dancer Press.

Sex Discrimination Act (1975) *Part 1. Section 7(2)* United Kingdom Legislation Sex Discrimination Act 1975 (legislation.gov.uk). Accessed 29 August 2023.

Taylor, J. (2022) *Implementing Trauma Informed VAWG Services*. London: Victim Focus Publications.

Chapter 6

Community Housing and Therapy

Andreas Constandinos, Anthony Jones, Jalil Kane, and Iwona Munia

Organisation Overview

Community Housing and Therapy (CHT) is a registered charity based in the United Kingdom that provides residential therapeutic environments for those with long-standing mental health problems.

At CHT, we work with and support individuals with a history of multiple and prolonged hospital admissions or social care placement breakdowns, who are often unresponsive to treatment, and who may have very complex needs and histories of trauma.

Our residents typically have a diagnosis of personality disorder or psychosis and experience the most debilitating mental health symptoms including self-harming, suicidal behaviour, social isolation, and a lack of independent living skills.

Our services provide both an alternative to hospital admission or the 'next step' after hospital. We focus on developing the skills and confidence needed for independent living, giving people a chance to live happier, healthier lives.

CHT currently has seven services in London and the southeast of England, supporting up to 70 adult residents in a range of high-, medium-, and low-support residential mental health recovery communities. CHT's high-support services are regulated by Care Quality Commission (CQC) to provide a community-based alternative to hospital admission.

Residents can enter different services depending on their needs:

- **Mental Health Recovery Communities – High Support:** providing intensive 24-hour support, these settings offer structure and routine for those experiencing severe mental health difficulties.
- **Mental Health Recovery Communities – Medium Support:** providing less-intensive treatments and a community-focused model to support individuals experiencing poor mental health back into independence.
- **Semi-Independent Move-on Flats:** These self-contained flats provide those who do not require high levels of support a way of transitioning to full independence.

DOI: 10.4324/9781003415053-8

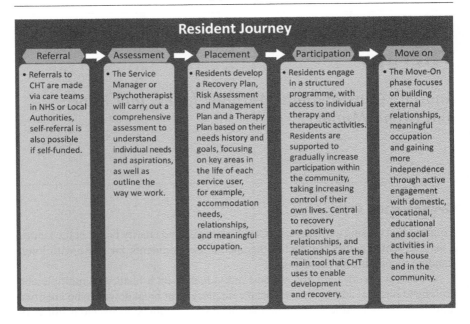

Figure 6.1 Resident Journey

Our current staff teams are made up of a Service Manager, Community Psychotherapist, Team Leader, and a team of Therapeutic Practitioners and live-in support workers. Each service is supported by a part-time Psychiatrist and Social Worker.

Residents typically stay for a period of 2–3 years, but treatment pathways are individualised rather than having a set period of treatment (Figure 6.1).

Background

Although CHT formed as a registered charity in 1994, it can trace its origins back to the therapeutic communities of the 1950s and 1960s, where a desire for more democratic, resident/patient-led forms of therapeutic environment was growing in an attempt to provide an alternative to the authoritarian practices of many psychiatric establishments of the time. At the heart of therapeutic community philosophy is that recovery can be found by allowing patients to participate in their own and each other's mental health treatment and that responsibility for the daily running of the community is shared among the patients and the staff. Social interaction and a sense of community is placed above medication as a treatment leading to the common description of the philosophy – 'Community as Doctor' (Rapoport and Rapoport, 1958).

Since its formation in 1994, when staff of an existing charity that was ceasing operation was granted control in order to form a new charity, CHT has traversed challenges that have seen many of the long-established adult mental health therapeutic communities cease operation. Over the years, CHT has had to grow and adapt to changes both politically, regulatory, and operationally in order to continue to provide an alternative model of care and treatment to those experiencing severe mental distress.

By far one of the most fundamental changes has been the incorporation of the Psychologically Informed Environment (PIE) framework into CHT's clinical model in 2017. Up until this time, CHT had operated with a Psychoanalytically informed Therapeutic Community model that latterly drew heavily on Lacanian Psychoanalytic and Group Analytic theory as the backbone to the model, although the majority of CHT's staff team was, and always had been, made up of lay staff with little or no background in Psychoanalytic theory. Working in CHT required a steep learning curve as staff struggled not only to apply complex theory to their work with residents with complex presentations, but also to be able to clearly articulate its model of practice to commissioners, potential residents, and other stake holders.

By 2016, with austerity measures adding to an already pressurised wider system, commissioners, concerned with ever tighter budgets, looked for placements that took people off their caseloads and could be justified to the scrutiny of funding panels. Higher levels of distress were being seen in CHT and the wider community as the threshold for hospitalisation increased ever higher, leaving many in the purgatory between hospital care and cheaper community support. CHT, like many residential mental health providers, had seen numbers of residents dropping to unsustainable levels as commissioners were forced to cut costs and struggled to be able to understand the cost benefit of a complex clinical model alongside a lack of clear methods for measuring outcomes.

PIE Implementation

In 2017, following the retirement of CHT's long-standing CEO and a period of change in senior management, the appointment of a new CEO entered CHT into an ambitious five-year plan in order to reinvigorate the charity and become a sustainable, successful, vibrant, high-quality provider of Psychologically Informed Therapeutic Environments for people experiencing complex and severe mental health conditions. This plan included remodelling CHT services using a PIE approach adapted to the existing therapeutic community settings, and the redefinition of the therapeutic model, basing it in relational psychodynamic theory and modern developments in interpersonal neurobiology.

This top-down approach ensured that CHT benefited from Senior Management buy-in, as the framework was being driven by the new CEO, who had been employed by the Trustees with a remit of reinvigorating CHT so that it would have a clear future within the wider Mental Health system. However, as CHT already worked within a psychological framework, much of the culture change work was helping staff to redefine some of what they were already doing and the introduction of new structures to train and support staff, a key principle of PIE.

One of the first measures was to introduce a new role – Community Psychotherapist – by recruiting qualified and accredited Psychodynamic Psychotherapists to offer individual psychotherapy to residents and to support the staff teams in understanding and implementing a psychological formulation-based approach rather than relying on psychiatric diagnoses to direct their interventions.

Formulation can be defined as the process of co-constructing a hypothesis or 'best guess' about the origins of a person's difficulties in the context of their relationships, social circumstances, life events, and the sense that they have made of them. It provides a structure for thinking together with the client or service user about how to understand their experiences and how to move forward (Johnstone, 2018).

Each of the service managers was supported by the new Community Psychotherapists to produce PIE implementation plans that the community would hold and work collaboratively towards. By using each of the principal areas of PIE, the communities were able to identify where existing areas of practice fit within the PIE framework and identify areas that were missing. Existing practice was analysed through the lens of the PIE framework to establish meaning and intentionality. Through this process staff were able to join in with the change and receive targeted training in order to be reskilled in the use of psychological formulation to help unify the support residents received as well as to understand and manage risk. Focus was also given to the social spaces, and improvements were co-produced with residents.

Change – A Service Manager's Perspective

Change is always difficult. For the staff team in particular, the early days of PIE implementation felt similar to playing as part of a rugby team: exciting, energising, rewarding, but also a surprisingly bruising affair, as we were asked to look at what we had been doing and were proud of previously through a critical lens. It's a bit like one day you are doing your job and then the next, you realise that you have got it all wrong. Perhaps not so brutal and not quite that quick but there is an impact, and it gets felt. I remember not long after we had launched PIE, about a year into my management career, introducing the changes that were coming to staff and residents. The wider organisation had been through a difficult period but at service level I had a good team, our occupancy numbers were good and our CQC rating was on the up; we had been weathering the storm and the staff were up for the change.

One day the new CEO and the Head of Services came to meet the residents. That made good sense, as there had been little or no interaction between the residents and the previous CEO, until, on the hour, the reality of the staff being uninvited started to land. Even now, all these years later, I feel the defences rising at the exclusion. The meeting took place in 'our' living room – the community's living room – where we held all of our groups; the room with the TV and the piano where we could step back and unwind or marvel at each other's talents; the room we would one day paint together as a community (claiming our environment in proper PIE fashion, but much to the dismay of CHT's head of maintenance). Now the staff had been turfed out and we feared that all that history, all that shared context, was going too. The more enlightened among us would have realised this was a good opportunity to catch a break while the rest of us sat waiting for the kicking that would, in our minds inevitably, follow.

The symbolism was stark and predictable. Of course, if you shut the staff out and the residents in with the CEO, the staff are going to get a pasting. And so, I guess it came to pass. My arguments were well prepared; old habits die hard. Our resident population was changing. A lot of the new residents were young, they were bright, and they were articulate. The voice of the community was much stronger, much quicker into fight or flight responses, much less fragmented now than it had been in the past. If and when we got things wrong the residents would let us know about it and in no uncertain terms. The power dynamics were shifting. Newly protected private spaces were emerging; the threshold of the bedroom door was becoming newly significant at the intersection between the individual and the group. It was not enough anymore for the staff to be thoughtful and caring. We were starting to do something different with the way we occupied the space.

Pride would hope that nothing new was learned that day – except maybe be more careful about who you invite for tea – but that would not be true. Nobody lost their jobs as a result of the uproar. There were no stern words sent down the hierarchy. A split had been manufactured but still it was recognisably ours. We definitely had a 'new' CEO. Maybe there was less to fear. As tempers calmed the community came back together again. There was room for reparation and soon after the community started work – this time in an ever so slightly changed frame of mind – on a process of review that would feed into our PIE implementation plan.

We had been stuck in a loop. Rethinking the place of the complaints seemed key. Kept 'out there' somewhere in the community, hidden in plain sight, bundled up in a mixture of guilt and shame, the complaints had become the community's lament: "all we ever do is sit here and talk", "you don't do anything", "you're not listening". That had to change. We had to change our place in the system. We could not go on repeating these positions, so current throughout adult mental health services. We had to start listening differently.

Over time these implementation plans became continuous improvement plans as PIE, rather than something new, became what we do.

The Treatment Model

CHT – Where Relationships Are the Treatment!

At CHT, we like to say that 'Relationships are the Treatment', but it's more than just a catchy motto, it goes to the heart of our model and ethos. Managing relationships is central in the PIE principles and the phrase was brought in as the subtitle to our logo as part of the PIE implementation. It was a perspective that CHT already held, but it became more overt, more clearly formulated, and more directly articulated with the introduction of PIE: it became easier to hold our approach up in public.

As humans we live in a social world: subject to social rules, social norms, support or the lack of it, stigma and relational trauma. On joining CHT, residents are invited to establish relationships within the community, both with fellow residents and staff members, with the hope that those relationships in time can enable the reshaping of their previous relational experiences.

CHT's psychological framework is based in Psychodynamic theories of human development and attachment. Rather than relying on psychiatric diagnosis, by using a formulation-based approach residents and staff are able to share an understanding of how someone's past is affecting their present, providing meaning to their presentation and allowing us to co-create interventions and positive risk-taking strategies.

We work with individuals within a social setting and much of the day-to-day life of each service is trying to share the work of maintaining the community, including cleaning, shopping, budgeting, as well as maintaining agreed boundaries, all framed by the therapeutic programme with a large proportion of it given to groups. Residents are encouraged to build relationships with each other and actively participate in each other's recovery journey, this enriches the view of each person's situation, giving different perspectives, feedback, suggestions, but also a feeling of belonging.

Two Resident's Journey' – The Model in Practice[1]

Alan and Mary were both referred to us in early 2021. Mary had spent over 30 years in prison while Alan had spent just shy of 20 years on a secure psychiatric ward. For both of their respective clinical teams, finding a placement for clients who, on paper, presented with high levels of risk, presented a no doubt daunting challenge.

Our clinical model has at its heart the principle of relational treatment which attests to the power of reparation. Central to this is creating safe spaces (environments!) where residents can learn to re-orient their relational styles, form beneficial attachments to both peers and staff and develop a sense of agency through activities of day-to-day living, voluntary work, education, training as well as social and recreational activities. Consequently, both Alan and Mary moved from environments where their lives were heavily restricted and where they could be and were, on occasion, physically restrained to a community where they were each given two keys, one to the front door and one to their respective rooms. Apart from being asked to abide by the house rules that every community has in place, no other restrictions would be placed on their freedom. This difference is enormous and one could argue that both Alan and Mary were about to enter very different worlds.

Positive risk taking is an important aspect of working in a psychologically informed manner as the more we allow residents to get in touch with their vulnerabilities, within a safe and contained framework, the more the fear of doing so diminishes. CHT knows that by accepting referrals such as Alan and Mary it is taking a risk, as for some, the transition from a highly restrictive and regulated environment to one of comparative freedom can be overwhelming. However, our model, underpinned by evidence from the latest advances in neurobiology, informs and empowers our staff to understand that, despite the appalling traumas most of our residents have experienced, it has been demonstrated that later positive life experiences and relationships can, over time, help restructure the brain thanks to the wonders of neuroplasticity.

Both Alan and Mary had experienced traumas during their early life experiences which would have shaped their internal worlds. This in turn impacted their perception and prediction of future experiences, their sense of self, and the overall direction of their lives. In both cases, this was then compounded by their experiences in both prison and hospital.

Managing relationships is a key principle of working in a psychologically informed way and this can include pets. Early on in her time with us, Mary acquired a rescue dog and the two would soon become inseparable. As with every decision of such consequence, this needed to be discussed within Mary's community and the dog was quickly embraced by the other residents. From pet insurance to what happens on those rare occasions where Mary and her dog were not together were thoughtfully and compassionately discussed and it is fair to say that the dog became not just Mary's dog, but the community's therapeutic pet. Having the experience of such devoted and unconditional love supported Mary through some difficult periods when the transition from prison was at its most challenging. Tasks that others would consider trivial, but at times seemed unimaginable to Mary, such as going to see the GP, were made possible by going with her dog.

A further crucial component of a PIE is having access to therapy. All of our communities are run by a leadership dyad which comprises a Service Manager and a Community Psychotherapist. The latter acts as the clinical lead for the service, providing clinical support to the staff, leading on meetings such as formulations and reflective practice, as well as providing weekly individual therapy for residents. Both Alan and Mary consistently engaged in individual therapy with their respective Community Psychotherapist, largely from the outset, building powerful therapeutic alliances that contributed to both being able to feel safe in their new environments. Our psychotherapists all work with a high degree of flexibility within the boundaries of psychodynamic thinking. They are willing and able to work with what the residents bring, and do so without being constrained by specific timeframes. All of this is vital when working with a client group that has been socially excluded.

When Alan and Mary entered their communities, it enabled our staff teams to formulate, formulation being another key component of our approach, their past experiences and better understand both Alan and Mary's psychological and emotional needs. By providing holistic community spaces, both could develop important connections, build their confidence, and gain independence. A PIE acts as a framework to ensure the day to day running of both Alan and Mary's respective communities provided a psychologically and emotionally safe environment for both of them to make sense of, better understand, and learn to live with, their past experiences.

All of the above equips our staff teams to essentially understand and be able to apply the principles of PIE as one great risk management tool. This not only bestows our communities with a theoretical model but also the practical skills to work in a therapeutic manner with highly traumatised individuals who, on paper, present with a high amount of risk. To date, both Alan and Mary have embraced these new worlds and are both preparing to move into more independent accommodation. Mary will be taking her dog with her.

As well as individual formulations, our Community Psychotherapists and Service Managers take part in Community Dynamics supervision and in turn are able to support staff to hold the community in mind, ensuring joining the community and any planned treatment interventions are carried out with both the individual and community in mind.

Managing Risk through Co-creation

Co-creation is a key part of how CHT approaches risk management, in line with the PIE principle of client involvement. Risk assessment is seen as a dynamic process with a human being at the heart of it. By taking a formulation-based approach to risk management, both residents and staff try to make sense of risk in order to devise and agree on interventions by bringing together an understanding of the residents history, mental state, current environment, key relationships, and other protective factors, as well as keeping in mind changes in any of these areas.

Jane's Story – Positive Risk Taking[1]

In 2020, Jane moved into one of our communities. She had been hospitalised for almost a year following an initial overdose and subsequent serious incidents of self-harm. When she first arrived, she was withdrawn and it took some time before she felt safe. This included the weekly psychotherapy space and so it became vital to Jane to be able to access alternative spaces of a therapeutic nature. All our communities embrace creative therapeutic spaces such as Art Therapy, Body and Dance Movement Therapy, as well as activities involving exercise. Last year, we also hosted a trainee placement during which a weekly journaling group was facilitated. It was in these spaces, some of which had only come into existence due to the suggestion and then prompting from Jane herself, that she was able to express how she was feeling and ultimately rediscover a voice that had been lost for too long.

Last year, Jane, accompanying her Community Psychotherapist, travelled to Greece to speak at a conference about her experiences. She stood in front of an audience of enthralled delegates and spoke eloquently about the power of being given the role of helping design her own recovery. Being given support to plan, to monitor, and to assess how she wanted to live her life as well as having open and honest conversations around her areas of risk had helped Jane have the courage to speak about some of this in front of a room full of strangers. At the end of the presentation, one of the delegates approached Jane and said, "I think you are very brave".

While our residents live in our communities, we have a duty of care towards them. This is not just a legal duty but also a moral and ethical one. The potential organisational risk of supporting a resident to travel abroad for four days needs to be acknowledged. The fact that she went with her therapist, with whom she had been in individual therapy for two years, can be interpreted as both a further risk or, conversely, as an empowering embrace of the concept of positive risk. Once more, this is an example of how the principles of PIE furnished us with the ultimate risk management tool which no doubt contributed to the trip being a success. For Jane, not just being asked but also being actively listened to helped her to feel safe and ultimately build the confidence where she now feels ready and able to move into her own accommodation.

The Physical Environment and Social Spaces

Our relational work takes place in a specific physical space – often a house with a garden, with a number of bedrooms and shared spaces, some of them with a specific purpose, like a medication room or staff office. Walls, floors, ceilings and fences set limits to this particular space, designate a boundary, become a container for the group of people that come together for a very specific purpose. This physical space becomes a social and emotional space for everyone invited to share it, whether through living or working there.

Come for a Visit – Social Spaces

Welcome to one-any-all of CHT services. It is a house surrounded by a local community, a short walk from a train station and shops. It may have from 6 to 18 bedrooms, with or without ensuite bathrooms.

When you enter the premises, you may notice that the front door is propped open; that there is a note on it making you aware of a resident dog; there is an empty coffee cup on the doorstep.

There are people in the building and at times you may not know who lives here and who works here. People approach you and ask you who you are and what you are doing here. The resident dog may also appear. You are glad you were warned about the dog's presence, considering the size of him.

There are shared social spaces: living room, dining room, kitchen. They all look lived in, well used, sometimes worn out. There are some paintings and art on the walls created by the community, some notice boards have a selection of photos from trips and activities, mixed with copies of policies or the recent CQC rating. Someone has crossed the 'GOOD' rating and replaced with handwritten 'BAD'. You can hear a discussion of a group of people trying to decipher whose writing this is. There might be a coffee or tea stain on the wall/floor/furniture.

The Therapeutic Programme displayed on the notice board tells you that in 15 minutes there is a community meeting. If you want a drink, you may need to wash a cup first (maybe the one you found on the doorstep!) and you are likely to struggle to find a teaspoon. Someone has left a half-eaten sandwich next to the kettle.

There is a nice garden at the back of the house, with a summer house and a smoking shelter. If you came for the annual BBQ, apart from great food, be aware of the water balloon fight, which in this service is now an annual event. Maybe you are here for the bake sale, finding yourself amazed by the variety of cakes you can choose from.

You are taking it all in and think that this place has a great potential.

The ongoing daily work of all our communities is to create a therapeutic, social space that will serve the therapeutic purpose of establishing and maintaining reparative relationships, to create connections between individuals and groups.

There are a few maps and signposts visible throughout the building to help navigate this space – there is a therapeutic programme reminding everyone where they are expected. There is a laundry room schedule, cooking and shopping rota. A white board available to all establishes expectations and rhythm of the day, including visits and one-to-one sessions. Boundaries help all feel contained and in the right place, not lost.

The Art group can be the source of paintings and drawings that are displayed on walls. The community decides to refresh the living room, choosing a rather eccentric green colour and catching bits of floor in the process of painting.

Since introducing PIE principles, social spaces in most of our services expanded. We added therapy rooms in all services, some created out of space that was previously used as a dumping ground. Communities may argue that they are still a 'dumping ground' for emotional difficulties and pain, recognising how necessary those spaces are. Two services expanded and added summer houses to their spaces, spacious enough to create a meeting or sensory room.

All communities started to build bridges with the wider community they are located in and all try to establish relationships with local areas. We have had very successful bake sales and art festivals, with amazing cakes, curious activities, and conversations with local people.

Working in a 'CHT way' is at times challenging and complex. We establish relationships with adults that often do not have the experience of secure attachment. On the contrary, they have experienced others as rejecting, threatening, unpredictable. Feelings of anger, shame and emotional pain are often externalised.

Coffee and tea stains on the walls, smashed and broken frames, cups and paintings, are often the evidence of someone's distress and extreme struggle. A satsuma decaying under the sofa, a dirty and unclaimed t-shirt in the corner of a living room, cigarette ends on the ground a short distance from the bin or bite marks on a block of cheese in the fridge, can be seen as reflection of experiences of physical and emotional neglect that most of the community members faced in their life.

We offer the experience of accepting those difficult feelings as a part of healing and recovery. A process that often is not easy to be a part of whether living or working here. Difficult feelings can at times be projected and located in the physical space. In a few of our services, we had/have a narrative of a 'mad room'. 'This is the room where people become unwell', where they struggle to 'get better' and instead 'become mad'. In one community this narrative was so strong that the living-in staff room was moved there with the hope of shifting this and reclaiming the struggles and the deterioration of mental health back to becoming part of a dialogue between people.

Sharing and negotiating a living space is not easy. With as many as 20 points of view on how a new sensory room should look like, it feels impossible to get a final decision and agree with each other. And another month passes by without a sensory room. Yet we get there in the end.

Lack of teaspoons in communities is a source of a lot of projections. One community was struggling to explore the idea that some of the residents relied on drug taking as a source of support and established a comfortable split, where all that is 'bad' was located in those that use drugs. They were responsible for the lack of teaspoons ('well, you know what they are using them for' was said at a community meeting). Teaspoons are still the desired, yet missing, item despite a change in the community with less, if any, drug taking behaviours.

We work with defences from staff members against difficult projections and dynamics taking place in the community. This can be expressed in a tendency to see tasks as concrete 'to do' activities, in effect losing the meaning behind them. Staff members seeing cleaning as just cleaning are struggling to see the crucial symbolic task of getting together, and how central their role is in maintaining the relational work with a group of people that see relationships with others as a threat. "I didn't cause the mess so why should I clean it!" is an often heard sentence of expression of exhaustion from any community member – staff and residents alike. Staff teams can find it difficult to remain the container, especially the container for the disturbance and pain. This can be particularly heavy if teams need to deal with very concrete consequences and expressions of disturbance and pain – for example faeces or blood. One resident was not able to reach the toilet on time due to severe obsessive compulsive disorder (OCD) behaviours and needed staff's support in dealing with this. Blood stains resulting from self-harming behaviours are often a visible reminder of the levels of distress being expressed by residents and their need to have a witness to their experiences.

With all incidents and events involving property, social spaces, etc. taking place in the community we are always looking into the context, trying to understand the meaning. During one community meeting a few residents told staff about the reasons why the bathroom door was kicked in: a female resident could not release the lock on the door and a male resident, in an attempt to rescue his peer, kicked the door in before any staff was alerted, before someone could find a maybe less emergency-style solution. This all took place while the community has been discussing care-seeking and care-giving dynamics, residents expressing their worry that there is not enough care and love to go around.

When we started working with PIE principles, all services had PIE implementation plans in place. The environmental plans reflected the hope of communities that they can live and work in beautiful, clean, almost pristine spaces. Since then, we experienced that the social spaces are a container for the relational work we do, and as such they will always reflect the work that we do. We like to think about social spaces and the environment as interwoven with the daily work and as an ongoing process of communication between people occupying those spaces and their communication with a wider world.

Reflective Practice

Reflective practice is fully embedded not just within each of our therapeutic communities but across the organisation as a whole. Every week, the respective Community Psychotherapist facilitates a 90-minute reflective practice group with the staff team. They also facilitate a weekly community reflective space which both staff and residents attend together. Further, on a monthly basis, all of our Community Psychotherapists and Service Managers attend their own reflective practice group in a neutral venue which is externally facilitated. Additionally, for the past year, our Central Office team has attended a monthly reflective group which is also externally facilitated. Finally, CHT offers an externally accredited Diploma in Relational Practice to all of its frontline staff which includes a seminar on reflective practice, and all training seminars attended by our staff are followed by a 90-minute reflective practice group.

All of the above helps ensure we are committed to creating spaces within our organisation where we can think about our work, assess how and why we have done or thought about something in a specific way, and create an environment in which we are continuously learning. What we are hoping to develop is a specific way of working, namely thoughtful and reflective interactions across our organisation. It is arguable that this is even more important in a charity such as ours where we work with and are confronted by the impact of trauma on a daily basis; this will inevitably have consequences and if not acknowledged and worked through can result in an inability to think clearly, therefore potentially function poorly and generally leave the organisation in a position where it is unable to achieve its charitable aims. After all, an organisation is nothing more than a constructed community of individuals all working towards the same goal.

One of our biggest challenges when it comes to reflective practice is in ensuring there is a collective understanding of the fundamental purpose of these spaces. Our therapeutic communities promote a group-based approach to treatment and are demanding and challenging spaces to work in. It can be tempting for staff to want to exclusively place any kind of difficulty within the framework of the weekly reflective practice session. This can range from fairly trivial daily disagreements between staff and residents to more fundamental issues such as serious incidents. What this does is to, in effect, create a pressure cooker within a staff team where everyone has to wait for their weekly space: this is not conducive in any way to the creation of a reflective discussion. Reflective practice is not a container for a staff team's difficulties but a space in which staff can learn to hone the skill of thoughtful and reflective interaction which they can then adopt within every other aspect of the work on a daily, and hour-by-hour, basis.

A further challenge is the perception of the staff reflective practice space from the resident's perspective. The perception can easily develop that for these 90 minutes no care is being given towards the residents and this can only be avoided through open dialogue within our communities; failure to do so can result in residents being seen to 'attack' the space which can subsequently lead to a dynamic where staff feel the need to 'protect' their space. One of the aims of CHT's model is to create a living-learning experience so that our residents can be supported to recognise and experience their own capacity to be both a care-seeker and care-giver, the two faces of attachment. By staff being able to articulate why the staff reflective practice group is important in their own care, and how it contributes to our staff being able to act as care-givers, they are powerfully modelling something within our communities.

As aforementioned, our Central Office reflective practice group, in its current guise, is a relatively recent addition within the organisation. It is attended by our Senior Management Team as well as those who lead on fundraising, human resources and business development. The creation of a group which includes clinical, operational, finance and administrative staff engenders a fascinating multitude of different perspectives on the work in the organisation. Nobody embodies this more than our Head of Maintenance, Pavel.

Rupture and Repair – Head of Maintenance Perspective

Pavel spends his working week travelling across our four communities in order to repair, restore and unblock. He is confronted by the wear and tear, damage and sometimes wanton destruction that is part and parcel of working in an environment such as ours. It can be soul destroying returning to the same community week after week in order to be confronted with the same problem over and over again. Conversely, it can also be immensely satisfying starting your day with a specific issue and then leaving knowing it has been resolved. At first glance this may seem a far cry away from the clinical work that is taking place every day within our communities, but what Pavel has shown the rest of us in our reflective practice sessions is that he is simply addressing and fixing problems from a slightly different perspective, showing that things can get better with a little bit of work.

Moving on, Moving Forwards

The Greek philosopher Heraclitus is credited with saying that the only constant in life is change. Whether one is creating something from scratch, developing an existing structure, or implementing something new, change will only happen if there is a clear vision of what is changing and if those asked to work within this vision see its value. For CHT, the challenge in making the organisation a PIE was creating a shared understanding of a concept that had originated in another sector, and enabling staff who had previously worked in a specific way to be engaged and empowered to see the value, and to see that they were not completely changing what they were doing but complementing their vision of how to support those living in our communities. You could argue that this is the very definition of the process of change, namely finding the right way in which to manage the back-and forth between at times letting go and at times holding on.

Within any change process there will be resistance, which will often have at its root fear. Introducing a new clinical model was daunting to many of our existing staff yet some of the key principles of PIE have created the necessary framework to make staff feel more contained and supported, thereby alleviating some of the fear and with it some of the resistance.

Central to this vision of change are our residents, and ultimately, CHT is in the business of helping people move forwards towards their goals by supporting them to understand themselves and how to do things differently in the future. Change is complicated and in the process of implementing PIE, as our residents do, CHT underwent a period of reflection and learning in order to develop a new way of being; and, also like our residents, the forward momentum is a continuous process not a simple act.

As an organisation, CHT is committed to continuous improvement and our model of work is always being tweaked and improved. Modernising CHT's clinical tools and systems is an ongoing process. The Covid pandemic offered numerous challenges, forcing us to embrace the online world as well as change the physical environments that we live in as we experienced quarantine and 'lock down'. Coming out of this, CHT is currently focused on improving the physical environments of our communities, on ensuring our staff and residents are further empowered and supported, as well as increasing the focus on our residents' bodies and physical health.

CHT is well into our next ambitious five-year plan that focuses on being able to offer more training, more services, and more opportunities for our residents and staff, and that we are more PIE. By working towards ensuring every aspect of our organisation is as psychologically informed as it can be, CHT embraces the notions that change is not always easy, but that growth and constant development are necessary for both whole organisations and for the individuals, staff or residents, management or frontline, who live and work within them.

Note

1 For the purpose of concealing resident's identities, names as well as some aspects of their stories have been changed. This has been done to respect the privacy of those residents mentioned below. The essential part of each story remains unchanged.

References

Johnstone, L. (2018). Psychological Formulation as an Alternative to Psychiatric Diagnosis. *Journal of Humanistic Psychology*. 58 (1), pp 30–46.

Rapoport, R., & Rapoport, R. (1958). Community as the Doctor. *Human Organization*. 16 (4), pp 28–31.

Chapter 7

Enabling Horizontalisation

Doing the Dance Differently

Natasha Berthollier, Geoff Dennis, and Rex Haigh

This book is about leadership in psychologically informed environment (PIE) and trauma informed care (TIC) and here the authors take this far beyond the usual concepts of a PIE and TIC by thinking about whole communities as they are and where they are. They give fascinating perspectives on the roots of and application of enabling environments, PIEs and trauma informed approaches, and then take them into a whole new area of development, applying a psychologically informed enabling approach to whole systems rather than individual services within systems. They also challenge concepts of hierarchical leadership by considering whole communities as leaders in the change process. The authors look at the creation of an 'enabling town' and indeed a complete enabling district.

Introduction: Creating an 'Enabling Town' – The Background

Therapeutic Communities

Looking at a broader canvas as the background for this narrative, the British model for Democratic Therapeutic Communities has undergone gradual but substantial change over recent decades, most particularly by reduction of therapeutic community (TC) programme availability in the NHS (Pearce & Haigh, 2017). This has been through both considerable reduction of the number of TCs available in the NHS (in the 1970s, most county asylums had a TC facility) and the proportion of people's time spent in the programmes (from fully residential in the 1960s to one day per week or less now).

In America and the rest of the world, the term 'Therapeutic Community' more commonly applies to a concept-based programme specifically for addictions, also known as hierarchical or behavioural TCs (De Leon, 2000). These are still mostly residential, but the length of admission has been substantially reduced. Their sanctions have become less harsh in recent decades, and they have become more connected to other community services. Although they come from very different origins, it has been recognised that 'democratic TCs are more hierarchical than they say, and hierarchical TCs are more democratic than they say' (Winship, 2004).

DOI: 10.4324/9781003415053-9

Having more in common than what divides them has been described as the 'Fusion Model' (Vandevelde et al., 2004; Haigh & Lees, 2008).

The development of this 'whole town' macro-TC approach takes some elements of both, but also makes a radical departure from both. This is similar to the ideas of 'TC in the Head' (Haigh, 2018), 'TC without Walls' (Dennis, 2018) or buildings – by being held and owned by the members themselves, and distributed across different services and sectors across the town. The rest is a 'felt experience' of *being-in* and *belonging-to* a coordinated network of relationships and services that offer companionship, emotional safety and opportunity for development and growth.

Enabling Environments

The 'Enabling Town' initiative is closely related to the aspirations of the Royal College of Psychiatrists' national 'Enabling Environments' programme, which can be seen as taking the interpersonal characteristics of a therapeutic community – particularly the *quality of relationships* – and recognising them through an accreditation process. It is based on ten relational values which are operationalised into standards, and then measured in a process of engagement and collaboration (Haigh et al., 2012; Royal College of Psychiatrists, 2016).

BELONGING: The nature and quality of relationships are of primary importance.
BOUNDARIES: There are expectations of behaviour and processes to maintain and review them.
Communication: It is recognised that people communicate in different ways.
Development: There are opportunities to be spontaneous and try new things.
Involvement: Everyone shares responsibility for the environment.
Safety: Support is available for everyone.
Structure: Engagement and purposeful activity is actively encouraged.
Empowerment: Power and authority are open to discussion.
Leadership: Leadership takes responsibility for the environment being enabling.
Openness: External relationships are sought and valued.

PIPEs and PIEs

In other settings and sectors, this process has led to psychologically informed planned environments (PIPEs) in the criminal justice sector (Benefield et al., 2018), and psychologically informed environments (PIEs) in the homelessness sector (Johnson & Haigh, 2010; Keats et al, 2012) and beyond into young persons' services, mental health, registered care, women's refuges, etc. as evidenced in this book and elsewhere.

Relational Practice

Research is now identifying 'Relational Practice' as an underlying concept behind this approach, and it is applicable in many other settings (Haigh & Benefield,

2019). Relevant work includes a large multicentre study into using the 'Open Dialogue' approach to crisis interventions (Seikkula & Olson, 2003), and the critical 'Power – Threat – Meaning Framework' (Johnstone et al., 2018). Experiential training for staff working in TCs and other therapeutic environments has been available for many years, in the UK and overseas, as 'Living-Learning Experiences' (Rawlings, 2005).

Greencare

Another relevant area is that of incorporating nature into therapeutic programmes, of which the importance is re-emerging (Burls, 2007). This is in keeping with a growing evidence base for the value of nature-based activities for mental health and well-being, as well as concerns arising from unsustainable lifestyles causing climate change. The field was described and operationalised through an EU COST programme called 'Greencare', which has produced a conceptual framework (Sempik et al., 2010).

In this programme, a weekly optional greencare group became an important and much-valued element of the community (Ansell et al., 2019). It was organised through a social enterprise partner, Growing Better Lives CIC, whose founding vales are stated as:

> Greencare is a holistic and economically viable alternative to treatment with medication and hospitalisation. Sustainability is about connecting people to each other and to nature, helping people to see that there is a life worth living, and on a planet that is worth living on.

It took place in a group-maintained therapy yurt in a local environment centre and mixed the normal TC-style groups with horticulture, growing our own food, maintenance, and other relevant activities.

Constructing the Actuality

To enable relational practice at a system level, we needed to prepare the ground using a field perspective (Lewin, 1939). This implies that the whole is greater than the sum of the parts, but some of the parts contribute to the whole. In this project, each development contributed incrementally to the overall transformation and was a part of the dynamic process – which also built on relational foundations. In this organic and fluid space, novel and invaluable synergies emerged, which would not be possible in a traditional linear planning of development.

In our experience, relational practice is not an intellectual exercise, it is an experiential learning process. People need to feel and emotionally understand what this means, working relationally with self and other. It is a felt experience. Without any of that, there is no ownership as it is not understood at an emotional level.

This challenges an institutional mentality, and it exposes the limitations of hiding behind institutional policies and procedures. It allows people to connect as people. Traditionally, in institutions, people aim to protect themselves in a 'bubble' in their 'comfort zone', feeling they are too busy to think and act differently and are actually disabled by the organisational procedures. To work effectively, different parts must be influenced into different ways of thinking and brought together over time. That requires a consistent, dynamic and active approach. It is a multi-layered process of working with the relational field.

It allows for the individual and collective to have confidence and assurance to challenge the orthodoxy and have confidence to find new ways of working and relating: this is 'doing the dance differently'. Enabling environments may exist spontaneously, otherwise they require incremental co-creation of the relational field. A collective of well-engaged people allows for connectedness and relationship development, rather than individuals functioning within their own bubbles.

To accomplish this, it is vital to consider issues of ownership and power. In our project, we consider ourselves as the custodians of the service: we are here to serve people, not the other way round. We host the space for the service, but need to establish, promote, and maintain a sense of shared power and joint ownership. This allows for 'horizontalisation', through which people engage with underlying hierarchical structures in a way that feels less threatening. Changing the power dynamic in this way can create a rich and nourishing environment, which is radical and emancipatory.

Co-production is not the 'end product', it is not a 'task and finish' initiative, but the journey and ongoing process of co-creating relationally enabling environments which allow the culture to be embedded. Before authentic co-production can start, a culture shift needs to take place to provide a sense of being and belonging, whilst developing social connectedness. Without sufficient understanding of co-production and without the field conditions which nurture co-production, there is a risk of it being tokenistic and experienced as somewhat patronising. The process requires fluidity and experiential opportunities to learn together and make meaning out of the *present* relational environment *present*. This requires deep immersion and presence, and it evokes Keats' 'Negative Capability':

> When a man is capable of being in uncertainties, mysteries, doubts, without any irritable reaching after fact and reason.
>
> (Keats, 1899)

We believe that this open-minded vulnerability of 'not knowing' is the prerequisite for opening up the space in which genuine co-creation can successfully emerge. Thus, we provoke knowledge by allowing for relational encounters and understanding the community from the standpoint of its relationships.

Enabled by this, we have adopted an 'asset-based' approach. This allows us to recognise and enable people's potential on the basis of their strengths and capabilities; this supports people to experience being valued and contributing to their individual and collective well-being.

This is underpinned by 'salutogenesis', which is the opposite of a deficit model, 'pathogenesis'. Salutogenesis is a term coined by Aaron Antonovsky, a professor of medical sociology (Antonovsky, 1996). It describes an approach focusing on factors that support human health and well-being, rather than on factors that cause disease or 'pathogenesis'.

The drawbacks of the deficit model encouraged us to develop a different way of understanding 'treatment'. Developing a sense of purpose on the basis of people's strengths allows for co-production to become a 'treatment' in itself. This is exactly what the people who use our services stated clearly, and with passion, in their co-produced service philosophy: 'We are not a diagnosis, we are people, and we would like to be involved in decisions around our mental health, and when this is not possible – to still be treated with utmost respect. Please do not concentrate on 'un-wellness' and find at least a small bit of 'wellness' each day'.

What emerged from this field is the sense of passion and energy which attracted people to contribute to further developments of their relational matrix. We focused on developing numerous opportunities for people to do so, including the training to join us as peer mentors and lived experience practitioners. The acquired sense of ownership, and what it brought, stimulated 'a buzz' and a continuing energy with the promise of boundless growth. As described, this defines 'horizontalisation' in a way in which work is done 'with' people, rather than working 'on' people.

To achieve the necessary paradigm shift, we had to move towards more collaborative and empowering approaches that prioritise co-creation, participation and an openness to new and diverse perspectives. This requires health to be seen as a social movement and, as such, is everyone's responsibility. It involves collective efforts aimed at promoting well-being and preventing illness – at individual, community and societal levels. As the concept of health has evolved, from a treatment of illness to a broader social and political phenomenon that encompasses a range of factors beyond medical treatment, our approach sees individuals and communities as the co-producers of health and well-being, rather than the recipients of services. This is the essence of asset-based community development.

> A health asset can be defined as any factor (or resource), which enhances the ability of individuals, groups, communities, populations, social systems and/or institutions to maintain and sustain health and wellbeing and to help reduce inequalities
>
> (Morgan & Ziglio, 2007)

Making It Human

Trauma informed approaches acknowledge the intricate and pervasive impacts of trauma on a person's outlook on life, relationships, and interactions with services and staff (Sweeney et al., 2016). Effective services are organised and delivered in a way that encourages 'choice, trustworthiness, collaboration, and empowerment' (Blanch et al., 2012). Through the use of relational strategies, people should be able to interact with 'the right services at the right time', however high level of demand on statutory services does not allow this. In this project, a new way was developed to promote mental health through positive relationships and compassionate interactions. 'The right services' needed to be flexible and more in tune with the person's strengths and abilities, and not just focusing on what was 'wrong'.

People who required support from our services often experienced deep pain which brought them to consider taking their lives. Joiner's Interpersonal Theory of Suicide (Joiner, 2005) provided a framework for understanding the complex interplay between interpersonal factors and individual vulnerabilities that contribute to suicidal behaviour, and it has been supported by various studies (Van Orden et al., 2010; Franklin et al., 2017). Joiner's psychological framework emphasises the significance of perceived burdensomeness, thwarted belongingness, and acquired capability, and each individual's recovery planning ensured people's needs were met within these three areas. By addressing these factors, we developed interventions and prevention strategies to reduce suicide risk and promote mental well-being.

Perceived burdensomeness refers to a person's perception that they are a burden to others and that their existence creates excessive difficulties or demands on their loved ones or society. To address this, we worked on supporting people to develop a sense of purpose. People's strengths are identified and they are given opportunities to develop recognition and confidence to build on them. Coproduction is the main vehicle for these opportunities, and we believe that, as such, co-production becomes 'the treatment'.

Thwarted belongingness refers to the feeling of social isolation and the perception of a lack of deep connections or social support. To counteract this, everything we do is based on the development of a strong sense of community (Pearce & Pickard, 2013). The relationally enabling environment of a therapeutic community, and the social connectedness that is nurtured within, helps members to develop a sense of participation, ownership and agency and demonstrated how community becomes 'the treatment' itself (Haigh, 2013).

It reminds us of the powerful and beautiful message by Christian African philosopher, J. S. Mbiti's: 'I am, because we are; and since we are therefore I am', and how this Ubuntu philosophy was used poignantly in South Africa in moving on from its troubled past (Mbiti, 2015), as well as by UNESCO (Nderitu, 2020).

The last element of Joiner's theory (Joiner, 2005), acquired capability, refers to a person's capacity to overcome their inherent fear of physical pain and death, in order to take their life. By developing individually tailored, psycho-social, formulation-driven evidence-based recovery plans, we support people to acquire the opposite capability. The requirement to share responsibility for others, as well as to take responsibility for oneself, is supported by the structure of the community and its various groups and activities. We have aimed to change the expectation of 'dis-ability' to 'response-ability'.

Capturing the Dance Differently

Over the years, we have undertaken numerous co-produced research and audit activities. Examples include a partnership with our public health colleagues led by our service users, small projects for students, national projects such as CofC (Haigh & Tucker, 2004) and EE (Haigh et al., 2012), and the development of our innovative website. Importantly, it includes economic evaluation to demonstrate considerably reduced NHS costs in the year after being in the treatment programme. In addition to routinely using standard quantitative outcome measures, we recognise the intrinsic value of qualitative co-produced research that captures the essence of how people benefit from relational practice and an enabling environment. This is an integrated approach in which the study of the process is a part of the process itself.

Our qualitative outcome data includes patients' feedback, carers' involvement, continuous and returning input and service co-creation as peer mentors, to meaningful activities following discharge, such as training and work, as well as the Care Quality Commission (CQC) inspection report on 'Outstanding Patient Engagement' and the NHS Trust's award for the 'Best Patient Experience'.

When people recognised a need to have an online presence, the extensive project of co-producing the website involved numerous voices from our communities. Those involved chose to have a relational website that does not just offer information but evolves in response to the continually developing conversation about mental health across the town; in this way it represents the philosophy, culture and values of the overall community. It was launched in 2020 and continues to respond to people's changing needs: www.EnablingTownSlough.org.

Our model, based on principles of therapeutic communities, enabling environments and 'health as a social movement', has received local, national, and international recognition: we have presented our work at numerous conferences, seminars and webinars 'Local commendations include in 2017 the CQC highlighting the inherent value of patient's voice, in 2018 the Slough Partnership Award for community integration and the local Healthwatch commendation as an example of excellent patient experience, and in 2019 being the National Positive Practice in Mental Health Awards winner for addressing inequalities.

Creating an Enabling Town – The Practice

Over the last few years, we have transformed services in a town which was struggling with mental health provision. Alongside engaging with people who required services, this initially required defining and scoping the task with key stake holders, including Berkshire Healthcare clinical staff, community mental health teams, local authority directors and staff, commissioning colleagues, senior managers, and public health.

Some traditional institutional processes were soon identified as obstacles, with poor access to accessible services. A different concept of working with people was introduced, based on 'relational practice'. Our central tenet, of co-design and co-production, was applied across the system. This challenged inequality in the health system by creating opportunities for all; by minimising the 'us and them' dynamics, we could work 'trans-diagnostically' and make formal diagnoses and their pathways into a secondary issue. For this, we developed a non-diagnostic and inclusive pathway, which aspired to meet the needs of all those requiring mental health services. It relied on co-produced interventions, jointly delivered by people with lived experience, in different settings, across the town. We believed that taking services *out into the community* was a more positive and responsive development than *bringing people into the service* and its buildings.

One of the requirements for a more inclusive system was to bring about a cultural change to enable people to receive services that they needed. As 'custodians of the service' (Dennis, 2011), we had to shift the power dynamic – but in full collaboration with all those who should be involved in deciding what was needed. This sounds like a simple process, but it required a complex approach on a systemic level. This included frontline health and social care professionals, staff at director and commissioning levels, and at its core, the local community.

System Change

To successfully achieve this, the development required attention to the relationships with all the key stakeholders. It needed a consistent approach which included bringing groups of people together, to work as part of relationally enabling groups, as we describe the process 'Doing the dance differently' (Dennis & Berthollier, 2020) across the system, over a long period of time. This is different from a usual consultation structure, which relies upon a standard and formulaic way of gathering information and processing it in a short period of time. We believe that this is not an effective way of using the rich assets that people with lived experience bring. It results in the 'top-down' production of action plans, which are not embedded within the existing relational environment.

The approach that we implemented introduced relationally enabling groups, at different levels, and initially specific to particular groupings. Once these were set up, a wider group was run regularly, across organisational structures and levels. In this way, people who use services were brought together alongside commissioners and directors, as well as clinical staff. The groups operated in such a way to remove the expectations of a power hierarchy, and they empowered people to connect and to recognise the humanity in each other. Physical objects (including tables and digital devices), behind which some professionals can hide and avoid direct and open communication, were removed, thus allowing for a 'circle of connection' to form.

Moreover, regular events with a common sense of purpose were organised across the town. This involved numerous people, from various backgrounds and at all levels, contributing to the wider community. This in turn created a sense of being a part of and belonging to this community, across a widely spread and diverse population.

The work took 12 years of gradually developing these co-produced and asset-based services. It is important to state that each development, in its own field and space, as described below, was related to the others as part of the relational and incremental developmental synergy. The starting point was with the most important people, those who use services. Their needs and experiences were placed at the heart of service design and delivery. The amount of creativity, dedication and energy that comes from those who use services was – and still is – remarkable. It highlights the question of who is teaching and who is learning (Dennis, 2004).

By rejecting the usual engagement structures, such as consultation surveys and focus groups, we required attention to the task over a long period of time in order to form the bedrock of meaningful relationships. This is not a quick fix, and it is worthy of mention that the longer process allows for a high level of trust to be built which is sometimes lacking for users of mental health services.

However, the process has not always been met with willingness and optimism: embarking on the change process also created tension, conflict, and challenge at times. As in any change process, there are always people who struggle to see the benefits and focus on protecting what they currently know within the narrow window of what is going on in front of them. Only by being persistent and open about creating a different way of functioning, by involving people and engaging them to contribute and experience the relational process, did they come to see the value of it.

Field Elements

Our concept of synergy illustrates that the combined effect of multiple components working together is greater than the individual contributions of those components. Our collective interactions and interdependencies between the component elements have given rise to 'Enabling Town Slough' and demonstrates the emergence of complex and often unexpected benefits. The elements below are described in chronological order.

The Circle Works

From the beginning, the process of change started by working relationally. The first opportunity to do this was by introducing The Circle Works (Geoffrey Court, 2002). This is a forum for people to come together in a way where everybody has an equal voice, and it was created for teachers. The creator Geoffrey Court realised there was no space for the teaching profession to reflect on the complexity of their work. The key concept is that the facilitator is the host of the hosted space, whilst ownership is with participants. Utilising The Circle Works allowed us to give voice to those who had not previously have a voice – to express and describe their needs and views. Allowing this space and process empowered the first authentic co-production of the town's services. Later in the process it was introduced and incorporated into the structures for development of the local community. The process allowed us to start a programme design with a different vision to develop more appropriate recovery-focused programmes.

Recovery Team

The second clear gap that became apparent was, on examining what recovery workers within the local Community Mental Health Team actually did, it became clear that it was not effective and had little therapeutic value. There was little understanding of the importance of the person's psychosocial needs, so the work only focused on practical tasks. The recovery team was therefore developed in a way which brought all the recovery workers together under clinical leadership which concentrated on therapeutic aspects, including strength-based recovery planning. This required a change in the way that recovery workers were treated and valued.

Singing for Health

Mobilising professional staff was equally important. We invited nurses, social workers, doctors, and psychologists to participate in one of the first group activities, *Singing for Health*. People who used the services and clinicians were invited to be a part of this: it horizontalised the power dynamic and allowed them to have a common sense of purpose. The choir was named 'One Voice' and focused on practising together for performances at public annual events which supported mental health, such as World Mental Health Day on 10th October each year.

ASSiST (Alternative to Admission)

Following the closure of local hospital psychiatric beds, funding was made available for an alternative to admission service. Different proposals were considered, including a crisis management service and commissioning private hospital beds. However, our psychologically informed proposal was accepted, and a team focusing on supporting people with at least 20 bed days of admission was developed. The team worked with people on psychiatric wards, who were considered by the system to be presenting with 'high risk' behaviours. People were supported to be discharged by focusing on individual's needs based on psychological formulation, rather than the diagnosis. The focus on the Joiner's Interpersonal Theory of Suicide model (Joiner, 2005) was used to ensure that safety plans were based on the biopsychosocial needs of the person, whilst considering their strengths. People were supported to develop a sense of purpose and belonging. This is described in more detail below.

A concerted effort was made to meet people where they were, and to support them with their needs in a relational way whilst they were still on inpatient wards. It connected to other wider community opportunities, and it worked across sectors. People were supported for at least three months to develop their own individualised plans, and the programme was based on therapeutic community and enabling environment values (Royal College of Psychiatrists, 2016). However, it became apparent that, with the success of first year of ASSiST, more was required: continuing the principle of a therapeutic community approach, development of a novel therapeutic community was the next step.

EMBRACE Therapeutic Community

A therapeutic community was developed to allow the person to move forward within its enabling environment, which provided a continuity of care with the AS-SiST therapeutic culture. EMBRACE is a modified asset-based therapeutic community. The modification is based on a number of important areas. Firstly, fusion between Democratic Therapeutic Communities and Concept Therapeutic Communities was established (Haigh & Lees, 2008), which was based on the values of each, and which allowed the service to develop in a distinctive and innovative way. In addition to this 'fusion model', it could also be described as a 'therapeutic community without walls', as it is based on connecting the core weekly group to the wider system that was being developed alongside and across the town's mental health and social care services.

EMBRACE developed a four-phase programme, based on people's individual needs and assets (strengths). It became clear that people who used the service were in those phases; the needs identified themselves through the co-production itself, and continues to do so. EMBRACE has been recognised as a modified therapeutic community by The Royal College of Psychiatrists (Haigh & Tucker, 2004). The model of fusion and modification has been recognised by two three-year cycles of formal accreditation as meeting the College's Community of Communities' standards and values.

EMBRACE has been actively involved and contributed within the field of therapeutic communities by widely sharing its structure, processes, and outcomes. Presentations at conferences and engagements with a wider field are always co-produced, are designed specifically for each occasion, and creatively involve participation of diverse audiences.

Hope Recovery College

It became apparent that the recovery team's therapeutic work also required a different way to work creatively, for certain groups of people. Hope recovery college is a co-produced service with a curriculum being developed by people who use services and their carers, alongside staff: it is forever changing, dependent on the needs of people who use services at the time. The success of co-production within Hope College has allowed people who used services to deliver courses themselves. It has open days each semester, which become a part of the wider community. People who used services are involved in talking to the wider community about the college and promoting it.

Peer Mentors

With the success of EMBRACE and people going through phases and moving on from the TC programme, the graduates were offered opportunities within Hope College – and peer mentor training was born. This was also offered to everyone using mental health services, and an impressive group of volunteers was supported to develop their own personal skills. The value of volunteering became apparent, and it empowered people to seek wider employment opportunities. Once people come to the end of their pathways within standard service provision, people are offered different opportunities, including 'Helping Hands' and the peer mentors programme. Peer mentors and Helping Hands contribute widely to the recovery pathway and are called upon to engage with, and present information to, people who use services, service providers, organisations, and commissioners.

After peer mentors have completed their therapeutic programmes and have undergone specific training, they become equal members of the team alongside other professionals. The service has now reached a stage where they are being employed in substantive posts.

The key to all of the above was the collaboration between the local authority and health services with a strategic understanding of the need to incrementally develop mental health provision in a cohesive and planned way. There was an annual schedule of developments based on what had been successfully achieved and what the next development needed to be. None of the developments were in isolation, but it involved collaboration with all parts of the system. The positive outcomes and evidence for successful services, all working within the framework of relational practice, helped to develop trusting relationships with commissioning decision-makers and other key people, who could then support further consistent and progressive developments.

Hope House (Supported Living)

The next target within the development was supporting a more meaningful supported living accommodation for people within the locality. The vision was supported living accommodation at Hope House, a ten-bedded unit, with a six-bedded move-on block of flats. This allowed a two-year programme for people with supported living needs to move on into more independent accommodation. Partnerships were developed between the mental health provider, the local authority commissioner, and a supported living provider called Look Ahead, who offer Care Support and Housing. The contract was set up to allow for co-production of the supported living needs with a direct link to mental health services as developed above. A clinician occupational therapist based within the Recovery Team was dedicated to supporting the residents and supported living colleagues. Other teams were working closely to support staff and people who use services according to the needs identified in the collaborative partnership. The success of Hope House led to a further development of a higher needs supported living house, called Hope Place. This is an eight-bedded unit using the same model.

BRAVE (Domestic Abuse Programme)

Another example of collaboration and incremental development of services with the local authority and health was the development of the BRAVE project. This came about through conversations including those who use the services, about what was missing. This led to an understanding of how we could start a project to address the psychological impact of domestic abuse. From the initial conversation and finding common ground, a project proposal was developed and accepted. The initial pilot ran for three years and was so successful that it secured The Police and Crime Commissioner Ministry of Justice funding, and it expanded to the rest of the county. The model has in itself become another therapeutic community-based service, following key relational and enabling values, and including people with lived experience in its co-production.

Public Health Partnership Working

Public Health is a part of the local authority provision, and it has always been an important collaboration for mental health services. Only by working together can prevention and health promotion be properly addressed. Mental health services have been a part of the overall health strategy and have incrementally developed strategies which promoted key messages and values for the locality. The partnership with Public Health was an important part of developing key strategies and events to share and promote across the town. Again, trusting relationships were built, which formed the basis on which funding was allocated for further development. This included the design of the website, and funding for a person who used services to be employed in a role to lead on this co-production.

Enabling Town Slough Website

This year-long project was managed by mental health services in collaboration between Public Health, the local authority, and those who use services. The web design company were brought in to learn about the way we worked; this resulted in co-production for the web design, again showing the value of working in a fundamentally relational way. 'Enabling Town Slough' became the umbrella term for all the work, across sectors, that was being co-produced across the town. It gathered together the relational, enabling, and all-encompassing model that ran like a golden thread through all that we had been implementing for the last decade. It also allowed interested people to have one place to find out all about services and the strategy. Since its launch, it has continued to grow and adapt according to needs. A special area, with a log-in for carers and people who used services, was built, bringing together various useful resources as well as information on services and support in the community. It became a particularly important resource during the Covid pandemic.

Leading Co-Production across the County

Based on the success of Slough's co-production model, external partners have often become interested in learning more about the model. For example, we were invited to lead on the development of co-production across the county – to explore what people needed, and for the development of the pathway. Slough citizens and staff welcomed the opportunity to share this experience across the whole county, and further afield. It contributed to a sense of pride, meaning, and purpose for those who had previously received little of those benefits from the statutory services.

Flagship Events

As a part of our development, to reach the wider community, we introduced an annual gathering on 10th October, World Mental Health Day. These themed events have been so successful, truly including the whole community in coming together to promote better understanding of mental health, and celebrating all the work that had been done by people who use services. One of the events was a 'Slough Fest', in which local people provided all the food for hundreds of people who attended. The celebration included adults and older adults who use services, as well as their carers, family, and friends – with art exhibitions, a play, a film, music, dance classes, poetry reading, and a choir. Everything was co-produced and developed according to strengths our community members had at the time. Peer mentors were the key 'meet and greet' people and worked tirelessly to make it all happen.

Another year brought the theme of *suicide prevention*. The key play included 'What's Left Behind', which highlighted the issues surrounding bereavement by suicide. Songs within the theme of 'I can't keep quiet' in both poetry and singing allowed people to experience the depth of despair and desolation that can be part of mental health issues. It allowed participants to form a new understanding, and to start talking more openly about suicide in our communities.

The theme of *social isolation and loneliness* brought another year's celebration, called 'Being and Belonging'. Our peer mentors were commissioned to do a research project on the views of communities about what it meant 'to belong' and its importance. Key findings were presented by the peer researchers on the main stage.

Further years promoted co-production and its impact: togetherness, connectedness and being stronger together. Despair in our communities was named and a dialogue started to reduce the stigma and feeling of the need to keep quiet about mental health issues. The theme of *the sound of silence* was used for this, and it included a dance performance portraying, through movement, feelings of despondency, and the need to talk and connect.

Therapeutic Philosophy

Our service philosophy was co-produced using The Circle Works: This is text that was created by the process:

Compassion is the foundation of our philosophy and combined with trust and honesty we can thrive in our community together. We want to be allowed to find our own voices and for our own unique individuality to be heard and seen. We would like to be empowered to help ourselves based on support, acceptance and kindness which will enable us to grow as people. We can all learn from each other and we don't always want advice, sometimes it is to be non-judgmentally listened to and validated as human beings. We are not a diagnosis we are people and we would like to be involved in decisions around our mental health, and when this is not possible – to still be treated with utmost respect. Please do not concentrate on 'un-wellness' and find at least a small bit of 'wellness' each day.

Conclusion

It is important to emphasise 'the paradigm shift' which has allowed the Enabling Town Slough project to achieve so much has been primarily based on changing the nature of relationships across the whole system. We believe the success and growth of Enabling Town Slough is that it is not constrained by walls, or limited by set structures: it is because it is a living, breathing, growing and expanding process, which requires alignment of the interdependent elements described above.

In adopting the therapeutic community model we enabled the community of the town itself to be therapeutic. This change embraces the increasing complexity of community and society and highlights limitations of the current treatment system.

Berkshire Healthcare legally owns IP (Copyright, Designs and Patent Act 1988) arising from the delivery of patient care, the education and training of employees and R&D programmes undertaken by its employees in the normal course of their work for Berkshire Healthcare. The programmes of work have been delivered in collaboration with system partners.

References

Ansell, L., Haigh, R., Hamilton, S., Lomas, F., Tizzard, S. & Welsh, H. (2019) Existential settings and groups: Our weekly Greencare Group. In: *Wiley World Handbook of Existential Therapy*. Chichester Sussex: Wiley. p. 656.

Antonovsky, A. (1996) The salutogenic model as a theory to guide health promotion. *Health Promotion International*. 11 (1) pp. 11–18.

Benefield, N., Turner, K., Bolger, L. & Bainbridge, C. (2018) Psychologically informed planned environments: A new optimism for criminal justice provision. In: *Transforming Environments and Offender Rehabilitation*. Akerman, G., Needs, A. & Bainbridge, C. (Eds). London: Routledge. pp. 179–197.

Blanch, A., Filson, B., Penney, D. & Cave, C. (2012) *Engaging Women in Trauma Informed Peer Support: A Guidebook*. Rockville, MD: National Center for Trauma-Informed Care.

Burls, A. (2007) People and green spaces: Promoting public health and mental well-being through ecotherapy. *Journal of Public Mental Health.* **6** (3) pp. 24–39.

De Leon, G. (2000) *The Therapeutic Community: Theory, Model, and Method.* Berlin: Springer Publishing Company.

Dennis, G. (2004) *Trading Places: A Peer Research Project with Drug Users in South Gloucestershire.* Kingswood: South Gloucestershire Local Authority.

Dennis, G. (2011) *Custodians.* Halifax: The Circle Works.

Dennis, G. (2018) *Without Walls.* The Consortium of Therapeutic Communities Conference.

Dennis, G. & Berthollier, N. (2020). *Doing the Dance Differently.* Quing International Conference Recovery to Discovery, Isle of Man, 6 March 2020.

Franklin, J.C., Ribeiro, J.D., Fox, K.R., Bentley, K.H., Kleiman, E.M., Huang, X., Musacchio, K.M., Jaroszewski, A.C., Chang, B.P. & Nock, M.K. (2017) Risk factors for suicidal thoughts and behaviors: A meta-analysis of 50 years of research. *Psychological Bulletin.* **143** (2) p. 187.

Geoffrey Court (2002) *The Circle Works.* https://theimaginationacts.co.uk/tales/tales-circle-works-celebrating-30-years/

Haigh, R. (2013) The quintessence of a therapeutic environment. *Therapeutic Communities: The International Journal of Therapeutic Communities.* **34** (1) pp. 6–15.

Haigh, R. (2018) Therapeutic communities for the future: Surviving modernisation and staying at the radical edge. In: *The Neurobiology-Psychotherapy-Pharmacology Intervention Triangle: The Need for Common Sense in 21st Century Mental Health.* Pereira, J.G., Gonçalves, J. & Bizzari, V. (Eds). Wilmington, DE: Vernon Press. pp. 111–126.

Haigh, R. & Benefield, N. (2019) Towards a unified model of human development. *Mental Health Review Journal.* **24** (2) pp. 124–132.

Haigh, R., Harrison, T., Johnson, R., Paget, S. & Williams, S. (2012) Psychologically informed environments and the "Enabling Environments" initiative. *Housing, Care and Support.* **15** (1) pp. 34–42.

Haigh, R. & Lees, J. (2008) Fusion TCs: Divergent histories, converging challenges. *Therapeutic Communities.* South Gloucestershire Local Authority **29** (4) pp. 347–374.

Haigh, R. & Tucker, S. (2004) Democratic development of standards: The community of communities – a quality network of therapeutic communities. *Psychiatric Quarterly.* **75** (3) pp. 263–277.

Johnson, R. & Haigh, R. (2010) Social psychiatry and social policy for the 21st century-new concepts for new needs: The 'psychologically-informed environment'. *Mental Health and Social Inclusion.* **14** (4) pp. 30–35.

Johnstone, L., Boyle, M., Cromby, J., Dillon, J., Harper, D., Kinderman, P., Longden, E., Pilgrim, D. & Read, J. (2018) *The Power Threat Meaning Framework.* https://cms.bps.org.uk/sites/default/files/2022-07/PTM%20Framework%20%28January%202018%29_0.pdf

Joiner, T.E. (2005) *Why People Die by Suicide.* Cambridge: Harvard University Press.

Keats, J. (1899) *The Complete Poetical Works and Letters of John Keats.* Boston: Houghton Mifflin Company.

Keats, H., Maguire, N., Johnson, R. & Cockersell, P. (2012) *Psychologically Informed Services for Homeless People.* (Good Practice Guide) Southampton: GB. Communities and Local Government.

Lewin, K. (1939) Field theory and experiment in social psychology: Concepts and methods. *American Journal of Sociology.* **44** (6) pp. 868–896.

Mbiti, J.S. (2015) *Introduction to African Religion.* 2nd Edition. Long Grove: Waveland Press.

Morgan, A. & Ziglio, E. (2007) Revitalising the evidence base for public health: An assets model. *Promotion & Education.* **14** (2_suppl) pp. 17–22.

Nderitu, D. (2020) The meaning of human person in the African context. In Wariboko, N. & Falola, T. (Eds). *The Palgrave Handbook of African Social Ethics.* London: Palgrave Macmillan. pp. 93–102.

Pearce, S. & Haigh, R. (2017) *A Handbook of Democratic Therapeutic Community Theory and Practice*. London: Jessica Kingsley Publishers.

Pearce, S. & Pickard, H. (2013) How therapeutic communities work: Specific factors related to positive outcome. *The International Journal of Social Psychiatry*. **59** (7) pp. 636–645. https://doi.org/10.1177/0020764012450992.

Rawlings, B. (2005) The temporary therapeutic community: A qualitative evaluation of an ATC training weekend. *Therapeutic Communities*. **26** (1) pp. 6–18.

Royal College of Psychiatrists (2016) *What Is the Enabling Environments Award?* https://tinyurl.com/EEatRCPsych.

Seikkula, J. & Olson, M.E. (2003) The open dialogue approach to acute psychosis: Its poetics and micropolitics. *Family Process*. **42** (3) pp. 403–418.

Sempik, J., Hine, R. & Wilcox, D. (2010) *Green Care: A Conceptual Framework, a Report of the Working Group on the Health Benefits of Green Care*. Loughborough: EU COST Action.

Sweeney, A., Clement, S., Filson, B. & Kennedy, A. (2016) Trauma-informed mental healthcare in the UK: What is it and how can we further its development? *Mental Health Review Journal*. **21** pp. 174–192.

Van Orden, K.A., Witte, T.K., Cukrowicz, K.C., Braithwaite, S.R., Selby, E.A. & Joiner, T.E. Jr (2010) The interpersonal theory of suicide. *Psychological Review*. **117** (2) pp. 575–600.

Vandevelde, S., Broekaert, E., Yates, R. & Kooyman, M. (2004) The development of the therapeutic community in correctional establishments: A comparative retrospective account of the 'DEMOCRATIC' Maxwell Jones TC and the hierarchical concept-based TC in prison. *International Journal of Social Psychiatry*. **50** (1) pp. 66–79. https://doi.org/10.1177/0020764004040954.

Winship, G. (2004) Democracy in practice in fourteen UK psycho-therapeutic communities. *International Journal of Therapeutic Communities*. **5** (4) pp. 275–290.

PIE and Organisational Development

Part III

RIR and Organizational
Development

Chapter 8

Reflective Practice – Contributions to Practice Development and Leadership

Ali Curran

Introduction

In this chapter, we examine reflective practice as a core component of psychologically informed environments (PIEs) and the contribution it makes to trauma-informed practice. We consider reflective practice in general before outlining typical individual and group responses to reflective practice at different stages and ways in which the practice invites individual, group, and organisational leadership. The processes, reflections, and understanding described here arise from my experiences over many years of facilitating reflective practice groups, and leading a team of facilitators, across a large multi-site, multi-layered organisation providing services for homeless people.

A Brief Introduction to Reflective Practice

Reflective practice involves paying attention to thoughts and feelings which arise in the context of work so that these may be observed, thought about, and considered as to whether they were helpful responses to the situation. Grounded in self-awareness, the practice of reflexivity is developed at the level of the individual and practised in a variety of contexts. It can form part of a team meeting, individual and group supervision, or in a reflective practice group. Dedicated reflective practice groups are a central element in a PIE working model: they offer an intentional space in which reflectivity can develop through the sharing of experience and peer learning.

Founded on trust and confidentiality, the reflective practice group is a safe place in which to explore how you are in your work and the highs and lows that naturally occur as a result of interactions with clients and colleagues. An original concept of theorist Donald Schon lays the foundation for what today is at the core of reflective practice:

> Just as reflective practice takes the form of a reflective conversation with the situation, so the reflective practitioner's relationship with the client takes the form of a literally reflective conversation. Here the professional expertise is

DOI: 10.4324/9781003415053-11

embedded in the context of meanings. He attributes to his client, as well as to himself, a capacity to mean, know and plan. He recognizes that his actions may have different meaning for his client then he intends them to have, and he gives himself the task of discovering what these are. He recognises an obligation to make his own understandings accessible to the client, which means he often has to reflect anew on what he knows.

(Schon, 1984)

Schon's seminal text referred to reflection in the context of a variety of professions from law and medicine to urban design and psychiatry. His core theory, regardless of profession, proposes that in order to remain attuned to our professional practice we must reflect on the exchanges and interactions we have with clients and colleagues to continuously learn about ourselves as practitioners in action. Although the inclination towards reflection is a character trait, it is also a skill which can be developed by conscious and intentional action.

In the context of social care, working as a PIE with reflective practice groups offers staff at all levels a space to think about complexity, to consider factors of influence and what might be going on beyond what is initially apparent in an interaction or situation. The act of reflection helps to slow down thinking, enabling some distance, and creating space to consider ways our professional selves react and respond to individuals and situations: it is a vital part of developing professional practice especially in sectors offering services to vulnerable clients and working with compound trauma, where interactions need to be responsive not reactive. Aptitude for reflection is greatly enhanced by being part of a regular reflective group meeting weekly, bi-monthly or monthly, as a minimum; reflection also often forms part of supervision and is a central element of mentoring and coaching.

There are several studies specific to social and homelessness services which draw out these findings that can be found on PIElink, a dedicated practitioner portal for organisations and professionals working within the PIE framework (also see Cockersell et al. for further references; Cockersell, 2018).

Reflective practice differs from group supervision which is framed more explicitly by the client work. The reflective practice space is available to a wider range of considerations provided they are relevant to work and the professional self: the group's purpose is to explore together experiences, incidents, or topics in a reflexive manner and to benefit the group members by working things through together. It is the working through with a group of peers which is the important characteristic of group reflective practice, and which makes it an important factor at all hierarchical levels of an organisation, especially one that aspires to being psychologically or trauma informed. The important and sometimes difficult work which is done by the group will ultimately help to maintain best practice and client-centred services for those experiencing compound trauma and/or the challenges of homelessness.

From a leadership perspective, being prepared to take stock, share learnings, and consider things from other perspectives are actions which communicate that reflection is welcomed, that it is valued, and that it is an integral part of the organisational culture. Reflective practice accelerates the process of introducing psychologically and trauma informed practice in an organisation as it provides a regular space in which the day-to-day demands of the work can be thought about from a psychologically and trauma informed perspective within a group, engendering or enhancing the process of peer learning.

Observations on the Reflective Practice Group Process

Reflective practice in groups requires time for the group members to settle into the work together, to establish a sense of connectedness, and for members to find their voice. It is a process which rewards on the basis of the inputs from its members and as such it is best for members in the early stages of group work, for example the first 10–12 sessions, to attend reflective practice with an open mind: this means thinking about what you might bring to the group which would be useful to hear colleagues' reflection on, and, of equal importance, showing up as an attentive listener to what other group members bring.

Participating in a group process can evoke new and challenging feelings. This is not only true of the beginning stages of being in a group: it is the nature of group dynamics regardless of how long the group has been gathering. Silences can evoke anxiety in some and not others, for example, or it can be difficult to be honest in our reflections and open about some of our more vulnerable moments in our work: this is normal and part of building our confidence as a more reflective practitioner.

However, the more time spent in reflective groups the greater the capacity to tolerate these responses and understand them as an integral part of the learning becomes. While reflective practice groups are often established to support frontline staff in the client work, they also provide a space in which teams and individuals can reflect upon all aspects of the work which may not comfortably belong in other settings such as team or business meetings, or group supervisions. This is particularly important for managers and senior staff who may not have other forums where the impact of the work and the working environment on them and their capacity for effective action can be discussed.

With this in mind, this can give rise to pre-group anxiety or in-group tensions as the notion that something unspeakable might be given voice and the fear that the group might implode (Hartley and Kennard, 2009). Furthermore, organisational anxieties can manifest in ways which seek to undermine the group boundary: for example, a manager might ask a group member about things that come up in the group, which places the group member in a difficult position as to whether or not to break the group's boundary; or individuals may become hostile to the group itself as the reflective space becomes the locus of negative projections. Certain groups then become the subject of "good group – bad group" projections as a result of leaky boundaries, which threatens to undermine the reflective group process. That each reflective practice group holds a certain mystery to those who are not present in it (Gilbert, 2001) is unavoidable, and therefore individual and organisational leadership is required to take up the practice and adhere to, and protect, the simple but critical boundaries within which the practice can be maintained and grown.

As group members this simple boundary requires showing up regularly, and participating actively and authentically. Organisationally, leadership in the reflective capacity of the whole organisation is enacted through executives and managers putting practice development over externally imposed organisational outcomes. Most organisations operate on a transactional basis, providing services measured by outcomes for funders and, while outcomes are quantifiable and valid as a form of measurement, in social care professions which operate on a relational basis, such as PIEs, the reality of practice is actually more complex. Often it is less about concrete outcomes such as reducing numbers entering homelessness and rather about investing in understanding and working through the complex needs of the client within supportive working partnerships.

Psychologically informed organisations operating a model of trauma informed care (TIC), are relational rather than transactional. By acknowledging and overriding the desire for simplistic concrete outcomes, decision-makers with operational and budgetary responsibility demonstrate trauma informed leadership when they allocate adequate resources for staff teams to participate in reflective practice groups, and actively encourage them to do so, including by example. This in turn achieves positive organisational outcomes by way of building resilience against vicarious trauma, reducing burnout and lowering staff turnover (McFadden, Campbell and Taylor, 2015)

Furthermore, psychologically and trauma informed culture is enhanced when management and executives participate in reflective practice themselves, recognising that organisational trauma is relevant to the whole system. Connecting to the practice of reflection can be challenging for those working further away from direct client contact. However, developing an aptitude for reflection is at least as important in these roles as in any other as it will then inform whether decisions are made and policies formed in a psychologically informed, trauma informed, client-centred way, which in turn affects the tone and culture of the whole organisation.

If this describes the optimum starting position for reflective practice in an organisation – that reflective practice permeates all levels of the hierarchy – let's next look at some of the conditions and phenomena which require conscious and intentional leadership in order to establish and keep reflective practice going.

Creating the Right Conditions

There are some critical factors to consider when establishing reflective practice within an organisation, some of which on the surface have the appearance of being simply practical and administrative. However, these factors form the foundation of the work and are fundamental to creating the best possible beginning for the group to act as a safe container for its members. We will look at these factors in turn before considering the effect of the factors in combination with each other.

Environment

Environment is a primary consideration in working as a PIE. Being aware of the physical space in which we invite people to engage in intimate client work and their own professional development suggests certain conditions which are conducive to reflection. Firstly, the space in which the group is due to meet needs to be large enough to hold all group members comfortably: that is, to accommodate a circle of chairs with adequate space between each so that group members can experience connection without crossing into their neighbours' personal space. If the room is very large, the facilitator will need to create a section of the room that can emulate a more intimate area in order to create that quality. The space should have adequate natural light and sufficient heating: 90 minutes is a long time to sit in one place, and if it is dark and/or cold, it is likely to distract from the task of reflection.

Location

The space needs to be located somewhere that is private: that is, for the duration of the group anyway, not a shared or transitional space where other people are moving through or around. Ideally, the space will be away from common areas such as a canteen or staff kitchen to ensure that there is no opportunity for the discussion taking place in the reflective group to be overheard as this can cause group members to become self-conscious and silent. Universal accessibility should also be taken into account.

Timing

The reflective group should be scheduled at a time that is most conducive to the group members' schedule so as to remove as many barriers to attendance as possible from the beginning. The facilitator will not know the unique patterns of each team, or individual group members' schedules, so it is therefore incumbent on the manager or the group members themselves to liaise with the group facilitator to identify a day and time that they feel will be (most) convenient for all the group members to attend.

Consistency

The space in which the group meets should be the same every month (or week, etc., depending on the group frequency, which we touch on later in this chapter). This consistency is an important cue that underpins the regularity of the practice and develops unconscious associations between space and practice which support the development of reflective capacity. Holding the space is an important unconscious part of the containment the group can offer its members.

Initiating the Group and the Role of the Facilitator

Typically, groups are requested from within the organisation, perhaps by the services division, the practice development team, or human resources. This will be based on an assessment of need which the facilitator should sense-check initially with the original point of contact. It is an important part of the initial psychological contracting process to also check the perceived purpose with the group itself and to deal head on with any issues which are immediately apparent before moving into a more expansive reflective process. Often there will be dominant themes which group members wish to discuss in early sessions which need to be aired before practice reflection is possible.

It is worth bearing in mind when introducing reflective groups for the first time that in many organisations, especially those of scale, this will be the first confidential space without a specific agenda that will have been offered to staff teams: naturally, there may be a desire to offload a little. The facilitator should be practised in managing this, allowing for the need of the group to do so before bringing the group back to the primary purpose of reflective practice and professional development.

Clarity on Approach and Process

Reflective practice and indeed many group processes are responsive to the group members' engagement and interaction. Whether working in a structured format or a more open, associative way, group members should be part of the discussion with the facilitator as to how the group intends to work together. This is particularly important at the outset to differentiate the group process from another other type of team and group meeting where hierarchy or agenda takes precedence. In reflective practice groups, all members are equal and the facilitator is in service to the group, so establishing the members' intention to be present and open to participate is key. This intentionality forms part of the psychological contract, as is the adherence to confidentiality and respect for fellow group members.

Homogenous versus Non-Homogenous Groups

Team members already know each other. This can escalate the connection but can also silence those who don't feel comfortable opening up in front of colleagues; similarly, intra-team dynamics influence the unconscious group process, and where there are tensions things may come to a head in the group. The reflective space can become a dumping ground for frustrations between staff and management with individual reflection and learning absorbed into 'group-think' and oppositional positioning.

On the other side, members of more diverse groups may be tentative about reflecting with people they don't know. There may be unconscious envy or competition between teams or individuals, with members feeling unable to present honestly from fear that they are exposing themselves and/or their colleagues, or in some way appearing as failing or less than if they are honest about difficulties in practice.

Either way, without accepting pre-conceived positions/projections from the manager or whoever is identifying members of the reflective group, the facilitator needs to consider the group membership and their relationships to each other, from whether they work together outside the group to the sequence in which group members arrive.

Attendance

While group members may not always feel like attending a reflective practice group consistent attendance pays dividends for the individual and for the group. Understandably, in a busy, often pressurised work environment, members can feel that they are "too busy" to take the time out for the group or perhaps that they have little to contribute or are unable to share what's going on for them. It is in these moments that it is especially important to attend, and it is especially important that there is an organisational culture, from senior leadership down, that attendance is assumed. Choosing to override these resistances can offer learning about what the resistance might be telling us, unlocking a deeper understanding of what is going on for us in our working lives. Being present to the experience of others and contributing to the group as an attentive listener is an equally important role in the group. The cohesiveness and level of participation in the groups says something about the cohesiveness and level of participation in the psychological and emotional life of the whole organisation.

Confidentiality

There are limitations to the confidential boundary of the reflective practice space, but this should only happen in consultation with the group, by their request, and by agreement with all group members present. For example, the group may decide that they wish something that has come to light through reflective practice to be brought to the attention of colleagues who are not part of the group; or there might be concerns surrounding an incident, individual, or situation that affects the group and the group members may want this to be taken outside the group and, for example, be brought to the attention of management.

Paying attention to these factors is a helpful familiarisation exercise for the facilitator as they learn much about the organisational culture and system in co-ordinating these elements. For group members (and their managers) it positions the reflective group as requiring to be thought about differently to other team or group meetings, demonstrating the care and attention which is a characteristic of the practice and of the quality of facilitation the group will be receiving.

There is a considerable amount of thought put into starting a reflective group which the facilitator holds in their role as the person primarily responsible for the group's dynamic administration, that is to say the apparently practical elements, such as setting a schedule of dates and times at which to meet, securing a space which is consistent and suitable, and maintaining communication and coordination with group members and the relevant person in the organisation (i.e. manager, team lead, staff development lead, etc.). From a group analytic perspective, the outputs arising from attentive and considered dynamic administration are the foundation on which the group can form safely and securely, and be felt as containing. These apparently tangible details pertaining to things such as room size, natural light, convenience of location, and consistency of access are indeed practical but they are also emblematic of the psychological investment in the group members by the facilitator as a supportive resource invested in, but independent of, the organisation.

These considerations and conditions within which reflective practice has the best chance of establishing itself can be counter-intuitive to the organisational drive for ad-hoc solutions and "fixes", tangible results, and concrete outcomes. As discussed previously, psychologically and trauma informed practice is relational rather than transactional and group member interactions dictate process and progress. Therefore, forming a safe space of genuine support and practice development for group members to work with what is present, regardless of timeframe or external contexts, requires ongoing commitment and leadership from all involved.

Leadership in Reflective Practice

The role of the facilitator is in establishing an authentic space, operating without agenda, in which "humble inquiry" can prevail; that is to say, the means by which questions for which answers are not yet known can be put to the group as a whole, in order to promote reflection on what might be occurring beyond surface appearances (Schein and Schein, 2021). This active learning experience is both cerebral and physical, encouraging members to work with all available sources in information including what their body might be telling them in terms of feelings of anxiety, unease, or general disturbance. Often it is not necessarily about knowing exactly what is the right or wrong of a situation but rather becoming open to the sensations that something is not sitting well with you in the exchange, whether that be with a client or a colleague, and that is perhaps the most valuable area of focus of our reflections as it offers the greatest potential for deeper learning.

The practice of balancing measurable outputs with the less definite areas of social care, which are more process than outcome and contain many factors which are beyond the control of the social care professional, examined through the group process and shared experience of the group members can inform a more accurate perspective on the work which is both task and process based. This is true at all hierarchical levels of the organisation.

The group facilitator at this stage is considering the roles taken up in the group, not so much as identifying individuals with behaviours, but rather the ways in which the group dynamic motivates individuals to unconsciously take up certain roles and enact these roles in and for the group. For example, in an early-stage group, it would be common to observe group members not listening to each other or cutting each other off, dominating, making inappropriate jokes or being very silent. These are ways in which the group facilitator can think about the needs of the individual-in-the-group and what are known as "anti-group" behaviours: behaviours which can be the actions of the individual or a presentation of the unconscious dynamic of the group or both. The group facilitator can consider what role this and each group member is taking up for the group.

This stage of helping the group form involves tuning into the group energy and interpreting the verbal and non-verbal cues. Initially, giving time to a perceived "non-doing" space can feel counter-intuitive to the task-oriented staff member or manager; it takes time for the practice to embed and to take up a position of priority in the weekly or monthly schedule. For that reason, any in-group or external review is conducted at the earliest after ten–twelve group sessions, to allow for the group members to experience their own journey into reflection and to establish "groupishness" (Adlam and Scanlon, 2009).

While the focus may be on the facilitator in early group stages, often with group members directing reflections and comments through the facilitator, as the group matures reliance on the facilitator lessens. What emerges is group member "ally-ship" from shared intimacy relating to the challenges of their work, and appreciation for support in navigating organisational dynamics. Ally-ship is the active state of looking out for each other in the workplace, attending to inequity, and upholding a level playing field. It is critical to establishing and maintaining workplace equality. The principle and practice of ally-ship is a cornerstone of trauma informed and PIE ways of working because attunement to the disenfranchised and marginalised is key. These principles are also germane to the conditions of a reflective practice group, which should strive to be a space founded on equality and inclusion for all members. Ally-ship is shown to be a powerful consequence of safe, trusted space in which to share around the work: deepening empathy, emotional literacy, and sharing of practical supports occurs as ally-ship increases (Lambert, Egan and Thomas, 2021).

As time in reflective practice accumulates, the group matures and it is the members who set the tone and energy of the group. This ownership of the group process is an important transition in leadership. The facilitator continues to contribute to the sense making process, offering observations to the group for reflection, but the group no longer needs the facilitator to keep the group "on track" but rather the members take up leadership of the group collectively in reflection and exchange.

Leadership is therefore crucial to the reflective atmosphere. Modelling a reflective stance within the group increases levels of reflexivity for all members within the group and outside the reflective group environment, infusing the team culture which in turn contributes to the collectiveness and effectiveness of organisational culture.

Evidence of this is more likely to show up in behaviours, attitudes, and the way in which people speak about the work, rather than as a single uniform response. For example, practitioners demonstrate greater awareness of the nuances of the client (or funder or management) relationship, develop increased capacity and tolerance for working with uncertainty, and include reflection as an integral part of how to approach challenges and problems as they arise. Furthermore, team members develop an appreciation for each other's practice, greater tolerance for difference in approaches, and are more attuned towards colleagues' needs for support outside of the group setting.

Between group sessions, reflective practice is encouraged in other settings. For managers of teams and those in senior roles, reflective practice, whether in a closed group, supervision or team context, signifies a certain type of leadership and communicates organisational values which are psychologically and trauma informed. For those in leadership positions, actively supporting reflective practice and attending a group oneself encapsulates internal and external messaging which reflects positively on the organisation. It says:

- This organisation is pro-enquiry, recognising reflective practice as a tool to appreciate the complexity and nuance of the work.
- That to reflect in order to learn is a strength; no one is expected to know everything and learning-in-action is encouraged.
- The organisation is a learning environment regardless of perceived levels of experience, expertise, or position.

This is not to say that training and experience does not accumulate in ways of knowing that allows the practitioner to be confident in assessing the needs of a situation or interaction, determining a course of action, or determining the strategic direction of the organisation: confidence and agency in a role is supported by the reflective practice and the benefit of consideration of the perspective of colleagues.

Whether we choose to share within a particular reflective group or not is an individual decision, a preference of learning styles as much as anything. However, everyone in the group benefits from another's reflection by association: internal resonances can echo beyond the boundary of the allocated. It is a generous process which, when entered into fully, offers learning that is not always found in dyadic exchanges or formal learning environments.

Reflective Practice in Wider Context

Among the positive impacts possible for a client–practitioner relationship founded on trauma informed and psychologically informed care is the opportunity for the client to establish a secure attachment with the caregiver, which becomes an experiential reconsideration of earlier, often childhood, experiences when safety and security were unpredictable. The relational nature of working in a caregiving capacity with trauma is part of the emotional labour invested in by staff teams. Reflective practice provides a safe and consistent space for processing the emotional response to the work: a parallel process to the working dynamic of client and caregiver. By caring for the caregivers' capacity and tolerance for working with the clients' trauma experience and corresponding behaviours, their effectiveness, and so the whole organisation's effectiveness, is increased (Hopper, Bassuk and Olivet, 2010).

A review of the literature provides clear evidence for the value of reflective groups as staff support, with groups experienced as beneficial provided they are set up properly and run well (Hartley and Kennard, 2009). The same authors describe ways in which groups are experienced as helpful and the characteristics of groups which are likely to be experienced as unhelpful. This analysis provides useful insight when considering reflective practice in a whole system, recognising diversity of experience in groups and the reality of group benefits and perceived outcomes, which mirror the client experience with some interventions resulting in positive outcomes and some appearing to be less effective or ineffective.

As outlined earlier, suitably trained facilitators are important to the success of reflective practice groups as they are capable of identifying and working with unconscious processes within groups and considering ways in which they can help the group overcome group "basic assumptions". Basic assumptions – a theory of group behaviours originated by British psychoanalyst Wilfred Bion – describe tendencies within groups to revert to unconscious positions which get in the way of the group working together as a whole on the task at hand. Basic assumptions include an over-dependency by the group on the/a leader; preoccupation with an internal or external perceived enemy giving rise to fight or flight responses; a pairing response where two members of the group seek support in each other outside of or in opposition to the group; or when something or someone internal or external to the group is identified as a potential saviour who will solve the problems of the group or make the situation go away (Stokes, 2019). In essence, these are avoidance techniques to distract from the principal task of the group, which, in the case of reflective practice groups are the sometimes difficult feelings and thoughts which arise from professional practice within often conflicted organisations and antagonistic or simply failing systems.

"Leaders and members of groups dominated by basic assumption activity are likely to lose their ability to think and act effectively" (Stokes, 1994). Identifying when groups are working out of a basic assumption or have a tendency for adopting a particular basic assumption on an ongoing basis can be very helpful to unlocking what might not be being talked about, or what is being avoided, so that the facilitator can offer an intervention which will usefully move the group forward towards addressing the issue.

Furthermore, it is not uncommon within organisations delivering humanitarian services such as charities and health and social care providers, that power and ambition are seen as negative attributes. Organisations split off "competitive, and ambitious strivings" (Roberts, 2003) to the detriment of affective and creative leadership. Safe reflective spaces allow group members, in particular those in senior management and executive positions, to work with these kinds of dichotomies in the organisational system to reflect on the kind of leadership which can hold both the successful running of the business and its humanitarian objectives in balance.

TIC and PIE principles are by their nature client-centred, and the reflective practice space allows members to consider themselves in relation to the work, their clients, and the hoped-for restorative outcome. However, it is important to think about the way in which the whole system is part of the culture, and those without direct client contact are still in relationship with their colleagues, as well as with other departments of the organisation and the wider system. Integrating PIE and TIC principles through reflective practice at all levels in the organisation establishes the practice of thinking and acting in a psychologically informed/ trauma informed way and helps integrate the organisational response. Social care teams sit within the complex system of their own organisations while in service to a disenfranchised population within a complex social system. Belonging to an integrated organisation is arguably the greatest potential of reflective practice in a move towards being a learning organisation.

Systems theory proposes the baseline state of complex systems is in fact dis-integration. The nature of teams with a variety of team-specific goals results in a fragmentation of purpose within the overall organisation which informs a constant dynamic of disintegration (Warren, Franklin and Streeter, 1998). Reflective prac-tice builds capacity to transition between these ever-evolving organisational dy-namics, offering spaces which maintain our ability to think and make connections between everyday client interactions and unseen or unconscious organisational changes (Scanlon and Adlam, 2012).

In practical terms, these phenomena show up in referring to the organisation in the third person as if individuals are a passive component in a system over which they have no control, or in locating "the problem" within one team or division. Adopting PIE principles unlocks the opportunity to develop as a whole thinking system, and to recognise in each specific area of work the parallel process of the disempowered client within the network of services. Interfacing with external agen-cies, funding challenges, and resources shortages manifest in frustrations whether working at the frontline of homeless services or in property acquisition or execu-tive functions. Reflective practice is a space in which to reflect on the organisation as we may hold it in our minds (Armstrong, 2005), confront the reality of how we contribute to organisational culture and to consider individual and team roles as part of the wider system.

As reflective practices build trust across the organisation, members try out their voice, revealing thoughts and feelings which may be vulnerable-making. The experience of these being accepted within the group promotes an organisational configuration that is not fearful of contrary perspectives. Working with dissent and defences as naturally occurring phenomena allows alternative perspectives to be present without them overpowering the system (Armstrong, 2011).

Organisational defences frequently revert to unconscious cycles whereby the organising work happens at executive management level, with frontline workers delivering on the task feeling deprived of initiative. In homeless services each client needs a bespoke response, while the organisation is contracted to deliver a standardised response, placing the worker in a confusing space between client-centred practice and organisational loyalty. Report and audit procedures may be experienced as organisational control, and statistical reporting as a denigration of the client–practitioner relationship to a number, where success is based on simple binary metrics. Reflective practice across all areas of an organisation, front line to executive, develops a culture of inquiry, opens up this tension to creative discourse, and creates and recognises the benefit of whole system learning (Schein and Schein, 2021).

Reflective practice assists group members to work effectively in processing feelings of helplessness and frustration, creating a non-hierarchical temporary learning system within traditionally vertical organisational structures. If "the right kind of space can be created, the team may notice the levels of fear and arousal it has been doing its best to disregard" (Adlam, 2019, p. 180); these phenomena are at the route of traumatised teams and organisations.

At an individual level, vicarious trauma negatively impacts personal resources and erodes resilience. A workforce in which vicarious trauma is a significant factor results in trauma in the organisation, which can manifest in a number of ways in the reflective practice space: for example, resistance in the form of voicing discontent within the group, where the topic becomes what is wrong with the organisation rather than the circumstance, creating a consistent heaviness in the group; or consistent absenteeism, which is in essence avoidance, silencing group members and avoiding hearing the unthinkable. There are many ways in which a traumatised organisation defends against the perceived threat of being consumed by the trauma it is processing with the client group and on behalf of society.

Presentations of this nature can feel destabilising after the initial flurry of connection and concerted effort towards synergy. Despondency arises in members as they navigate the group's journey which mirrors the unpredictability, disappointment, and disempowerment of the clients' experience in homelessness (Scanlon, 2017). If the team can recognise these feelings as arising from the inherent challenges of the work and connect to the emotional highs and lows, mitigation of consequences of working with trauma is available. Social care teams and their parent organisations grapple with survivor's anxiety in the face of complex trauma: as a consequence "anxiety and blame are pushed around the system like a pinball bouncing back and forth between the different areas of responsibility" (Evans, 2015; Adlam, 2019).

Establishing a PIE can evoke unexpected reactions at different levels in the organisation. Groups operate within a confidential boundary in order that the organisational system may learn to tolerate not knowing what arises in the group and not being in control of the outcome. This parallel process mirrors the political and economic environment in which homeless services operate and the societal and community contexts in which clients of these services are located. Fantasies about power and leadership surface from the group conscience, which can help group members to consider alternative perspectives and examine their role within the wider organisational system. As a result, reflective practice groups can symbolise "the renunciation of power and the sharing of responsibility" (Adlam, 2019, p. 179). Acknowledging these dynamics supports movement from a position of fear, resulting in rejection, towards recognition of interdependence and acceptance. Reflective practice at this stage of maturity ignites distributed leadership without fear of displacement of responsibility or position.

Conclusion

Reflective practice is a space neutral of hierarchy. It is an inward-looking space in which the members organise their own dynamic. Within an organisation this offers a space in which the sharing of responsibility can unlock avoidance of facing the reality of working with trauma and promote learning from experience, creating "a clearing in the forest" (Adlam, 2019). The cornerstone of working as a PIE, this simple yet powerful tool develops trauma informed skills and capacity at individual, team and organisational level. Reflective practice supports the working-through of trauma events which are abundant in the client experience, and by extension in the homeless services which support the journey out of homelessness. Reflective practice offers a frontline defence against vicarious trauma for staff teams, creating effective protection for the organisation so that it may function as an un-traumatised, thinking system capable of responding to the vagaries of providing service to societies' most vulnerable as an emotionally intelligent organisation.

References

Adlam, J. (2019) '"Scallywag battalions": Reflective practice groups with multidisciplinary teams in mental health and social care systems', *Organisational and Social Dynamics*, 19(2), pp. 168–185. https://doi.org/10.33212/osd.v19n2.2019.168.

Adlam, J. and Scanlon, C. (2009) 'Disturbances of "groupishness"? Structural violence, refusal and the therapeutic community response to severe personality disorder', *International Forum of Psychoanalysis*, 18(1), pp. 23–29.

Armstrong, D. (2005). 'Using depictions of critical incidents for social constructions of reflective practice, conference presentation', *American Association of Colleges of Teacher Education*, Washington DC.

Armstrong, D. (2011) 'Meaning found and meaning lost: On the boundaries of a psychoanalytic study of organisations', *Organisational and Social Dynamics*, 10(1), pp. 99–117.

Cockersell, P. (ed.) (2018) *Social exclusion, compound trauma and recovery: Applying psychology, psychotherapy and PIE to homelessness and complex needs*. London: Jessica Kingsley Publishers.

Evans, M. (2015) '"I'm beyond caring"', in Armstrong, D. and Rustin, M. (eds) *Social defences against anxiety exploration in a paradigm*. London: Karnac, pp. 124–143.

Gilbert, T. (2001) 'Reflective practice and clinical supervision: Meticulous rituals of the confessional', *Journal of Advanced Nursing*, 36(2), pp. 199–205. https://doi.org/10.1046/j.1365-2648.2001.01960.x.

Hartley, P. and Kennard, D. (eds) (2009) *Staff support groups in the helping professions: Principles, practice and pitfalls*. Abingdon: Routledge.

Hopper, E. K., Bassuk, E. L. and Olivet, J. (2010) 'Shelter from the storm: Trauma-informed care in homelessness services settings', *The Open Health Services and Policy Journal*, 3(1), pp. 80–100.

Lambert, C., Egan, R. and Thomas, S. (2021) 'What does effective allyship between social workers and lived experience workers look like in the Australian mental health context?', *Qualitative Research in Psychology*, 18(4), pp. 459–472.

McFadden, P., Campbell, A. and Taylor, B. (2015) 'Resilience and burnout in child protection social work: Individual and organisational themes from a systematic literature review', *British Journal of Social Work*, 45(5), pp. 1546–1563. https://doi.org/10.1093/bjsw/bct210.

Roberts, V. Z. (2003) 'The organization of work: Contributions from open systems theory', in *The unconscious at work*. Abingdon: Routledge, pp. 48–58.

Scanlon, C. (2017) 'Working with disappointment in difficult places: Group-analytic perspectives on reflective practice and team development (RPTD) in organisations', *Group-Analytic Society International – Contexts*, (75), pp. 23–37.

Scanlon, C. and Adlam, J. (2012) 'The (dis)stressing effects of working in (dis)stressed homelessness organisations', *Housing, Care and Support*, 15(2), pp. 74–82. https://doi.org/10.1108/14608791211254207.

Schein, E. H. and Schein, P. (2021) *Humble inquiry: The gentle art of asking instead of telling*. Oakland: Berret-Koehler.

Schon, D. A. (1984) *The reflective practitioner how professionals think in action*. New York: Basic Books.

Stokes, J. (1994) 'The unconscious at work in groups and teams', in Obholzer, A. and Zagier Roberts, V. (eds) *The unconscious at work*. Abingdon: Routledge.

Stokes, J. (2019) 'The unconscious at work in groups and teams: Contributions from the work of Wilfred Bion', in *The unconscious at work*. Abingdon: Routledge, pp. 28–36.

Warren, K., Franklin, C. and Streeter, C. L. (1998) 'New directions in systems theory: Chaos and complexity', *Social Work*, 43(4), pp. 357–372. https://doi.org/10.1093/sw/43.4.357.

Chapter 9

Helping, Harming, and Being Harmed

Understanding Traumatised and Traumatising Organisations

Jo Prestidge

In this chapter, I will explore the idea that organisations can be both traumatised and traumatising and that recognising, accepting, and managing this is an essential part of any organisation's journey to become trauma and psychologically informed (TI/PI). As Brene Brown puts it, 'To build courage in teams and organizations, we have to cultivate a culture in which brave work, tough conversations, and whole hearts are the expectation, and armor is not necessary or rewarded' (Brown, 2018).

I have worked in the voluntary sector for almost two decades in both frontline services for vulnerable people and a national second tier organisation. Building on my experience in different service settings, I now have the privilege of influencing and supporting change in practice for people experiencing homelessness across the country. Part of my role has included raising awareness of TI/PI, and developing and delivering training and guidance to support organisations seeking to change their approach.

To improve the work I and my team do, I undertook a fascinating and challenging professional qualification in the psychological dynamics of organisations. It is through this that my understanding of the emotional life of organisations and systems grew, and where my thinking about trauma shifted. Where I had for many years considered trauma to be something experienced by individuals and sometimes groups, I now understood how whole organisations are affected as a result of the challenging work they carry out.

This chapter brings together a psychosocial and trauma informed perspective to organisational and system dynamics, drawing on literature and concepts from psychological and social sciences, as well as my own observations from practice. I have pulled out the information I think will be of most interest and use for leaders but of course encourage you to do your own learning and exploration.

The information within this chapter may initially spark concern about the harm that can be caused to people accessing and working in services. While most leaders, to a greater or lesser extent, are already aware of this they may not know how to practically address it. More often than not, acknowledging the reality can be too painful and may instead have been avoided or denied. These are normal human responses but nevertheless important to think about and act upon. Without doing so, as you will read below, organisations can adopt strategies that unintentionally make

DOI: 10.4324/9781003415053-12

things worse instead of better. Having a greater understanding of the dynamics of trauma within the context of organisational change is essential when embedding TI/PI, as part of the purpose of doing so is that services and workplaces can be as safe and empowering for everyone within them as possible.

What Is Trauma?

To understand what is meant by traumatised and traumatising organisations, I want to start by considering what is meant by trauma. Within the homelessness sector, this word is now part of the lexicon and used regularly within the context of service provision, commissioning and policy. But although easy to say, it is difficult to define as it encapsulates a broad range of experiences.

Most simply, my understanding of trauma is that it is the impact of experiences which are physically or psychologically harmful or threatening, and where an individual's ability to cope is overwhelmed. Not everyone will experience the same event in the same way, but those most affected will experience devastating impacts in many areas of their lives.

Trauma is used to describe the impact of one or multiple events. However while experiencing one single traumatic event can be life-changing, experiencing multiple and prolonged traumas such as abuse, neglect, or war is life-shaping. The affects are exacerbated when this occurs in childhood, and particularly within the context of a caring relationship. Childhood trauma has been found to have long-lasting impacts and those most affected are likely to require support for their health, care, and social need from services provided by the public and third sectors.

Although trauma is most commonly thought about in relation to individuals, trauma also relates to collective experience of distressing events and multi-generational adversity. This includes the experiences of terrorism and war, but also the trauma experienced as a result of one's race, culture, or ethnicity. Trauma is pervasive within society, for both individuals and groups.

So, in thinking about trauma as a collective experience, we can understand how people at work may be impacted. Organisations are not static or inorganic entities, they are groups of living and feeling people that come together to achieve a stated purpose, and which adapt and respond to the contexts within which they operate. People within organisations, as a result of distress and adversity, can become traumatised and organise themselves around their trauma (Bloom, 2011).

Traumatised and Traumatising Organisations

There is a rich literature from the fields of social science and psychology that explores how organisations become traumatised and what happens as a result.

Before delving deeper into experiences that result in organisational trauma, it may be useful to have in mind how a traumatised organisation can function. Many

How people feel	o Staff feel overwhelmed and unable to cope
	o Staff feel attacked or are aggressive and attacking
	o Staff feel stuck, hopeless and believe things cannot change
	o There is a sense of loss, mourning and unresolved grief
	o People are paranoid
	o Services feel unsafe
	o Staff feel vulnerable and disempowered
	o People cannot name their feelings
What people think	o Staff are disconnected and detached from their work
	o Distressing experienced are minimised or discussing/thinking of them avoided
	o Experiences are forgotten and confused
	o Reality is both known and denied, and people collude to 'turn a blind eye'
	o There is stereotyping, scapegoating and depersonalisation of others
	o There are unrealistic beliefs and aims about risk management
	o There is defensive grouping and 'gang' like mentality
How people act	o Practices within services are unsafe
	o Historic experiences are repeated and re-enacted
	o Services are reactive, driven by crises and deprioritise planning/thinking
	o There is 'tough' management
	o Boundaries are either too loose or too tight
	o There is splitting and fragmentation: between teams, agencies and within organisational hierarchy
	o There is ineffective communication
	o There is increased routine and robotic-like behaviour, at the expense of relationships and common sense
	o There are difficulties making decisions
	o It is difficult to manage conflicts and challenges
	o Workers are silenced and not consulted
	o The organisation does not adapt to its external environment and declines
	o Leaders may be seen as celebrities, charismatic and consider themselves to 'know best'
	o The sharing of power and information is limited
	o At the extreme, there is systematic abuse or neglect

Figure 9.1 Symptoms of a Traumatised Organisation. Adapted from the work of Bloom (2011), Hinshelwood (2012), Long (2012), and Treisman (2018).

of the symptoms of a traumatised organisation are similar to those we see in individuals impacted by trauma, the difference being that these symptoms are not isolated to one or two individuals but are experienced collectively by teams, services, or the organisation as a whole. Symptoms are shown in Figure 9.1.

Let us now think about the types of situations that can be trauma-inducing for organisations.

Trauma as a Result of Unprocessed Past Events

It can be useful for leaders to think about the history of their organisation and whether there were any distressing events which are having a residual impact. Experiences such as constant change and transformation (Wilke, 2012) and the loss of an esteemed leader (Reed, 2012) may have been experienced by organisational members as harmful or threatening. If space was not given for these experiences to be processed, it is possible that the trauma may be embedded in the culture of the organisation. People within the organisation can unconsciously re-enact patterns of behaviour or relational dynamics as a result of past experiences.

For example, take an organisation that has a significant restructure and enforces change on its members without care or transparency. This leads to feelings of unsafety, disempowerment, and a deep sense of betrayal in those affected by the process. A collective belief grows amongst staff that leaders cannot be trusted and do not care about them, and leaders feel attacked and anxious when communicating with staff. There is a slow breakdown in working relationships which further embeds the beliefs and feelings on either side and creates a divide between senior management and operational staff. Over time, others join the organisation and experience a lack of connection with senior management. They begin to question whether senior management understand or have interest in their work and find communications from them disconnected and overly authoritarian. They slowly become accustomed to the unspoken beliefs, culture and working dynamics at play.

After several years a new leader joins the organisation and decides to propose a small change to the flexible working policy. They are met with overwhelming resistance which feels disproportionate to the suggestion being made. The new CEO finds the extreme reaction by staff difficult to understand. Had they been more aware about how the previous restructure affected the organisation and was continuing to play out within the culture of the organisation, they may understand that dynamics of the previous trauma were being re-enacted.

Understanding the history of an organisation, and the events which may have adversely impacted its systems, processes and culture can be extremely useful for leaders, especially where there are challenges or change is being introduced. Taking time to understand, observe, and think about the story of the organisation will enable you to plan carefully for any potential issues which arise as a result of past experience.

Trauma as a Result of Difficult Work

If your organisation works with a population of people who have experienced trauma, there is a risk that those in contact with them will individually and collectively experience trauma-related stress. While I want to predominantly focus on how collective trauma in organisations manifests, it is important for managers and leaders to understand the different types of stress that can be experienced by individuals. I recommend a paper by Newell and MacNeil (2010) which explores many of these, and how to prevent them, in more depth. Individuals may experience:

- **Primary trauma** as a result of extremely distressing events such as assault, serious accidents and the death or serious harm of people accessing services. Severe and prolonged trauma can result in Post-Traumatic Stress Disorder (PTSD), with one in three individuals generally developing the condition (NHS, 2022). Research into the direct trauma experienced by staff working in homelessness services found that 23% of participants met the PTSD diagnosis threshold (Lemieux-Cumberlege et al, 2023). It is important to recognise that people accessing the service may also be exposed to further direct trauma within the service.
- **Secondary trauma** symptoms are similar to those experienced by individuals with PTSD and result from knowing about the trauma experienced by another with whom you have an empathic and helping relationship. For example, a worker who supports a victim of sexual assault may develop images and nightmares about their client's experience and may feel panicked and unsafe in their personal life.
- **Vicarious trauma** similarly occurs as a result of empathic relationships, but involves changes in worker beliefs and thoughts rather than PTSD-like symptoms. For example, the worker described above may have instead started to consider certain locations unsafe or certain people or agencies untrustworthy.
- **Compassion fatigue** is the result of prolonged exposure to others' pain, chronic use of empathy, and needing to balance these emotional demands alongside administrative ones. Compassion fatigue 'disturbs the ability to think clearly, modulate emotions, feel effective and maintain hope' and can result in withdrawal and disconnection (Stoewen, 2020).

The underlying motivations for why people work in certain types of services and with certain client groups may further exacerbate the adversity experienced at work. Quite often, people are attracted to health and social care roles because of their early life experiences (Roberts, 1994a) and there is a growing trend in most sectors to intentionally employ people with a shared lived experience to the client group. The reasons why people take up certain careers will inevitably impact how they feel about what happens in their roles. And those with histories of trauma, or existing anxiety disorders, are more susceptible to trauma-related stress and burnout (Newell and MacNeil, 2010). Taking a TI/PI approach must consider the trauma that staff carry with them from their past and present, and how this shows up in how they carry out their work and engage with the organisation.

Staff working with particularly challenging and traumatised client groups are thought to be more likely to experience compassion fatigue because of the relational dynamic between them and their clients. Psychotherapists and social scientists, Christopher Scanlon and John Adlam, have for many years worked across fields such as criminal justice and homelessness. They suggest that the disconnect between staff who want to help, and clients who explicitly or implicitly refuse help, leads to difficulty and distress, which is heightened by unrealistic expectations set by the system (e.g. funders, government, the public). Staff who are driven to help others are not only psychologically affected by having their help refused, but are also affected by the scrutiny and pressure to achieve outcomes for clients who do not share the same goals (Scanlon and Adlam, 2012).

In order to feel they are helping, workers may then begin to consider small changes made by their clients as significant measures of improvement, such as someone turning up to an appointment or changing their clothes. However these small changes are usually not considered a measure of success by those who want to see more obvious progress like reduction in anti-social behaviour or decreased levels of rough sleeping. The expectations and demands placed upon the service do not align to the reality of the work, and staff feel they have failed their clients and others (Hinshelwood, 2012).

In such challenging situations, teams may begin to mirror the distress experienced by their clients (Scanlon and Adlam, 2012). For example, take a team that provides assertive outreach to severely marginalised clients with significant health and care needs. They are funded to proactively support their clients into housing and health services. The clients do not prioritise their health and are not willing to meet with workers. Referrals made within the same organisation for housing are rejected due to the complexity of need and 'non-engagement' of the person being referred. The team make repeated Safeguarding referrals which are ignored or rejected. They begin to feel helpless and abandoned by others within and outside their organisation. They experience a sense of being shut out of a system that is not meeting their needs. Their experience parallels that of those they attempt to support (Bloom, 2011). This affects the morale of the team and their ability to creatively work with others who can help them achieve the aims of their service.

'Taking on' the emotional experiences and adopting similar behaviours and attitudes of others have been described by Moylan (1994) as a 'contagion' that can pass through whole staff teams and services. She suggests that negative emotions are passed from clients to staff through a similar process of emotional and non-verbal communication that exists between a mother and baby (projective identification). As a result, teams become immobilised and unable to think, problem solve, or find effective solutions. 'The more distressed the client group, the more likely these communications'.

Unless there is effective support for those dealing with work experiences which are consciously and unconsciously challenging, the emotional and psychological strain will remain unaddressed and can lead individuals and groups to adopt alternative strategies. Quite often, this too will involve unconscious processes and result in the development of coping mechanisms which are themselves problematic.

Putting on Armour to Cope

When people at work are not safeguarded, and distress and trauma goes unprocessed, 'armour' is unconsciously utilised. Freud called this armour 'psychological defences' and identified mechanisms like avoidance, denial, splitting/projection, and repression as strategies that are unconsciously used by individuals to keep themselves emotionally safe.

Psychological defences are also found to operate amongst groups of people at work (Menzies, 1960) who begin to organise themselves around the stressors experienced. Processes and systems can be designed, unconsciously, to help people at work manage their anxiety, uncertainty, helplessness, and guilt. Some of the symptoms in the table above, such as reactive or robotic service delivery or difficulty making decisions, may be the result of collective defences against these emotions.

However, these paradoxically often provide false hope and may in turn create problems. There may be a significant impact on an organisation's ability to deliver services (Bloom, 2011) and positions taken that work against what the service aims to do (Roberts, 1994b). An organisation, as a result of its trauma, can become traumatising.

For example, consider an accommodation service which has dealt with high instances of self-harm. If this is not effectively acknowledged or processed, staff affected by repeat exposure may begin to develop behaviours which are not helpful to the residents and which may unintentionally cause more distress. This might include avoidance or overuse of room safety checks, or adopting blanket risk management policies which are intrusive and unnecessary for everyone living there. The frontline staff and managers may become preoccupied with the completion of tick box checklists and risk assessment, as though this in itself will result in fewer incidents. The service may begin to refuse referrals for people who have a history of self-harming behaviour, and collectively the team may begin to adopt blaming attitudes and language towards their clients. Because of the distress experienced, the staff and service begin to function in a contrary and potentially harmful way because painful emotions are avoided or split off and projected onto the clients.

Many of the policies, practices, and procedures that can be adopted to defend against emotionally difficult work can unfortunately trigger or replicate the dynamics of trauma for those who engage in services for support. Although not always directly harmful or threatening, they can be experienced as re-traumatising by a client who feels as if they are experiencing another traumatising event (SAMHSA, 2014). This may include:

- Breach of boundaries, e.g. neglecting to respect an individual's space or requests, being inconsistent in how rules are enforced, expecting the individual to meet the demands of the service but there not being fair reciprocation
- Coercive or disempowering practices, e.g. a confrontational approach to engagement and support, expecting an individual to do something specifically in

order to receive a service, not involving people in decisions about their care, not allowing individuals autonomy to meet their basic needs

- Restrictive (as opposed to protective) policies and procedures, e.g. rigid, blanket and punitive rules, not allowing people to challenge or question the status quo, use of isolation and restraint;
- Deficit-based and stigmatising attitudes, e.g. not recognising current needs and behaviours as trauma related, ignoring and discrediting people, discounting reports of abuse
- A lack of safety, e.g. environments which are insecure or threatening, changing support relationships, dysfunctional service dynamics which remain unaddressed

Bringing Down the Armour

Such is the nature of human existence that seeking to prevent traumatisation within organisations may be considered idealistic. However, there is much that can be done to mitigate against the impact of distressing and potentially traumatising experiences in order to protect employees, as well as ensuring that organisations limit their capacity for causing trauma to those who need their support.

Changing organisational culture and creating safe environments is an ongoing but essential journey which should be led from the top. Leaders and managers must be invested and make a continued commitment to drive it forward (Holly, 2017; Lemieux-Cumberlege et al, 2023). TI/PI frameworks provide several indicators for how positive change can be implemented, and the steps that can be taken to reduce the likelihood of traumatisation, and create safe and empowering cultures. However, there are a number of other recommendations from much of the literature cited in this chapter which can help to mitigate and disrupt the unconscious processes and dynamics described above. In summary:

- Allow emotional experience: ensure there is space for individuals and teams to connect and reflect on their experiences, create a culture where it is safe to discuss emotions, role model and allow staff to practice self-care.
- Develop supportive structures: meetings are TI/PI, managers are trained to supervise staff through a TI/PI lens, self and group reflective practice is encouraged and enabled.
- Ensure effective leadership: leaders are self-aware and role model vulnerability and self-care, they are confident and containing, have clear authority structures in place for decision-making.
- Acknowledge the impact of change: ensure change is managed carefully, that the emotional impact is not denied, and that there is space for feelings to be processed, including past experiences within the organisation.
- Foster collaboration and creativity: enable staff to participate and contribute, value creativity and initiative, aim for internal and external collaboration where difference is valued.

- Accept and make space for reality: acknowledge that there are conflicting priorities and tensions, ensure all parts of the organisation are connected to the reality of the work, accept that work-related stress exists.

As with frontline staff, leaders and managers must have the knowledge, skills and values to build resilient organisational cultures. Coaching, specialist training and support should be considered, and it can often be useful to bring in a consultant/facilitator who understands organisational dynamics. Someone external, who is not ingrained in the organisational culture, will be particularly beneficial.

Trauma as a Result of Difficult Working Contexts

In the section above, I predominantly explored the psychological impact of working with distressing and distressed people. We will now look more broadly at the contexts within which organisations work and the tensions that arise from conflicting stakeholder objectives, all of which may be felt as threatening towards the organisation's survival. The impact of this is exacerbated by the difficult work being done, and decisions can be made which often cause further traumatisation.

The expectations placed on health and social care services, to achieve certain outcomes in order to gain and retain funding, could be considered similar to the transactional nature that exists between businesses and their customers (Long, 2012) who often expect more for less. One study, commissioned by The Riverside Group, explored the impact of £1bn cuts to funding across homelessness services. The cumulated effect of increased targets, short-term and inadequate contracts, and a lack of quality control are considered to have created a 'traumatised system' (Blood and Pleace, 2020).

To obtain their grants, and increase their chance of repeat funding, providers must meet the outcomes expected by their funders. However, 'products' delivered by health and social care services are often far more complex to achieve than in other industries like manufacturing or hospitality. The reality of supporting people, especially those who are severely traumatised, is extremely difficult and results in disconnect between funder expectations and the reality of what is required by the people accessing the services.

This now often means that people requiring support find it more difficult to access the help they really need and, if they do receive support, may find that this is conditional on them meeting expectations that it is impossible for them to adhere to because of their trauma. For people accessing or being excluded from services, this can lead to feelings of abandonment and neglect (Long, 2012) which may lead to further traumatisation.

Although they are often thought to have more flexibility than public services, voluntary and community sector organisations are accountable to multiple stakeholders that sometimes have conflicting interests (Dartington, 2010). Trustees, funders, partners and the local community may have different expectations of the charity or make demands which are at odds with the main aim of the organisation. Because quite often meeting these demands relates to the organisation's functioning and survival, this can cause distress. Within organisations, there can also be conflicting priorities between teams or within services, e.g. housing management vs support work.

An example of this may be a small organisation with a precarious funding pipeline. Last year, it seemed as if the organisation would need to close as a substantial grant was coming to an end. However, the leader successfully applied for other funding which allowed the service to remain open. But the requirements of the new contract meant that the service needed to work with a broader cohort of people, and deliver support in a more flexible way than they had previously. Half of the staff were on board with this change, the other half were not. The second group criticised and accused the leader of putting staff at risk as well as calling for pay rises to cover what they perceived were significant changes to their jobs. Over time, the service delivery teams became fragmented, which led to a lack of coherence in how support was being provided to people accessing the service. Some disgruntled staff also approached trustees to make complaints about the leader, and trustees who had been risk averse towards the change started to side with these staff. It was as if gangs were forming across the organisation, and the leader found it difficult to communicate with those above and below.

Leaders manage conflicting priorities and tensions all the time, in order to ensure their organisation survives. But this, in itself, is emotionally charged and the consequences of decisions can be heightened because of the type of work that is carried out. Normal tensions, which may be easier to manage in different types of industry, have additional traumatic and traumatising aspects because of the contexts and purposes of the work and because often there can be an underlying sense of life and death – for the organisation, those working within it, and those they support.

It is important that leaders retain a capacity to think clearly about the difficult decisions they are required to make and take an approach to change management which makes space for the emotional and psychological impact of decisions to be thought about and processed. Taking care of yourself, as you also navigate the emotions of the situation, will also ensure you do not get 'caught up' in the emotions of others and act in ways that could be detrimental in the long run.

Reducing Burnout, Reducing Trauma

The contexts that many 'human services' organisations operate in have become extremely challenging and traumatic over the last decade. Many have been pushed to the brink through a gradual chipping away of resources despite increased need. As a result, the propensity for burnout is high, and, in many sectors, there are currently significant issues of staff retention.

Burnout leads to physical and emotional exhaustion and severely impacts staff well-being. In one study, frontline workers in the homelessness sector were found to experience higher levels of depression and stress than the general population, associated with burnout (Lemieux-Cumberlege and Taylor, 2019).

A number of organisational and contextual factors have been found to contribute to burnout (Newell and MacNeil, 2010; McKinsey, 2022; Lemieux-Cumberlege et al, 2023; Maguire, 2023). The contributing factors are both tangible (e.g. inadequate resource) and intangible (culture and power):

- Overwhelming demands without adequate resources, e.g. high caseloads, staff turnover, a lack of resources to meet client needs
- Limited autonomy and influence, e.g. oppressive hierarchical structures, a lack of co-design and consultation, an inability to make decisions around work
- Inadequate training and support, e.g. a lack of adequate management and direction, limited peer support, a lack of professional or clinical input
- Dysfunctional organisational culture, e.g. toxic work environments and others listed in the trauma symptoms table
- Unsafe working environments, e.g. unsafe service designs, environments which prevent healthy interactions, no space for staff to interact and work quietly as needed
- Unachievable goals: unrealistic targets, staff being required to focus on achieving outcomes instead of building relationships, a collective fear of failure

Organisations can become dysfunctional if burnout is not addressed. Like individuals who are emotionally and physically exhausted, services and organisations may move from a position where it is possible to think and find solutions, to one which is reactive, crisis driven, and where problems and conflicts are difficult to solve.

Finding ways to ensure that thinking and planning continues in teams, including at senior level, is crucial when facing such difficulties. Acknowledging and being transparent about the challenges faced by the organisation will help staff feel psychologically safe. This can be enhanced through effective support and supervision, the fostering of peer relationships, and a culture where self-care is encouraged. Leaders should also recognise their own vulnerabilities and seek out effective support, such as coaching, supervision, and peer support networks.

Holding the ability to think about the purpose of the organisation, and whether its aims can be delivered safely within the resource available, is an essential part of leadership, and even more important in organisations that are traumatised. The propensity for splitting and other psychological defences will be high, so ensuring that everyone is aware of the goals and pull in the same direction will help to reduce tensions and provide containment.

As we saw in an example above, it can be difficult to make changes to what a service does or how it operates, not least because this may be deemed by others as failing those in need. But evaluating whether the service can safely operate with the resources it has is essential for the well-being of staff and clients. Over the last few years I have come across several examples of leaders that have worked reflectively and made difficult decisions that have not always been popular, but which have reduced the likelihood of trauma and traumatisation as a result. This includes:

* Organisation A, which faced significant cuts to a supported housing contract. They renegotiated the contract with the funder by proposing a different service model which could be delivered more safely within the resource available.
* Organisation B, which was overwhelmed with increased demand at its community-based day service. They audited who was using the service and supported those who had other options to access them. They also changed the remit and working patterns of different parts of the organisation, so that responsibility for new clients was not situated with just one team.
* Organisation C was also overwhelmed with increased numbers of people needing their support. They worked strategically with other local providers to revise how they collectively offered services, which allowed each organisation to offer a more tailored service and ensured work was not being duplicated.
* Organisation D was a busy centre whose opening hours meant that staff worked directly with clients at all times of their shift, and where there was no protected time for staff development or team building. A decision was made to close the centre one afternoon a week and for this time to be used for staff well-being and self-care activities.
* Organisation E delivers a statutory service with increased pressures, which was having an immense impact on staff who were often having to undertake challenging assessments and deliver difficult messages to people seeking help. The manager decided to restructure the service so that individual staff members could move more easily between direct customer facing work and desk-based tasks. This allowed staff to take time out when needed, fostered team care and peer support, and offered more variety in people's roles.

Reflections on the Risks of Not Implementing TI/PI with Care

Accessing training is often an entry point for organisations seeking to adopt TI/PI. However recent research into the implementation of TIC has found that while training is an important part of the process, it does not constitute good practice by itself and must be complemented by wider cultural and systemic change for it to be effective (Burge et al, 2021; DLUHC, 2023). Many organisations invest in training and Reflective Practice Groups for their frontline staff, but not for managers or leaders. Funders and policymakers suggest or request that services are trauma informed, but don't often put the right conditions in place for this to be successful.

As I wrote this chapter I considered my own experience of supporting the implementation of TI/PI. More often than not, there is a perception that being TI/PI is only relevant to frontline service delivery, and there is little discussion about the broader applicability, and necessity, of these being implemented across organisations and systems. This may of course be because they're still relatively new, and there isn't a great deal of understanding about organisational trauma. There is also the question of resources, and what is required to embed TI/PI systemically. But when considering this through a TI/PI lens, could it be possible that there may be some 'armour' at play? And what are the consequences if that is not addressed?

Locating the responsibility for implementing TI/PI in operational staff (or perhaps in just one post) could be a way of others keeping their distance from the reality of the work carried out. By splitting this off, it might be considered that others in organisations, and the system, can disconnect from the pain and trauma that exists in the clients being supported. Given all the other challenges experienced in human services, it makes apparent sense that it may only be possible to carry the distress of one's own role; if you are worrying about the organisation's survival or a disgruntled partner agency, there is not much capacity for truly connecting to the pain of the client group too.

But the implications of only situating this in the frontline are risky, for the frontline staff and for others in the organisation. The chances of splitting and projection, avoidance, and denial of reality are high. Frontline staff may feel overwhelmed with the additional responsibility of implementing TI/PI, and angry that their wider organisation or funders are not creating the conditions that enable them to do this well. Others, like leaders, commissioners and policymakers, may make decisions which are not grounded in connectedness with the reality of the work and which cause more trauma and difficulty. And people who do not work frontline may be emotionally impacted by distress passing through the system, or because of the challenges of their own roles, without effective support. For this reason, there is a strong argument that we cannot just situate TI/PI in frontline services and that we should seek to enable these approaches to permeate whole organisations and systems. A TI/PI approach at all levels is essential to create organisational and sectoral cultures, processes, and systems which are not shaped by trauma.

Conclusion

Organisations as a whole, particularly those working with vulnerable and traumatised populations, are susceptible to trauma which can have significant impacts for staff and those they support. Although it may be individually and collectively challenging for organisations to fully embed a TI/PI approach in their culture and systems, it is essential to prevent and reduce harm. Leaders play a crucial role in creating the safety and space required for this, at all levels of the organisation.

As part of this journey, leaders should consider the implicit dynamics and processes that occur as a result of past and present trauma. While it can be difficult work, which may benefit from external support, unearthing and safely establishing less harmful ways of managing the emotions of the work, such as through reflective practice, is incredibly important for leaders seeking to implement TI/PI. The aim is to create organisational cultures that are thinking, connected, and creative. By not doing so, there is a risk that the organisation may begin to work in ways which induces trauma in those that access its support and work within it.

Although it won't be easy, and it won't happen quickly, the benefits for everyone should be evident in the testimonies of others within this book. As a leader, with a million and one other pressures and an ever growing to do list, this may seem like an impossible task and may involve facing up to things that have been avoided and denied. But small changes can have big impacts. With the right support, and in the right way, unhelpful armour can be brought down.

References

Blood, I. & Pleace, N. (2020). *A traumatised system: Research into the commissioning of homelessness services in the last 10 years*. New York: Riverside Group.

Bloom, S. L. (2011). Trauma-organized systems and parallel process. In Tehrani, N. (Ed.), *Managing trauma in the workplace: Supporting workers and organizations*. London: Routledge.

Brown, B. (2018). *Dare to lead: Brave work, tough conversations, whole hearts*. New York: Random House.

Burge, R., Tickle, A. & Moghaddam, N. (2021) Evaluating trauma informed care training for services supporting individuals experiencing homelessness and multiple disadvantage. *Housing Care and Support*. 24(1), pp. 14–25.

Dartington, T. (2010). *Managing vulnerability, the underlying dynamics of systems of care*. London: Karnac.

Department for Levelling Up, Housing and Communities (2023). *Trauma-informed approaches to supporting people experiencing multiple disadvantage: A rapid evidence assessment*. Accessed at https://assets.publishing.service.gov.uk/media/642af3a77de82b000c31350d/Changing_Futures_Evaluation_-_Trauma_informed_approaches_REA.pdf

Hinshelwood, R. (2012). Personal trauma and collective disorder: The example of organizational psychodynamics in psychiatry. In Hopper, E. (Ed.), *Trauma and organizations*. London: Karnac Books.

Holly, J. (2017). Mapping the maze: Services for women experiencing multiple disadvantage in England and Wales. In Department for Levelling Up, Housing and Communities (Ed.), *Trauma-informed approaches to supporting people experiencing multiple disadvantage: A rapid evidence assessment*. Accessed at https://assets.publishing.service.gov.uk/media/642af3a77de82b000c31350d/Changing_Futures_Evaluation_-_Trauma_in formed_approaches_REA.pdf

Lemieux-Cumberlege, A., Griffiths, H., Pathe, E. & Burle, A. (2023). Posttraumatic stress disorder, secondary traumatic stress, and burnout in frontline workers in homelessness services: Risk and protective factors. *Journal of Social Distress and Homelessness*. Advance online publication. Accessed at https://www.pure.ed.ac.uk/ws/portalfiles/portal/336701727/Lemieux_CumberlegeEtal2023JSDHPosttraumatic-StressDisorder.pdf

Lemieux-Cumberlege, A. & Taylor, E. P. (2019) An exploratory study on the factors affecting the mental health and well-being of frontline workers in homeless services. *Health & Social Care in the Community*. 27(4). Accessed at https://pubmed.ncbi.nlm.nih.gov/30864195/

Long, S. (2012). Trauma as cause and effect of perverse organizational process. In Hopper, E. (Ed.), *Trauma and organizations*. London: Karnac Books.

Maguire, N. (2023) Speaking on Understanding Burnout (Series 2, Episode 1). Going Beyond Podcast. *Homeless Link.* Posted 16 January 2023. https://homeless.org.uk/knowledge-hub/going-beyond-homeless-links-practice-podcast/.

McKinsey Health Institute, (2022). *Addressing employee burnout – are you solving the right problem?* Accessed December 2023. https://www.mckinsey.com/mhi/our-insights/addressing-employee-burnout-are-you-solving-the-right-problem.

Menzies, I. E. P. (1960) A case-study in the functioning of social systems as a defence against anxiety: A report on a study of the nursing service of a general hospital. *Human Relations.* 13(2), pp. 95–121.

Moylan, D. (1994). The dangers of contagion: Projective identification processes in institutions. In Obholzer, A. & Roberts, V. Z. (Eds.), *The unconscious at work: Individual and organizational stress in the human services.* London and New York: Routledge.

Newell, J. M. & MacNeil, G. A. (2010) Professional burnout, vicarious trauma, secondary traumatic stress, and compassion fatigue: A review of theoretical terms, risk factors, and preventive methods for clinicians and researchers. *Best Practices in Mental Health: An International Journal.* 6(2), pp. 57–68.

NHS (2022). *Causes – Post-traumatic stress disorder.* Accessed December 2023. https://www.nhs.uk/mental-health/conditions/post-traumatic-stress-disorder-ptsd/causes/

Reed, L. (2012). Trauma and leadership succession: Congregational leadership transition in the context of socio-cultural change. In Hopper, E. (Ed.), *Trauma and organizations.* London: Karnac Books.

Roberts, V. Z. (1994a). The self-assigned impossible task. In Obholzer, A. & Roberts, V. Z. (Eds.), *The unconscious at work: Individual and organizational stress in the human services.* London and New York: Routledge.

Roberts, V. Z. (1994b). The organisation of work: Contributions from open systems theory. In Obholzer, A. & Roberts, V. Z. (Eds.), *The unconscious at work: Individual and organizational stress in the human services.* London and New York: Routledge.

Scanlon, C. & Adlam, J. (2012). Disorganized responses to refusal and spoiling in traumatised organizations. In Hopper, E. (Ed.), *Trauma and organizations.* London: Karnac Books.

Stoewen, D. L. (2020) Moving from compassion fatigue to compassion resilience. Part 4: Signs and consequences of compassion fatigue. *Canadian Veterinary Journal.* 61(11), pp. 1207–1209.

Substance Abuse and Mental Health Services Administration (2014). Trauma-informed care in behavioral health services. *Treatment improvement protocol (TIP) series 57.* HHS Publication No. (SMA) 13-4801. Rockville, MD: Substance Abuse and Mental Health Services Administration.

Treisman, K. (2018). *Becoming a more culturally, adversity, and trauma-informed, infused and responsive organisation.* Winston Churchill Memorial Trust/Safe Hands Thinking Minds. https://media.churchillfellowship.org/documents/Treisman_K_Report_2018_Final.pdf

Wilke, G. (2012). Leaders and groups in traumatized and traumatizing organizations: A matter of everyday survival. In Hopper, E. (Ed.), *Trauma and organizations.* London: Karnac Books.

Chapter 10

Psychologically Informed Leadership in a Psychologically Informed Environment (PIE)

Learning and Reflections from Our Journey So Far...

Helen Miles

With Contributions from Joanne Wood, Marc Pescod, Leah Francis, Caroline Bradley, Nicole Samuel, Hara Sakellariadi, Sarah Keen, and Catherine Geddes

I don't want a massive house or loads of money in the bank. I don't want a second home and multiple holidays. I want to be able to live in safety with enough money for food and essentials. I don't want to panic every time I look at my smart meter or look in the fridge. I want to be able to access education fairly and equally with enough money to feed myself when I am there, have access to the internet and a laptop, to resources that others take for granted. I want to be able to feel comfortable applying for university without despairing at the thought of losing my benefits so loosely keeping me alive. I want the same opportunities as someone from an affluent background. I just want to be able to have aspirations instead of just being told to get a job and work a gig economy with very little pay. I want to be seen as a human being...

(Catherine Geddes – October 2022;
Ex Centrepoint Young Person, PIEineer & Youth Homelessness Campaigner)

Psychologically informed environments or PIEs are a relatively recent development for practice within the homeless sector (Keats *et al*, 2012; Westminster Council, 2015). They are 'intended to use the latest insights and evidence from the psychological disciplines to give rough sleepers and homeless people the best chance of sustainably escaping the cycle of poor well-being and chronic homelessness' (Keats *et al*, 2012, p. 4). For the homeless young people we support in our organisation, like Catherine above who makes this point so powerfully, this is about a meaningful life – the same as her 'housed' peers – where she is viewed as a human being with hopes and dreams, and with a future no longer dominated by the risk of being homeless.

This chapter is not, however, a chapter about what a PIE is, given the information already available on this: instead it is a co-produced reflection on our PIE journey to date in the UK national youth homelessness charity Centrepoint, focusing on what we have learnt so far about leading this journey across the organisation. We look at what has helped us start on this PIE journey and how we have tried to

DOI: 10.4324/9781003415053-13

embed PIE within the whole of the organisation by encouraging an understanding of psychologically informed leadership alongside delivery of the more typical 'ingredients' of a PIE (e.g. a PIE framework, staff support, training and reflective practice, improvements to the physical environment, increasing focus on the use of data, and evaluation to guide strategic decision-making). We also explore the concept of psychologically informed leadership and the importance of this in a PIE, with examples of how we have created, and are still trying to create, this within our PIE team as well as across the wider organisation, posing reflective questions for readers to consider for themselves on their own PIE journeys.

Learning and Reflections from Setting up and Leading a PIE

As an organisation, our PIE journey is far from completed, having only been on this road since 2019. Arguably, unlike the edible version, is a homeless 'PIE' perhaps never finished 'baking' anyway? In this sector, despite Centrepoint's longer-term strategy to #EndYouthHomelessness, there may always be challenges we need to address or modifications to the 'ingredients' of our PIE that we need to make. Moreover, as is noted in the Westminster Council (2015) PIE guidance, 'creating a PIE takes time, it's not an approach that can be introduced overnight simply through staff training or redecorating the building. Reflection and relationships are its cornerstones and these are both organic and ongoing processes' (p. 3). However, psychologically informed leadership of a PIE throughout is critical for its success. A PIE is something we have learnt that you have to 'live and breathe' every day: you can't turn your oven off and on willy-nilly and expect your PIE to bake!

Moreover, 'a PIE is likely to succeed if there is genuine and tangible backing from executive and senior management: creating a PIE is not the sole responsibility of frontline staff' (Westminster Council, 2015, p. 3) or indeed of any psychologists you might employ within the organisation to lead the approach. Instead, a successful PIE needs leaders from across the organisation to co-create a cultural change that is keeping 'people' at the heart of the journey, whether that is its staff or the homeless individuals, like Catherine above, that it supports. As a result, the starting point for our PIE journey at Centrepoint was to consider – Who are leaders within this organisation? Who needs to be part of our PIE journey to make it happen?

When we think of leaders, we often think of *the* leader, perhaps the CEO of an organisation, or even a Senior Executive Team. However, taking a less hierarchical, or perhaps a more psychologically informed, approach on our PIE journey at Centrepoint, we have reflected that within any organisation there may be many different 'leaders' at many different levels. During the COVID-19 pandemic in the early 2020s this was highlighted as many different individuals 'stepped up' to 'lead' on different projects or tasks (e.g. the distribution of food or Personal Protective Equipment (PPE) to frontline homeless supported accommodation services). Moreover, within different parts of a homelessness organisation, whether 'frontline' or back office 'support' teams, there are often many different leaders or 'subject matter experts' within their respective fields (e.g. fundraising, property management, policy, etc.), all working to improve the outcomes for homeless young people in different ways.

Therefore, it may be that there are individuals within an organisation in traditional positions of senior 'leadership' that may not really be 'leading', and others who may not hold a 'leadership title' yet are quietly leading their teams and inspiring others with great success. Consequently, 'leaders' within an organisation aren't always the ones necessarily at the 'top', and the term 'leadership' is a fluid concept depending on the situation or context. Thus, when considering how to create psychologically informed change, it can be helpful to take a system-wide view of an organisation to consider who the 'leaders' really are. Who are your potential change makers? Who can really help embed a PIE within an organisation? Whose voices need to be part of co-producing a PIE and how can we create psychologically safe spaces for them to be heard, especially if they aren't usually those who aren't listened to in strategic or operational decision-making? Moreover, this isn't just the employees within the organisation: this must also include those individuals, in our case homeless young people, using the services we provide. When we started our PIE journey at Centrepoint, the above questions were just those questions that it was key as the psychologist, the 'nominated' leader or 'custodian' of PIE within the organisation, to ask.

The first step of our PIE journey was therefore essentially a scoping exercise, wherein developing an understanding of all parts of the organisation, from the different frontline housing services to the support teams behind them, was critical. What was commonly highlighted at this stage, especially away from the frontline where potentially it is harder to embed a PIE, was the question 'why is any of this relevant to us?'. It was therefore important to consider how the PIE principles (e.g. training, reflective practice, physical environment, evaluation, relationships, psychological theories, or frameworks) uniquely applied to different areas of the organisation. This involved time and reflective discussions as well as a willingness to listen and learn from others but was critical to ensure that our 'vision of PIE' was appropriate to, and fitted with, our organisation needs. Like real pies, there are many different recipes that might be suitable. Whilst they all have core 'ingredients' (c.f. Keats *et al*, 2012), the 'fillings' chosen (or approach needed) may differ between organisations. Of course a PIE or psychology can apply anywhere that there are 'people', or where the primary task of an organisation (such as a homeless charity) is centred on people. It took us time to consider how PIE might apply in different ways to different areas, but this was essential to create a movement for psychologically informed change that everyone in the organisation could relate to and apply to themselves and/or their roles.

It also required a willingness to roll with resistance or defensiveness; and bucket-loads of humility as many teams were naturally anxious that some psychologist was coming along and telling them that everything they were currently doing was wrong! Instead, we found ourselves with the key mantra of 'evolution not revolution' which felt psychologically 'safe' to all staff within the organisation. It was highlighted that there was a lot of amazing work happening in the organisation already, and PIE was there to augment, highlight, share, and develop existing good practice rather than throw that metaphorical baby out with the bath water. The quote from the Westminster Council PIE Good Practice Guide, published by Westminster Council (2015) that 'the PIE approach is not about a whole new way of working but provides a framework, language and approaches to communicate, implement and enhance the good practice that already exists within homeless services' (p. 3) therefore became our second mantra. This reduced the organisational threat associated with changing from existing non-PIE approaches to a PIE approach to homelessness.

It was also key to engage with those that used our homeless services. We were able to work with an amazing group of young people in Centrepoint, including Catherine above, right at the start who helped co-produce key elements of the PIE. These self-named 'PIEineers' advised on our vision, processes, where they wanted to see psychologically informed change, what was important to them, and helped develop organisational wide communication materials. They challenged the narratives around youth homelessness and ensured that our PIE Framework was underpinned by universal relational concepts such as attachment rather than some of the psychological models found in clinical work that might unintentionally pathologise their homelessness experiences. They also came with curiosity, and together we asked questions of the organisation. For example, 'Why do we do it that way? What would be so negative if we tried this instead?' And a question that has guided every conversation we have had in the past five years about the physical environment: 'Would you want to live there, and if not, why is it OK that I have to?'.

From those initial scoping exercises, key potential PIE leaders from across the organisation were identified and invited to a regular PIE Steering Group, which became an ongoing place to regularly review the PIE journey and to plan next steps. Having this space to co-produce the PIE journey increased 'buy-in' from across the organisation – and as a psychologist in a new post it was also invaluable for understanding the wider system and building relationships with colleagues in order to get things done! It was clear that a psychologically informed approach is only possible if it is invested in by all, equally. It required a cultural shift in which all employees, regardless of background or professional discipline, would want to strive to think and act in a psychologically informed way. Time focusing on building quality working relationships with others was time well spent, as it empowered individuals from across the organisation to 'get involved' and make PIE changes that mattered to them.

This PIE steering group also helped create an understanding of PIE across different teams as leaders started to use PIE language or terminology within their own teams, slowly changing the culture of the organisation. Moreover, this group was vital to understand how PIE could be fitted into existing change programmes, strategies, or operational models to make them 'more PIE', for example where there were PIE gaps in a staff training offer that might need to be addressed, or where 'easy wins' could be implemented (e.g. changing the language of paperwork to be more psychologically informed, setting up staff well-being and inclusion focus groups), or where longer-term or larger projects were needed (e.g. in property maintenance projects), or where new initiatives would be required (e.g. setting up reflective practice groups), and/or where systems or processes that weren't 'PIE' could be modified (e.g. reviewing policies and procedures). Of course, this is not an insignificant task, so careful pacing and acceptance that not everything will happen immediately was, and still to this day has remained, essential.

There is also always the challenge of resources within the homeless sector, even in charities such as Centrepoint that have access to fundraising. Therefore, the PIE Steering Group also helped to consider the prioritisation of PIE (e.g. starting with frontline teams who had direct contact with service users before moving to support teams) so that it was possible to demonstrate early positive outcomes and get PIE approaches out to perhaps where they were needed most (i.e. the 'frontline' during the COVID-19 pandemic). It was often helpful to remember the systemic mantra 'push where it moves' in the early stages of our PIE journey to create continued momentum for change and to remain energised as a PIE leader when wider system issues could be challenging. Furthermore, the manta 'marathon not a sprint' became another useful viewpoint. Effective PIE leadership can sometimes require this ability to sit with the anxiety and the inevitable stresses or delays that may commonly arise in any cultural shifts within an organisation.

Additionally, celebrating the little wins that are a nudge in the right direction at regular intervals began to help all those involved, particularly those within the senior leadership of the organisation, to recognise that, even when it can feel like nothing is changing fast, there is value in the PIE approach so that they can make a continued investment in the process. It also helped to communicate regularly across the organisation about PIE. What are we doing? Why are we doing it? Why is it important? How does a particular aspect of a PIE, such as reflective practice, make a difference? In our organisation, this became the 'PIE Blog', which was part of the regular internal communications and documented our PIE journey, discussed psychologically informed issues, and gave a PIE perspective on different topics, whilst also becoming another co-produced space to hear different voices from across the organisation.

Encouraging good communication across the organisation generally was also a focus. It was clear that teams that shared decision-making, planning and problem-solving challenges had the best performance outcomes, and therefore using reflective practice spaces to encourage improved communication and solve team dynamic challenges was also time well spent. We found that, when ideas where shared, owned, and enacted together, outcomes were better than 'silo working' or an over-focus on an individual's performance, supporting Cooke's (2015) observation that 'teams with ideal knowledge but ineffectual interactions will not be effective as a team, yet teams with sketchy knowledge, but effective interactions, may succeed' (p. 418).

Psychologically Informed Leadership in a PIE

As well as considering *who* can help an organisation's PIE journey, how teams can work more effectively together, and how spaces for co-production of this PIE journey can be created, it can also be helpful to consider more specifically what psychologically informed leadership looks like in order to try to foster these characteristics in ourselves and others to further embed a culture of PIE. As a psychologist or evidence-based practitioner, it is essential to consider the evidence to guide a PIE approach to leadership. Therefore, leadership decision-making is arguably about the ability to seek out, understand, reflect on, and apply the evidence base (whether formal or anecdotal), and to use this to inform subsequent decision-making. Of course, there isn't space within this chapter to do a full literature review of the fields of management and occupational psychology, but interested readers can learn more in, for example, the reviews on leadership traits and attributes in Khan *et al* (2016) or Zaccaro *et al* (2018), and through looking up some of references throughout this book.

In summary, leadership theories have developed from considering leadership as something that one might be 'born' with, whether that be specific personality traits or 'rights' consequent of your parents status or class (see, for example, 'The Great Man Theory'), to suggesting leaders are better defined by the differences in emergent hereditary traits such as intelligence, gender, or attractiveness, or in acquired traits based on learning and experience, such as self-confidence and charisma (Ekvall & Arvonen, 1991). However, the failure in, or impossibility of, accurately determining which 'traits' were common in *all* leaders led theories to instead consider the role of situational/behavioural/contingency styles of leadership wherein leadership style is dependent upon a number of situational factors, i.e. 'what behaviour works' in some circumstances but may not be effective in others (Greenleaf, 1977). Nevertheless, these leadership models (e.g. Fiedler, 1967) were also inadequate because of the assumption that leaders can change their behaviour in different circumstances and are unaffected by unconscious beliefs or 'old habits'. Consequently, functional models (e.g. Adair, 1984; Action Centred Leadership or Kouzes & Posner, 1987; The 5 Leadership Practices Model) then suggested it was more important to focus on what effective leaders 'do' rather than how they should 'be', suggesting leaders can learn appropriate or functional behaviours through leadership training. However, this is arguably more about 'management' than 'leadership', the latter being what is actually needed to start and progress a PIE.

Most recently, leadership theory has moved to a more 'integrated' psychological model (e.g. Scouller, 2011; Three Levels of Leadership), which notes that an individual leader has public, private, and personal leadership roles. In other words, a leader needs to understand and perform as a leader in their public role, but also be aware of the importance of developing themselves personally and privately so that they can behave skilfully, flexibly, and authentically: e.g. 'values based leadership'. Moreover, it is argued that leadership is a process that involves (1) setting a purpose and direction which inspires people to willingly combine and work towards them, (2) paying attention to the means, pace, and quality of progress towards the aim, (3) upholding group unity, and (4) attending to individual effectiveness throughout.

This 'integrated' model also fits with the 'servant leadership' philosophy, which we have adopted within our organisation and underpins our PIE. This suggests that the leader of a PIE is merely the steward (or servant) of the PIE vision of the organisation, and their role is to clarify and nurture this vision with others, focusing on what others need to help them become more autonomous and more knowledgeable about psychological approaches. The 'servant leader' is also concerned with the 'have-nots' and recognises them as equal (Greenleaf, 1996) creating co-produced spaces within a PIE approach. Regardless of 'leadership theory', 'philosophy', or 'style', psychological research indicates those leaders who practise relational and transformational styles have better quality outcomes than those who demonstrate autocracy (Cummings *et al*, 2010), and transformational and relational leadership styles improve positive outcomes at individual and organisational levels (Khan *et al*, 2016). This again highlights the importance, as per a PIE approach, of the key role of 'relationships' in PIE leaders to bring about positive change, growth, and development within their organisations.

Consequently, we believe those leading a PIE need to hold a transformational and relational approach to their leadership rather than a reactive or autocratic style. To put this another way, 'psychologically informed' leaders are compassionate and display emotional intelligence or a psychological awareness of themselves or others. Within any organisation, there is significant interconnectedness between different services, departments, directorates, etc.: creating a PIE across a whole organisation requires us to see the 'bigger picture' of the whole system as well as the individual needs within that system in order to inspire that PIE vision. Understanding the Gestalt psychology principle that the 'whole is often greater than the sum of its parts' is key. A well-functioning PIE organisation is like this – whilst it may be made up of individuals or teams, the coming together of each of these creates something more than just those factors alone. That is the essence – or the 'magic' – of system-wide PIE approaches.

In addition, leadership of PIE requires passion and enthusiasm for the approach as well as a willingness to utilise PIE approaches to enhance efficiency, commitment, and outcomes of a team. There also needs to be space for intellectual honesty and humility so that truthful and useful information is passed to others, given that transparency and honesty are at the heart of relationship building and collaboration. However, a PIE is *not* the 'panacea of all ills' within the homeless sector. Having honesty about, and self-awareness of, the limitations of the approach – i.e. it can't solve wider system issues outside an organisation's control such as resource challenges within statutory services – as well as the limitations of our knowledge and experience, and being willing to seek out advice and support from others, is a sign of strength, not weakness as it can sometimes be perceived. Giving space to others to learn and develop, and in turn learning from them, is arguably also critical to unlocking the full potential of an organisation to become a PIE (alongside a healthy dose of persistence and perseverance!).

One example of humility that we have recently begun to consider further within our PIE team is that of 'cultural humility'. We have been reflecting on how we can ensure that as a team we create psychologically safe spaces for all those within the team, regardless of their background race, class, sex, sexuality, or any other protected characteristic, and we hope our learning from this internally within our team can then be taken out more widely across the organisation, which is beginning its own renewed focus on equality, diversity, and inclusion. Part of this learning has been the willingness to be open, to learn, to hear, to change and repair, and to acknowledge and address inherent power imbalances that can operate within any system, even one that is working towards being a PIE.

This can mean difficult conversations at times, making space for dialogue and acknowledging things that are unsaid. Moreover, working to understand our own unconscious biases and stereotypes with each other can then allow us to consider how this might be an issue within the staff teams we support, as well as the homeless individuals we, and they, work with. This is critical when considering how we take a psychologically informed approach to those who experience homelessness, a population who also experience disproportionately high levels of marginalisation and oppression compared to their housed peers.

We believe that additionally there are other characteristics, attitudes, or behaviours that are important to try to foster within yourself when leading a PIE. Role-modelling these as much as possible as PIE leader can encourage other leaders within the organisation to do similarly, both with colleagues as well as any service users you support. For example, being empathic, trustworthy (i.e. 'doing what you say you will do when you say you will do it, or saying why you cannot'), non-judgemental, and respectful are critical in building the relationships through which leaders create results. As noted above by Scouller (2011), leaders need to have awareness of not just the psychological needs of others but also of themselves; and being willing to reflect, learn, and develop, as well as being secure enough to give spaces for other voices to be heard within co-production, is critical. PIE leaders should provide others with self-confidence and self-esteem, give them that PIE sense of purpose and vision, encourage development and autonomy in others, and ensure that good communication, with an open and consultative approach, underpins all their actions (Khan *et al*, 2016).

This fits well with the work of Brown (2018) who argues that psychologically informed leaders have the characteristics of courage, vulnerability, and empathy. They keep the spaces for co-production open because they don't pretend to have all the answers and they don't avoid difficult conversations and situations. Brown (2018) argues that this requires being *brave* in our leadership, leading from clear values, and being open to feedback from others, as well as being compassionate to ourselves or others when we don't necessarily 'bake our PIE' immediately or we 'burn it'/have set-backs! This concept of 'B.R.A.V.I.N.G.' has been helpful to us in reflecting on our PIE journey. This is about holding clear 'B'oundaries of what PIE is, and what it isn't, as well as our own boundaries within the workplace of being a psychologist; being 'R'eliable and 'A'ccountable, as well as holding others' stories confidentially in 'V'aults to create that critical psychological safety across the organisation. Doing the right thing even if it's not the easy thing on our PIE journey (i.e. 'I'ntegrity) while holding a position of 'N'on-judgement and 'G'enerosity towards others.

Leading the Growth and Expansion of a PIE

Holding a 'growth mind-set' (e.g. Dweck, 2008) across an organisation can also be helpful in order to encourage others, perhaps exhausted and burnt out from their work within the homeless sector, to be 'open' to the idea that change is possible and success is the result of hard work, learning/training, and tenacity/perseverance. It is important that the organisation can see that failure is part of learning and improving. Growth in this context doesn't mean an organisation necessarily getting *bigger* in a concrete sense, i.e. winning more tenders, increasing income or expanding in size in terms of staffing; rather, we are considering it specifically in psychological terms, in the sense of growing as self-development.

Organisations that embody a growth mindset are more able to develop a PIE (and have better outcomes generally; Dwerk, 2016) because they encourage appropriate risk-taking as part of learning and reflective practice, and reward employees for important and useful lessons that may have been learned even if something does not work immediately. They also support collaboration across organisational boundaries rather than competition or silo-working amongst employees or departments, and they are committed to the growth of all of those within the system through development and learning opportunities via investment in staff with PIE training and reflective practice, trying out new strategies or ideas, and learning from challenges or setbacks through robust evaluation processes.

This 'growth' mind set can help build resilience in employees, and increase willingness and motivation to take on challenges and invest the time and energy needed to achieve the often challenging but vitally important positive outcomes or traditional 'Key Performance Indicators' (KPIs) required of the homelessness sector to demonstrate value to external funders or commissioners. It can be easy for an organisation, especially when starting on its PIE journey, to want quick results or to fall into the traps of insecurity or defensiveness when asked to reflect, which can inhibit its growth. If an organisational culture is one of 'talent-spotting' or 'blaming' rather than 'potential-spotting' or 'supporting', it can be harder for employees to share information, collaborate, innovate, seek feedback, or admit errors. Put another way, it is important that we create an organisational PIE culture that is based on trust and is 'psychologically safe' (Edmondson, 1999) without excessive hierarchy or silo-working that can be a barrier to inclusion or true co-production.

As a PIE leader, and holding a 'growth mind-set', it means sometimes being comfortable with ambiguity and uncertainty, being willing to take appropriate risks and find previously unseen opportunities to grow and expand a PIE approach into new areas. Examples of these are our developing 'Pre-16 Prevention' work, working with commissioners to develop new services such as our Lambeth Emotional Well-Being Services (LEWS), or considering new housing models such as our 'Independent Living Scheme'. Of course, this also requires PIE leaders to have strong situational awareness, i.e. the ability to see around, beneath, and beyond what is immediately obvious and, as noted above the capacity for 'bigger picture' strategic thinking in order to effectively utilise the resources and assets of the organisation to create positive change. If an organisation is a PIE, then it should always want to do better, to evolve and grow, and be accountable by evidencing what it is doing and why (Keats *et al*, 2012), rather than being complacent and simply doing things in a particular way because that's the way they have always been done.

One example of innovating our PIE to improve outcomes for the homeless young people we work with has been the identification of 'gaps' or 'needs' in services and careful consideration and reflection of what might be required to overcome these. Anecdotal evidence from reflective practice sessions across the organisation about possible undiagnosed neurodiversity or cognitive impairments that were underpinning challenging behaviours led the PIE team to develop a neuropsychology assessment pathway within the organisation. Often homeless young people have multiple and complex needs that can include mental health issues, substance use, disrupted attachments, and previous traumatic experiences (Centrepoint, 2021). These can be further complicated by specific neuropsychological challenges, which often remain unidentified due to young people being unwilling or unable to engage in statutory assessments. Through a PIE-led engagement approach to identification, assessment, and culturally responsive formulation(s) in context with their other needs and strengths, individualised care plans and interventions are developed and frontline staff can be supported to better understand and manage any associated challenging behaviours within services, whilst increasing a young persons' ability to function and move away from longer-term homelessness.

A PIE can also use psychological research methodologies to answer challenging questions in the homelessness sector. For example, we have carried out research with our education, employment, and training team (EET) to understand why homeless young people are not moving into EET. Not only did this show the value of psychology/PIE approaches to understanding issues in homelessness, but it has led to the development of a psychological model around the barriers to EET which we now plan to target through specific interventions for homeless young people as well as in future staff training and reflective sessions. In addition, a key part of this work was working with senior leaders in the organisation to have a more compassionate understanding of the underlying issues of complex trauma and previous adverse educational experiences that might be impacting on a homeless young person's willingness to engage in EET, as well as the need for long-term relationship building by frontline workers to overcome this – i.e. to help senior leaders understand why there is no 'quick fix' to improve KPIs!

How Do We Know Where We Are on Our PIE Journey?

Just like having a small child in the back of a car on a long journey, often those tasked with the leadership of a PIE get asked repeatedly 'Are we there yet?'. Clearly, improvements in KPIs such as reduced eviction rates and increased EET take-up or successful move on to own tenancies are important (Keats *et al*, 2012), but PIE leaders need to ensure that outcomes are not reductive to easily measurable targets that do not take into account the wider impact on client/staff relationships and personal development outcomes. It is important to not fall into the trap of believing that just because a building looks nice, it operates as a PIE.

We have found that whilst starting our PIE journey with a psychologically informed content within our training for staff, and creating spaces therein for relationship building, reflection, and learning, we have also needed to embed these new psychological skills and knowledge within regular team reflective practice sessions and make concrete changes to policies and procedures (e.g. risk management approaches). We have needed to be alert to more subtle but important changes in how staff might be interacting with those that use our services as well as each other, which links with Johnson and Haigh (2010) when they point out that 'for the moment, at least, the definitive marker of a PIE is simply that, if asked why the unit is run in such and such a way, the staff would give an answer couched in terms of the emotional and psychological needs of the service users, rather than giving some more logistical or practical rationale, such as convenience, costs or Health & Safety Regulations' (quoted in Keats *et al*, 2012, p. 5).

It is worth noting that sometimes it has been the temporary removal of PIE, e.g. a gap in reflective practice due to staff vacancies, that has highlighted the value of the approach; 'you don't know what you have got until it's gone'. Other observations that perhaps PIE is becoming more embedded in the organisation have been an increased focus on data and evidence for strategic decision-making in order to maximise outcomes with the limited resources available, a wider range of voices and opinions being heard and acknowledged with consensuses accommodating differing perspectives (i.e. 'doing with, not doing to'), and greater psychological safety in all 'business as usual' where trauma informed principles such as trust, safety, empowerment, collaboration, and control are enacted more regularly. This results in lower turnover of staff because a PIE approach can facilitate work engagement and involvement of staff in decision-making processes (Rondeau & Wagar, 2012) as well as lower levels of absence and 'presenteeism' (i.e. turning up for work unwell, or working unproductively; West & Davidson, 2012).

We have also found that the enablement of PIE approaches can be 'contagious'. Staff and clients having exposure to positive psychologically informed behaviours evokes positive emotions leading to further replication and more positive behaviour cycles being created (Seligman, 2002). As Cameron *et al* (2004) note; 'when organisations recognise and legitimise virtuous [or value based] behaviours (when courageous or compassionate acts are recognised and applauded), these become self-reinforcing and it fosters resiliency against negative and challenging obstacles' (p. 9). Consequently, in our organisation, as we are about to commence our first significant PIE evaluation, we will be considering a wide variety of both quantitative, i.e. primary KPIs, as well as qualitative, i.e. secondary relational outcomes, data to examine the success of our PIE approach to date.

Final Thoughts and Reflections

As a PIE leader and a psychologist, it has also been important to consider when to 'lean in' – i.e. offering psychologically informed ideas into strategic discussions or decision-making, focusing on key direct delivery activities such as training, reflective practice or property renovation work – and when to 'step back' to give others space to develop, innovate, or just run with psychologically informed ideas. As noted at the start of the chapter, creating a PIE is a shared responsibility across the organisation if it is to be most effective – no one person (or psychologist) is *the PIE* – no matter how good a baker they may be! Succession or longer-term planning is also important. We must always keep in mind how we can create, nurture, develop, support, and/or train the next generation of PIE leaders within an organisation so that a PIE journey continues even if employees move on to new roles.

Therefore it is important to consider: How do we create *inclusive*, psychologically safe spaces for those with potential to become future PIE leaders? How do we build the resilience of both our current and our future leaders, perhaps by sharing responsibilities, as well as providing the psychological support that they need, so that they can develop and support others? This last point is key, as increased psychological distress (e.g. depression, anxiety) amongst leaders leads to more abusive supervision behaviours and a reduction in capacity for future transformational leadership (Byrne *et al*, 2013), and may even undo PIE progress made to date.

Finally, and most importantly, we have found that leadership within a PIE often needs to hold onto those small 'glimmers' of hope or change. Working in the homeless sector can be challenging, frustrating, exhausting, and difficult at times: keeping our focus on those we are there to support, whether that is the staff within an organisation, or the homeless individuals the organisation is supporting, and keeping their voice central to everything we do, can help keep your eyes on the horizon and your motivation going, particularly if the non-people elements such as systems and processes can feel a barrier at times. It is important to remember that even a small change in how we interact with another person in a more psychologically informed manner can have a big impact on how they respond to others and what they do next – PIE in action!

Moreover, ensuring that our decision-making keeps, as its underpinning principle, what is going to be most beneficial or most PIE, even if that is not easy, can be a useful guide. Reflecting upon and evaluating what we are doing in order to always ensure achieving our mission or primary task is what underpins everything in our PIE means that there won't be a 'one size fits all' approach in every organisation, but that every organisation that is working in a PIE way will remain true to the fundamental principles of PIE. For us, that is trying to remember to hold our 'PIEineers' voices, like Catherine's, central as well as remembering at all times that a successful PIE is built around relationships with others, whether our colleagues, those we support, or those we interact with in the wider system such as statutory services, partners, supports, and donors. Successful leadership in a PIE is therefore arguably like successful leadership in many other sectors: [Leadership] 'is an art … more a weaving of relationships than an amassing of information' (De Pree, 1989).

Reader Reflective Questions

- Why PIE and why now, in your organisation? What is your organisation's vision for PIE?
- Who, within your organisation, can help with your organisation's PIE and how?
- How can you create psychologically safe and inclusive spaces to ensure your organisation's PIE works for your services, colleagues, service users, and wider partners if applicable?
- What 'ingredients' of a PIE might be a priority to set up first to build momentum for change? What 'ingredients' might come next?
- What organisation specific outcomes might show evidence of success of your organisation's PIE? How can you build these into the development of the PIE as you go along in order measure success or pick up and address challenges quickly?
- What do the different aspects of psychologically informed leadership mean to you and how might you apply this to yourself or others within your organisation?
- Where is your organisation's PIE similar to other organisations and where might it be different? How can you connect with others in the sector for learning and development?
- Is a PIE ever 'fully baked'? What is next for your organisation?

References

Adair, J. (1984) *The Skills of Leadership*. Aldershot: Gower.

Brown, B. (2018) *Dare to Lead: Brave Work. Tough Conversations. Whole Hearts*. London: Ebury Publishing.

Byrne, A. (2013) The depleted leader: The influence of leaders diminished psychological resources on leadership behaviours. *The Leadership Quarterly*. 25(2): pp 344–357.

Cameron, K., Bright, D. & Caza, A. (2004) Exploring the relationships between organisational virtuousness and performance. *American Behavioural Scientist*. 47: pp 766–790.

Centrepoint (2021) *The Mental Health Needs of Homeless Young People*. https://centrepoint. org.uk/research-and-reports/mental-health-needs-homeless-young-people.

Cooke, N.J. (2015) Team cognition as interaction. *Current Directions in Psychological Science*. 24(6): pp 415–419.

Cummings, G.G., Cummings, G.G., MacGregor, T., Davey, M., Lee, H., Wong, C.A., Lo, E., Muise, M. & Stafford, E. (2010) Leadership styles and outcome patterns for the nursing workforce and work environment: A systematic review. *International Journal of Nursing Studies*. 47: pp 363–385.

De Pree, M. (1989) *Leadership Is an Art*. New York: Crown Currency.

Dweck, C.S. (2008) *Mindset*. New York: Ballantine Books.

Dwerk, C.S. (2016) What having a 'Growth Mindset' actually means. *Harvard Business Review*. Accessed at https://hbsp.harvard.edu/product/H02LQX-PDF-ENG

Edmondson, A. (1999) Psychological safety & learning behaviour in work teams. *Administrative Science Quarterly*. 44(2): pp 350–383.

Ekvall, G. & Arvonen, J. (1991) Change-centered leadership: An extension of the two-dimensional model. *Scandinavian Journal of Management*. 7(1): pp 17–26.

Fiedler, F.E. (1967) *A Theory of Leadership Effectiveness*. McGraw-Hill Series in Management.

Geddes, C. (2022). Quote from Centrepoint Ex-Young Person/Youth Homelessness Campaigner.

Greenleaf, R.K. (1996) In Frick, D. M & Spears, L. C. (Eds.) *On Becoming a Servant-Leader*. Hoboken, NJ: Jossey-Bass.

Greenleaf, R.K. (1977) *Servant Leadership: A Journey into the Nature of Legitimate Power and Greatness*. New York: Paulist Press.

Johnson, R. & Haigh, R. (2010) Social psychiatry and social policy for the 21st century: Psychologically informed environments. *Journal of Mental Health & Social Inclusion*. 14(4): pp 30–35.

Keats, H., Maguire, N., Johnson, R. & Cockersell, P. (2012) *Psychologically Informed Services for Homeless People. Good Practice Guide*. London: Communities and Local Government.

Khan, Z.A., Nawaz, A. & Khan, I. (2016) Leadership theories and styles: A literature review. *Journal of Resources Development & Management*. 16: pp 1–7.

Kouzes, J.M. & Posner, B.Z. (1987) *The Leadership Challenge: How to Get Extraordinary Things Done in Organizations (1st Ed.)*. San Francisco: Jossey-Bass.

Rondeau, K. & Wagar, T. (2012) *Employee high-involvement work practices and voluntary turnover: Does human capital accumulation or an employee empowerment culture mediate the process? Examining the evidence in Canadian healthcare organisations*. Paper presented at the Organisations proceedings of the European Conference on Intellectual Capital.

Scouller, J. (2011) *The Three Levels of Leadership: How to Develop Your Leadership Presence, Knowhow & Skill*. Cirencester: Management Books.

Seligman, M.E.P. (2002) Positive Psychology, Positive Prevention & Positive Therapy. In Snyder, C. R. & Lopez, S. J. (Eds.) *Oxford Handbook of Positive Psychology*. Oxford: Oxford University Press.

West, M. & Dawson, J. (2012) *Employee Engagement and NHS Performance*. London: The Kings Fund.

Westminster Council (2015) *Creating a Psychologically Informed Environment: Implementation & Assessment*. Clevedon: No One Left Out Solutions Ltd.

Zaccaro, J., Green, J.P., Dubrow, S. & Kolze, M. (2018) Leader individual differences, situational parameters, and leadership outcomes: A comprehensive review and integration. *The Leadership Quarterly*. 29(1): pp 2–43.

Chapter 11

PIE as a Framework for Implementing Trauma Informed and Strength-Based Approaches in a Local Authority

Claire Ritchie

The Role of Leadership

"Will our managers be doing this training?". It's a question commonly asked at the end of a workshop and I appreciate why. Becoming a psychologically informed environment (PIE) is about changing the culture of an organization, and ultimately it is its leaders' responsibility to do this. They are the "cultural architects", continuously "radiating"[1] (Clark 2020) the values, beliefs, attitudes, and practices that guide and inform staff teams.

NHS Education for Scotland, who lead on the Scottish National Trauma Transformation Programme, have found through years of experience and research that "…it's really clear that leadership is essential…we know it has to happen at grassroots level and at leadership level. But I think the evidence over recent years really shows us that no matter how much we do at grassroots level, the leadership is crucial"[2] (NHS Education for Scotland 2023b).

In their video "What is trauma informed leadership and why does it matter?"[3] (Improvement Service 2023a) Hayley McDonald from the Resilience Learning Partnership states simply that leaders get to determine "What's valuable and what it makes space for". Leaders are who prioritise "…the time, money, and resources on what they feel is important." Anne Hyne from NHS Lanarkshire adds that it is leaders who "Permit and communicate the changes" who "Navigate troubled waters when sometimes there is resistance or stress is experienced" and who "Create the capacity to manage the changes and monitor the outcomes".

In October 2023, the University of Bristol issued a policy research report[4] (Lewis 2023) outlining the findings of their study on trauma informed approaches within healthcare. The recommendations (Table 11.1) are extremely helpful as, in my view, they confirm the need for PIE as an implementation framework and echo the importance of leadership within organisations, across regions, and from government.

The study acknowledges the role and impact of the political and economic environment, and organisational culture and resources, as important contextual factors impacting on effectiveness of change programmes and refers to a lack of leadership support at organisational and government levels as a barrier to successful

DOI: 10.4324/9781003415053-14

Table 11.1 Policy Recommendations Policy Research Report 88

1   Trauma informed organisational change programmes in adult primary care and community mental health require an allocated budget, involvement of all staff groups and people with lived experience, ongoing training and support for all staff, and safe physical and psychological environments for all patients and staff.
2   Every trauma informed organisational change programme should have an evaluation component to generate a UK evidence base. Current evidence is largely drawn from the USA, with limited evidence on effectiveness.
3   Bottom-up driven trauma informed initiatives need top-down support from organisational, regional, and national leadership.
4   Policymakers should support and join local and national trauma informed networks of professional and lived experience experts. These networks facilitate knowledge exchange and coordination of trauma informed initiatives.
5   Funders: commission a funding call to evaluate trauma informed organisational change programmes and initiatives.

implementation. I would suggest that to become a successful PIE, government support would add value but more important is support from senior leadership and, ideally, its commissioners. Additionally, the policy recommendation includes the statement that "Every trauma informed organisational change programme should have an evaluation component to generate a UK evidence base" which of course PIE does.

In Scotland and Wales there are key documents and road maps[5] (NHS Education for Scotland 2023b) to support implementation of psychological approaches, backed by government ministers. In England a working definition of trauma informed practice[6] (Office for health improvement and disparities 2022) was introduced in 2022 and a rapid evidence assessment of how the approach supports people experiencing multiple disadvantage[7] (Department for Levelling Up, Housing and Communities 2023). The report confirmed the value and importance of relational and person-centred approaches. We don't yet have a national framework: campaigning for this continues and the PIE framework would be a suitable place for the government to start.

Becoming PIE

Becoming a PIE is described as a journey – a journey which is non-prescriptive and unique to each service and organisation, and one that takes time and commitment, and is more likely to succeed with senior management support and participation. It's a model which puts the relationships, mental health, and emotional well-being of customers and staff at its centre. And it is one that is inherently trauma informed, asking us to see behaviour as communication and to consider what that behaviour is telling us, one which enables us to embrace the "why" of why we do what we do. It offers individuals who experience adversity and social, economic, and health inequalities access to services, and it encourages building a connection, however small, through unconditional positive regard.

This chapter will outline the PIE journey of Bournemouth, Christchurch, and Poole local authority Housing Directorate – the why and how, and the impact of doing so – and it also describes how a small group of leaders continue to keep the PIE fire alight despite other priorities and challenges.

The Journey

In 2018 the Homeless Reduction Act (2017) introduced significant new statutory duties such as a duty to prevent and assist with actual or threatened homelessness, and a duty on public bodies, such as health and probation, to refer and collaborate where there is a risk of homelessness. These fundamental changes mean that people previously ineligible for a homelessness duty assessment, those without priority need, are now eligible. These were positive and welcomed changes within the homelessness sector as it meant rough sleepers and single homeless people were now automatically eligible. However, it also meant housing department officials working more with people with so-called "challenging behaviours", and therefore it was also an opportunity to evidence how PIE can support housing department staff to work with the impact of trauma.

Research has consistently shown that people using homeless services are more likely to have experienced adverse and traumatic events in childhood. In 2022 Oasis Community Housing and Northumbria University concluded that "It's futile to try to solve the issue of homelessness without addressing trauma"[8] (Irving and Harding 2022). We also have clear examples, many included in this book, where becoming a PIE can offer staff confidence, competency, and consistency when supporting people facing the impact of trauma. Therefore, the PIE model is more relevant than ever.

For local authorities, however, the changes in law posed a number of risks and challenges (Table 11.2)

It was against this backdrop that I delivered my first workshop to members of the Poole Housing Options team and colleagues from the voluntary sector. Ben Tomlin, then Head of Housing Options and Partnerships, had commissioned the training for several reasons:

- Bournemouth, Christchurch, and Poole Councils were due to merge the following year, and Ben wanted to introduce a culture of person-centred approaches, as opposed to current process-led ones, prior to this

Table 11.2 Homeless Reduction Act (2017) – Implications for Local Authorities

- A significant increase in the number of referrals and assessments
- No increase in availability of affordable housing
- Introduction of a new recording system H-CLIC which brings an increase in administration duties
- Limited additional funding to respond to the changes

The accompanying code of guidance recommends training staff in an asset and strength-based approach, motivational interviewing and the impact of trauma

- To give housing staff "professional" skills, tools, and knowledge
- Consistency in approach to understanding trauma and communicating empathy
- Strategic and systemic thinking, to work collaboratively with colleagues in different directorates where people face multiple disadvantage such as social care

The training covered the five principles of PIE, providing a psychological framework through which the organisation could implement trauma informed care (TIC). Ben was also interested in how PIE principles could be applied to their physical environment, in particular their face-to-face customer hubs and enquiry spaces. It was clear the training resonated with him and others: I will always remember one passionate housing officer suggesting that an understanding of trauma should influence their decision-making when considering "intentionality" of homelessness – music to my ears! However, his, and the corporate, priority at the time was the imminent merger, and the implications of the Homeless Reduction Act (2017).

Later in the year, the Project Co-ordinator for Bournemouth Housing and Communities responsible for ending rough sleeping commissioned training to create a pathway of PIE services including housing options, supported housing, the outreach team, and voluntary sector organisations. The workshops were tailored to each cohort, but all included a focus on understanding the potential impact of trauma, consideration of the physical environment, and managing relationships via a strength-focused approach.

Although a strength-focused approach might not be considered a psychological approach by some, positive psychologists would argue differently: Martin Seligman, described by many as the father of positive psychology, suggests that to support people in distress we need to consider their character strengths and what helps individuals succeed, not just what holds them back and hurts them. His research into happiness and flourishing argues that people who know their unique mix of strengths and virtues, particularly if used in service to others, are the happiest[9] (Park et al 2004). In 2010 researchers attempting to identify common traits within trauma informed services identified a strength-based approach as one of them.

'TIC is a strength-based service delivery approach that is rooted in an understanding of and responsiveness to the impact of trauma, that emphasizes physical, psychological, and emotional safety for both providers and clients.'[10] (Hopper et al 2010)

The workshops were well received. However, staff were unsure how to commit to implementing the approach without leadership support and endorsement.

2019

In 2019 Bournemouth, Christchurch, and Poole local authorities merged to create BCP Council and introduced five core behaviours which easily align with the principles and practice of PIE and TIC.

i Listen – We understand the importance of being heard and value different perspectives.

ii Trust – We are empowered and empower others to achieve the best outcomes.

iii Act – We are positive and confident to take forward-thinking action.

iv Collaborate – We draw on our shared skills and strengths to learn together and achieve a common purpose.

v Aspire – Challenge ourselves to continually grow and achieve our potential and be the best.

Gary Pulman, Homelessness Partnerships Coordinator, approached me for support to pilot a strengths-based approach in his tenancy sustainment team. In the hope it would be adopted across the Housing Directorate, he presented my proposal to the senior leadership team who agreed for the training to be rolled out. We adapted the workshop content to take advantage of this and to encourage buy-in. This content included:

- the impact of trauma and how strengths-based assessments and conversations can avoid the re-triggering of negative feelings and emotions,
- how it aligns to the Homeless Reduction Act code of practice,
- where the approach is being used in other directorates, such as social work, and local voluntary organisations,
- experience of other councils such as Oxford, who were being supported by Crisis to implement the approach in response to the Housing Reduction Act,
- the added value, benefits, and impact of the approach in preventing and relieving homelessness with evidence from elsewhere,
- considering how staff attitudes and practice, particularly during initial contact and assessments, needed to change,
- how supervision styles can support practice,
- how a strengths-based approach can be used when dealing with difficult behaviour,
- the balancing of risk and strengths, and
- agreeing a tool to use with clients to measure progress.

Feedback from the sessions was positive and managers identified the next steps to include:

- a culture change and a new way of working, with relevant policies and process,
- a different approach to supervision and talking about risk,
- a top-down approach to implementation, and
- striking a balance of realistic and achievable.

Post training, I facilitated a reflective practice session with Gary and his team. We were scheduled to have three sessions over nine months to support implementation, develop tools, and adapt paperwork through staff experience and learning. Initially some found the change challenging as they were used to seeing clients through the lens of deficits and risks. Fortunately, a new team member, familiar with the concept, was willing to give it a go. His success gave the others the confidence to have different conversations with their clients which had such a positive outcome in terms of building trust for the next tranche of training that I was able to use their work as examples of how the approach can change the relationship between worker and client. The staff were genuinely surprised how small, simple changes in their own behaviour could have such an important impact.

2020

Covid19 brought unprecedented changes to working practices and a whole new set of priorities. Ben, now Head of Strategic Housing and Partnerships, and I discussed the impact of the training delivered so far, and what could support managers to keep strengths-focused conversations going with staff. As a result, I developed a template for 1-1's and appraisals. Having tailored tools to support the culture change was welcomed but it was acknowledged that across the directorate in fact managers were using a range of templates, in part because of the recent merger.

Gary and I reviewed the staff training content and agreed that 2020 workshops would consist of a session on TIC, followed by strength-based practice which would be framed to evidence how it can fit within the legal framework of the Homeless Reduction Act (2017), for example in the Personal Housing Plans. Gary was also keen for the role of reflective practice to be introduced and discussed in the managers' sessions.

2021

After delivering training for two years, it became evident that for staff to truly embrace and embed a strengths-based approach and to feel psychologically safe enough to adapt their practice within existing processes, managers and leaders needed a clear performance framework to model the approach. As a result, I developed a programme of six workshops, three for staff and three for managers (Figure 11.1).

The objective of the training for managers was to explore the benefits of a strengths-based approach, for themselves, their staff, and their clients or customers, and to create high-performing teams using the performance development framework. This would hopefully support a change in culture and provide psychological safety for staff to practise differently. For staff, the workshops introduced the concept of psychological trauma and of how using a different lens, language, and conversation, even slightly, could change the dynamic of interventions to avoid re-triggering trauma. It was also an opportunity to identify personal strengths and start to feel comfortable talking about their own and other people's in the group, and to support thinking about their personal development and to complete exercises they could take to discuss in supervision.

To date approximately 250 people have participated, and this training is rolled out each year to all new BCP staff and managers and has delivered tangible benefits.

Staff	Managers
Understand the potential impact of psychological trauma and how to use a strength-based approach with customers	Cultivating strength-based practice to support staff performance, development, and well-being
Trauma informed care	The business case for strengths
Completing a strengths profile, aligning work objectives and goals to strengths	Completing a strengths profile, aligning work objectives and goals to strengths
Strength-based practice	Designing your performance framework

Figure 11.1 Programme of Workshops for Staff and Managers

The Impact

Talking to Ben this year he described how becoming a PIE has had "Hoped for and unexpected benefits", but not to underestimate the challenges and time that it can take to implement. Outcomes he identified as attributed to PIE, include:

1 A change in language and conversations: approximately 50% of managers have regular strengths-focused conversations with their staff.
2 A change in staff behaviour as evidenced in the following email.

> Housing Options was inspected by the Housing Advice and Support Team at DLUHC. They spoke to different groups from politicians to senior leaders, team managers, housing support workers, apprentices etc. We've just received the headline report of their observations to help with our service development. Without prompting, they reflected the following within the summary of their findings and final report, which I thought I'd share with you.

- Prevention and strength-based approach of the service is evident.
- Strength-based approach evident throughout interactions with the team, with a positive approach to providing help rather than just an assessment service.

These reflections are referenced in the context of how the teams work together and the way in which officers work with residents. This would not have been evident prior to the focused training that you have helped to support us with, so thank you

(Personal communication, Ben Tomlin, 2022)

3 Using the performance framework has "fuelled personal development and sparked ambition": One manager has been motivated to study leadership and management, and an apprentice has been promoted to team leader, in part by demonstrating the behaviours promoted in the training.
4 A message I received as feedback after the workshops in 2022 also reflects how some staff have benefited.

The strength-based approach workshops were extremely useful for me as they helped me realise where my strengths lay and consequently what I was missing from my role. The workshops gave me encouragement to apply for a job that was a step up, hopefully an opportunity to use my strengths and to develop my unrealised strengths. The other elements of the workshops, using a strengths-based approach with people we are working with and supporting, can only be a good thing, as well as the increased awareness of the effects of trauma and the use of labels on people we are working with who have experienced homelessness.

(Personal Communications, BCP staff 2022)

5 The voice of lived experience is much stronger within the Homeless Partnership, challenging the conventional narrative.
6 A change in perspective: the narrative around homeless intentionality has changed. Where there are co-located multi-disciplinary teams, housing staff and care staff are talking the same language.
7 The annual appraisal has been replaced by the "BCP Staff Talent and Enablement Review" which includes the discussion topic of strengths.
8 Thirty properties housing homeless families have had physical changes to make them more welcoming environments.
9 Housing Options have introduced behaviour-led recruitment practices and value hiring people with lived experience.
10 The Homelessness and Rough Sleeping Strategy 2021–25 refers (briefly!) to both trauma and strengths.
11 In 2020 a Clinical Psychologist was employed by BCP for one year to help develop formulations for entrenched rough sleepers. She also facilitated reflective practice. Her work was considered a great success, and the intention was to continue when she left the post. Unfortunately, they failed to recruit.

Laura was funded through the RS funding we had back in 2016-18 as it was recognised several organisations were dealing with the customers, each with a part of the picture of what was going on. The psychological approach Laura used took practitioners through all the underlying issues that were in play with each customer that contributed to their homelessness and rough sleeping. It was a team around the customer meeting facilitated by a psychologist using trauma informed principles and diagnostic processes, a much deeper dive for practitioners into motivation and understanding the client. Outcomes were a shared understanding of the issues for each individual across the organisations and agencies involved, and agreement on a multi-agency support plan with an agreed lead professional – some agencies stepped back as too many involved.

As with any complex system it's not a straightforward task to attribute a specific input to an outcome, but some of the above examples can clearly be linked to the leader's commitment, and staff effort, to becoming PIE.

Learning and Legacy

Talking to Ben Tomlin recently he described how his current focus is on staff health and well-being, and how a group of managers are learning how to facilitate reflective practice.

We recognised we needed to improve our wellbeing and support offer to staff because of the increased complexity, and the traumatic situations, we ask our staff to deal with daily. We also recognised, via stress at work absences and staff retention issues, more effective support was necessary. Working alongside social workers and health colleagues it was clear that the more structured supervision and support in place for them was absent for housing staff, yet arguably housing staff were dealing with the same people and often equally traumatic and challenging situations. A handful of my team managers, with other team managers in services we typically work alongside with the people we help, i.e. community safety, anti-social behaviour teams, are learning how to become reflective practice facilitators. Our aim is to introduce a framework of reflective practice settings which all staff (including managers) can access and make use of.

BCP as PIE

BCP's journey started with a desire to create a culture of empathy and person-centred approaches, and to up-skill staff, giving them the confidence and recognition they deserve for working with people facing complex situations and multiple disadvantage. It progressed to understanding trauma and recognising strengths as part of their psychological framework and continues by embedding reflective practice skills in its managers. Leaders recognise the journey has been slow and challenging, that practice remains inconsistent across the organisation, but their resolve in recognition of its value in supporting and building on their good practice remains firm. Their commitment has helped unlock staff potential and brought about a change in language, perspective and behaviour which was witnessed and acknowledged by the Department of Levelling Up Housing and Communities in their Housing Advice and Support Team Report (2022). The journey continues and as more local authorities see the added value of becoming a PIE perhaps in time this will be the norm rather than the exception.

Notes

1 https://www.leaderfactor.com/4-stages-of-psychological-safety.
2 https://www.traumatransformation.scot/implementation/.
3 https://www.youtube.com/watch?v=Y9mxC496GP4.
4 https://www.bristol.ac.uk/media-library/sites/policybristol/briefings-and-reports-pdfs/2023-briefings/PolicyReport88_Lewis_trauma_informed_healthcare.pdf.
5 "A Societal Approach to Understanding, Preventing and Supporting the Impacts of Trauma and Adversity, for a wider audience" (2022).
6 https://www.gov.uk/government/publications/working-definition-of-trauma-informed-practice/working-definition-of-trauma-informed-practice.
7 https://assets.publishing.service.gov.uk/media/642af3a77de82b000c31350d/Changing_Futures_Evaluation_-_Trauma_informed_approaches_REA.pdf.
8 https://www.northumbria.ac.uk/about-us/news-events/news/homelessness-cannot-be-solved-unless-we-tackle-trauma/.
9 https://psycnet.apa.org/record/2004-20501-001.
10 https://scholar.google.co.uk/scholar?q=trauma+informed+care+Hopper,+Bassuk,+%26+Olivet,+2010&hl=en&as_sdt=0&as_vis=1&oi=scholart.

References

Clark, T. (2020) *The 4 Stages of Psychological Safety*. Oakland: Berret-Koehler Publishers, Inc.
Department for Levelling Up, Housing and Communities (2023) *Trauma-Informed Approaches to Supporting People Experiencing Multiple Disadvantage: A Rapid Evidence Assessment*. Gov.uk. Accessed at https://assets.publishing.service.gov.uk/media/642af3a77de82b000c31350d/Changing_Futures_Evaluation_-_Trauma_informed_approaches_REA.pdf
Hopper, E., Bassuk, E. and Olivet, J. (2010) *Shelter from the Storm: Trauma-Informed Care in Homelessness Services Settings*.
Irving, A. and Harding, J. (2022) *The Prevalence of Trauma among People Who Have Experienced Homelessness in England: A Report for Oasis Community Housing*. Northumbria: University Newcastle.
Lewis, N. (2023) *Trauma-Informed Approaches in Healthcare: Piecemeal Implementation Needs UK-wide Leadership, Strategy, and Evidence*. Bristol: University of Bristol.
National Trauma Transformation Programme (2023a) *What Is Trauma-Informed Leadership and Why Does It Matter?* Improvement Service. Accessed at https://www.traumatransformation.scot/resources/what-is-trauma-informed-leadership-and-why-does-it-matter/
National Trauma Transformation Programme. (2023b) A *Roadmap for Creating Trauma-Informed and Responsive Change Guidance for Organisations, Systems and Workforces*

in Scotland. NHS Education for Scotland. Accessed at https://www.traumatransformation. scot/implementation/

Office for Health Improvement and Disparities. (2022) *A Societal Approach to Understanding, Preventing and Supporting the Impacts of Trauma and Adversity, for a Wider Audience.* Gov.uk. Accessed at https://traumaframeworkcymru.com/wp-content/ uploads/2022/07/Trauma-Informed-Wales-Framework.pdf

Park, N., Peterson, C., & Seligman, M. E. P. (2004) Strengths of character and well-being. *Journal of Social and Clinical Psychology. 23*(5) pp 603–619.

Chapter 12

Commissioning for PIEs – A Journey, Involving Walking the Walk and Talking the Talk – Moving to Psychologically Informed Commissioning

Victoria Aseervatham

I was surprised to be asked to write a chapter: I don't feel like an expert on psychologically informed environment (PIE). But, on the other hand, I suppose I have been an agent of change and all those little steps, over time, do add up. In real life, you often don't see the changes fully until you look back and there's rarely a big bang, rather things evolve over time. So I said I'd have a go!

I like the phrase that PIE is a journey rather than a destination. I think that's the same with providers and in commissioning. If PIE is a journey, let me tell you about mine and share the things in my backpack that have helped along the way. Then I'll zoom out and think about the bigger picture enablers and challenges.

I may not be an expert but I do love to learn and triangulate and I collect quotes like a magpie. I have peppered quotes throughout the chapter that have helped me on the journey. As Lolly Daskal says, "quotations from other people are sources of guidance in times of need, they can give us inspiration in times of struggle, they can motivate us in times of tribulations - success is never final and failure is not forever" (Daskal, 2022).

The Beginning of the Journey

I've been in rough sleeping commissioning at Westminster City Council since 2004. We have the biggest numbers of rough sleepers of any UK local authority (the 'capital city' effect), which is very challenging; but if there's a silver lining, it's that it gives us the opportunity to spot trends in the rough sleeping population, make interventions that make a difference, and share them with the sector – and we've been able to do this a number of times, identifying new insights on things like brain injury, autistic spectrum, and gambling.

We commission a range of accommodation services for rough sleepers from outreach, hostels, and supported housing to Housing First and supporting health and well-being services. We've been promoting PIEs from the inception of the term (and we were quite into this sort of collaboration before we had the term 'PIE') and now the majority of our services would call themselves PIE services and we think of it as a PIE pathway and we attend to the ecosystem of interfacing services. All our commissioned services have features like reflective practice, we have a free

DOI: 10.4324/9781003415053-15

PIE training programme for all workers, and the majority have therapeutic services going into their services. They are all at different stages and there are ups and down, but all services are on the PIE train.

"There comes a point where we need to stop just pulling people out of the river. We need to go upstream and find out why they're falling in" Desmond Tutu (Goodreads, 2024).

The rough sleeping commissioning team has always had a strong component of people who previously worked in frontline services and that has been a huge benefit. It doesn't take long to work in the field of rough sleeping to realise how problematic siloed services are and the need for attachment and trauma to have a central appreciation. In terms of the river analogy there are so many earlier interventions and different approaches needed. The imperative to do things differently and take a systems lens has always been strong and our commissioning team had that shared appreciation as a team, even if we didn't know the exact route to take. I was designated the team investigator on PIE when the term emerged, as it immediately seemed such a good framework for what we knew needed attention.

To get to the stage of all services being on the PIE train, we have focused on four things: promoting, brokering, building it into procurement and bids, and wider system change work. The promotion was how we started, simply putting an emphasis on PIEs, creating networking opportunities, and creating and/or linking in with free training. We created a 'top down' clarity that we thought PIE was important while creating 'bottom up' agency to experiment, capture, and share emerging learning. We recognised early that staff engagement, morale, and well-being were crucial and made it clear to providers that that was where our gaze was. Then, casting our net wider, we started working on the eco-system of services, thinking about the joins with external services, and started brokering ways to forge connections across the gaps. As confidence grew in PIE we were able to build it into new procurement and existing contracts management and, crucially, bidding opportunities. Success bred success.

But I suppose it was a personal journey as well. I took an active approach in promoting and demystifying PIE and educating myself on what it actually means for a service to become psychologically informed. To authentically commission for PIE you have to understand it, you can't just "tick box it", and that fundamentally impacts on your approach as a commissioner for example to data collection, output measurements and everyday contract management, or looking at serious incident reports coming in. If PIE is a journey you need to walk the walk and talk the talk every day; but that can start with small steps.

The Benefits of the PIE Journey

For me there is no alternative – the more PIE a service, the better they are on quality and performance. Let me paint you a picture of what the fully fledged PIE projects share:

- Leadership from the manager of the service, and the backing of the organisation.
- Attention to detail of all aspects of the service, seeing it through the clients' eyes, and making every contact count.

- They are strong on coproduction.
- They are reflective and they network and seek out partners to meet need.
- They have recruitment sussed, the right staff and solid staff training and support in place, great team work, good self-care.
- Never give up, positive attitude of hope and unconditional positive regard.
- All took time to build.
- Key thing: definitely not above average contract values!

Our most developed PIE projects are delivering the best outcomes in hard and soft areas:

- Getting the long-term rough sleepers indoors.
- Less abandonments and evictions.
- Less serious incidents – PIE services do still get them but when they do, they are reflectively and skilfully handled, and exclusions/evictions are a very last resort, with sensitive touches like a goodbye letter to remind of all the achievements, or perhaps they've lined up someone to still work with the person to provide continuity, and they make sure that belongings and documents aren't lost.
- Good at stabilising the most chaotic – less nights sleeping out, less A&E, less self-harming, substance misuse and offending; and more working on their strengths and getting them involved and contributing.
- A powerful evidence base (which we hold) around savings to the public purse for high-cost clients.
- They don't just say no to referrals, and the quality of discussion at case conference is high, and they are good at smooth handovers between services.

But there are no quick fixes for people for whom so many hard experiences of trauma cast long shadows, and I don't have a neat formula to benchmark PIE vs non-PIE services. What I do know for sure is different approaches work for different people and we are still learning all the time, but that PIE has been and is a hugely helpful foundation every time and every day!

The Culture Clash between PIE Commissioning and a New Public Management Approach to Commissioning

Whenever I speak to other commissioners I always try and dispel fear and myths about PIE (like it costs big money). I think there can definitely be a mismatch with the traditional culture of commissioning which can feel like a technical space defined by jargon and bureaucracy. It can feel like PIE doesn't sit well with traditional key performance indicators (KPIs), contract price per hour, the Supporting People QAF, procurement codes, etc. and there's not a particularly neat ready evidence base. And there can be shadow issues: commissioners can feel out of their depth, that other external people will know more than them, and a fear that it will involve giving up control and power.

So I always advise that just because you are a commissioner you don't have to know best and know everything. I say, "I'm not an ologist", and I'm on a journey. Just like creating a PIE takes time, commissioning for PIEs takes time and grows. Our journey started years ago, with no money, and started small; as we got the wins it grew, and we invested more.

There is a phase "if something's worth doing, do it badly rather than not at all". I thoroughly recommend that. Sometimes you want to do something perfectly or at the perfect time and that can lead to procrastination, delays, stress, and anxiety. I feel like I've seen that with commissioners not wanting to venture into an area where they won't be an expert and they might not be able to do it 'properly' at the outset, or feeling that they need to wait until they can first secure psychologist funding. But "do it badly" as a motto can give you the courage to have a go; and more often than not, you end up not doing it that badly, and whatever you do today you can improve on tomorrow anyway.

I always recommend Collaborate's publications *A Whole New World* (2017) and *Exploring the New World* (2019) to all commissioners that I meet.

These reports make the clear case that:

- People are complex, issues are complex, systems are complex: so embrace complexity.
- We need 'whole person' responses, not siloed commissioning.
- Measure the right thing or not at all (it's very easy to inadvertently create 'gaming' with numbers).
- Involve people with lived experience: they have got to be at the heart of decisions.
- Commission via relationships.
- Support the workforce.
- Have commissioning cycles that allow for service flex and evolution.
- Recognise that learning and reflection drive improvements.

It's a leap, but so empowering and encouraging for commissioners to embrace vulnerability – you don't have to 'know best' and be in control at all times. It takes off the shackles and the straight-jacket in the way commissioners think that they "should be", and it promotes an altogether more productive approach that is so much more real and impactful. After meeting one of the authors, Toby Lowe, and reading *A Whole New World* cited above, I felt like I'd been on a mind spa. It was so affirming. "Finally", I thought, "that's me".

I knew I'd never been a conventional commissioner but I've had quite a bit of success over the years in one way and another, from helping people to collaborate and create flexibility, to recognising a gap and winning funding to fill it. The report helped me understand why this has worked. The focus on being human, learning, and nurturing the health of the system makes perfect sense, of course, and reinforced the focus I've always had on the importance of relationships at all levels from clients to workers, from workers to managers, from managers to commissioners, and so on.

As well as publishing the above reports, Collaborate host a 'community of practice': the community is growing and commissioners can join.

Getting Started

Helen Bevan (2022a) suggested in her improvement lessons that it is important to: "Ensure top-down clarity, bottom-up agency".

Going back to the beginning, we started with no dedicated money, rather making use of free resources and the interest of partners to start on the journey. But we were very clear that PIE was important and valued.

We started with a PIE forum, a totally free networking place to share ideas. Networking opportunities are so important and someone has to start the ball rolling, which can just mean booking a room or creating a virtual space. At the forum we celebrated all forms of connection and relationships rather that holding up psychologists as the sole experts in this domain. Some of the free resources we collaborated on, publicised, and explored include:

- Creating a Psychologically Informed Environment Implementation and Assessment – http://meam.org.uk/new-resource-on-psychologically-informed-environments/.
- PIElink Website – connecting people interested in PIEs – http://pielink.net/.
- Homeless Link Resources https://homeless.org.uk/
- Jay Levy's writings on Pre-Treatment. Not a lot is written about outreach: it seems to me it can feel like a 'dark art'. Jay Levy (2021) writes brilliantly and it's a great practical model.

We built on initial interest to create more networking opportunities by offering free training and workshops, building a coalition of the keen, and creating opportunities to learn, reflect, and train together. As well as the PIE forum for commissioned services a multi-sector Complex Personalities Network was created, chaired by a psychotherapist who was the lead counsellor for an NHS homeless psychotherapy service and coproduced with experts by experience.

Born from the necessity of having no dedicated budget, we didn't set out with a single psychological framework in mind to sponsor, and in many ways that stood us in good stead on the journey. Being open to the benefits of different approaches for different clients and promoting the development of an eclectic range of partnerships and psychological approaches has enabled a wide of approaches to flourish.

It always felt important to me to celebrate the non-theory based, practical, hands-on examples of PIE approaches which enhance relationships, things like the receptionist leading on mood music, a resident's favourite songs playing, scent diffusers in reception, having a cat or chickens in a hostel, gardening and dancing and music groups, etc. PIE has always instantly appealed to the psychology graduate workers but making sure the less academic workers, who generally stay in post longer (which has significant advantages), feel celebrated at the PIE table is crucial. We were keen to make sure we sent the message that our appreciation wasn't all for new therapeutically clever stuff – the old-fashioned good stuff that good workers have always done is really important and clearly PIE too: things like empathy, creativity, great teamwork, positive regard.

Equally we have had a variety of approaches to reflective practice over the years. This started off modestly with services typically buying it in an hour a month. As confidence has grown in the benefits, and more resources have been secured, this has 'staircased' up so that now the majority of services have psychology input from a central team commissioned by the council. Psychologists/psychotherapists certainly have a great all-round training for this but other disciplines can work very well too, and the 'fit' of the facilitator/style to the team seems most crucial.

Linking Up with the Existing Eco System for Quick Wins

Looking outside homelessness services we were able to broker relationships with NHS services who were willing and able to deliver light, therapeutic, pre-treatment interventions. This was so much easier to broker from our position at the council rather than for individual services to attempt. The classic problem with the mainstream treatment services is that they tend to be geared towards people who have one issue at a time, in the 'ready for change' step of the cycle of change; accessing the service involves a referrals process, often being abstinent, and usually attending a fixed appointment. However we have had good success in creating something accessible for people in the earlier stages of change by bringing the service to where the people are, making it lighter and drop-in based, where you don't have to be abstinent (just not under the influence for the session), and then creating a 'trail of breadcrumbs' back to the service. Gambling support, anger support, and a discussion group, and IAPT 'Stress and Worry' and 'Mood Boost' services, have been brought to day centres using this formula.

Another neat formula we developed is "Clinics for workers", and we have done this in relation to autism, brain injury, occupational therapy: you can't always get people to groups or services, but an effective way to unlock NHS expertise is to create clinic opportunities for workers to go and discuss their client with the experts, where they can get new ideas and strategies.

In the last few years we've got better awareness of the prevalence of autistic spectrum disorders amongst rough sleepers. We worked with PHD students to survey long-term UK rough sleepers, and they came up with a 12% national prevalence of autistic spectrum features (Churchard et al, 2019). Very few rough sleepers are going to go and get assessed; creating a clinic opportunity for workers to go and meet with an autism psychologist and discuss cases and get tips and strategies has made a huge difference. Often it is the permission for the flex that is the crucial thing to radically change the approach, ditch normal hostel ways of working (for example assessment and sign-up paperwork that can become barriers), and take positive risks. We have seen again and again the enormous difference the new lens and flex has made. All local authorities have an autism assessment service and I would recommend any teams working with rough sleepers to hold autism in mind and seek to link up with these services.

Free to Dream

"Creativity is essential for improvement. It needs two things 1) time and 2) space" – Helen Bevan (2022b).

"You've got to have a dream, if you don't have a dream, how you gonna have a dream come true" – Happy Talk, South Pacific (1949).

When we want to understand an issue better, we focus on building relationships and bringing together knowledge from different parts of the system. We book a big room and invite people to map services, understand gaps, and consider creative solutions. In some cases, we work with people who understand multiple issues and the interconnections between these, for example, about brain injury and rough sleeping, gambling and rough sleeping, domestic abuse and multiple disadvantage, or autism and rough sleeping. These people can act as a bridge, joining up different islands of knowledge to help us bring together actors across the system to go on a journey together, with lived experience at the heart.

Once we've identified solutions, we typically divide these into 'cost nothing', 'cost a bit', 'cost a lot', then run a low-cost 'experiment' trying things out. We choose experienced people to run it, and then see what they find out and can achieve. Typically the experiments work well, so the task is then to build on the learning and look out for opportunities to expand. For this reason the approaches and tools in *A Whole New World* and *Exploring the New World* felt familiar, like roadmaps that we'd travelled.

Two major gaps we had were around female rough sleepers at both ends of the spectrum of age. On one hand, there was a younger group of women with so much going on, from chaotic drug use, VAWG, some with no recourse to public funds, perhaps with a dog too (for company and safety), who were very hard to engage with and very caught up in life on the street. Often, when opportunity arose and they did actually want to come in, there was nothing available on that particular night. At the other end of the age spectrum, we had a gap regarding elderly ladies with mental health needs, often with trolleys and bags and wandering across various London boroughs, who were very guarded, not looking for help, and rarely in the same place twice.

Over the years we completed a regular audit and mapping and action planning process for female rough sleepers, and we got people together to reflect on these gaps: What have we got? What could we remodel? What could we do differently? What's our dream? How could that work? Who could be our partners? This process has paid dividends and meant we were really ready if any quick turnaround bids or underspend opportunities came up. For these two gaps for women, we got funding for a pan-London mental health nurse whose role was tracking ladies down and problem solving, and a little hybrid refuge/night centre just for the young women with complex needs. Both have generated great outcomes and learnings.

PIEing Up the Old Supporting People Norms

We opened up the conversation on how we in commissioning could support PIE in services and it became clear some of the familiar rules needed to be tweaked, and others broken, for example replacing a deficit-based model of referral, assessment, and support planning with a strengths-based approach.

Some services felt weighed down by what they said felt like Supporting People shackles such as the Quality Assessment Framework expectations, conventional needs assessments and risk assessments, and support plans that they felt just didn't work for some people. We encouraged services to move to strengths-based approaches and to find alternative ways to evidence their work and to do what works for the person, emphasising trauma informed, person-centred, strengths-based approaches.

Another change was making it clear what we were willing to fund and that we were actively supportive of multi-disciplinary teams rather than standard hostel teams' make-up. To support this we have promoted both pilots and student placements to brings skill-sets including Psychology, Speech and Language Therapy, Occupational Therapy, Nursing and Social Work into the workforce mix.

Linking Up with Universities

Another rich vein of free resources centred on linking up with Universities, facilitating PHD students to undertake real-world research. This enabled a number of academically published studies to document new understandings and develop practical tools for frontline workers on areas including gambling, autism, communication, and brain injury.

Investing More in PIE

As our confidence in PIE has grown we've invested more and seen the multiplier effect.

We started with a mixed economy of PIE approaches, with some buying in a psychologist or therapist on a per hour basis monthly or fortnightly (either just for staff, or to work with clients too) and with some services having an in-house psychologist. More recently we have been very fortunate to staircase up using funding opportunities across the system (NHS, Public Health, Rough Sleeping Initiative) to build up psychology coverage across Westminster services.

As well as therapeutic resources we have invested in projects dedicated to creating an 'eco-system' of services and promoting PIE across sectors. Our Homeless Health Coordination Project leads on PIE training (alongside a wide range of physical health training) across the commissioned pathway and its partners, raising the capacity of supported housing providers to support service users to improve their health outcomes through training, information toolkits and directories, and facilitating a range of health events. They also have a systems role, improving awareness amongst statutory health providers around holistic health needs in marginalised groups.

Systems Lens to Multiple Disadvantage

The field of rough sleeping, homelessness, and multiple disadvantage can feel so knotty: it is such a multi-faceted, complex problem that's hard enough to define and much harder to address. It has both structural and individual causes, and a national and local policy context. It requires brilliant, caring, innovative PIE organisations to make a difference, but it's impossible for any organisation to solve on their own. And it's impossible for organisations to solve together if they're not collaborating.

What is clear is that we need fresh perspectives in terms of thinking and a wide-angle lens that sees beyond an organisation and makes the whole system visible.

The need for this lens led us to becoming a making every adult matter (MEAM) coalition member and now a Changing Futures area. Both programmes focus on the need for systems change to better meet the needs of people facing multiple disadvantages. These have been good structures to accelerate collaborative working relationships across systems so as to better serve people who have experienced the effects of homelessness, trauma, and loss. It's a work in progress, but as noted earlier, small creative steps are always better than nothing.

Commissioning Tools, Tips and Behaviours That Promote PIE

Because commissioners can have such power and impact, simply endorsing PIE in an authentic way (that's avoiding a tick box approach) can be a first and easy step – simply putting word out that PIE is valued and important round here. Moving on from that first step, the following ideas break down approaches to step up PIE commissioning.

You Don't Have to Be an Expert to Be a PIE Change Agent, but It's Good to Know Some Experts

Waiting until the moment has come when you feel you've researched enough on areas of PIE and mental health means the moment is likely to never come. It seems to me that the mental health world is on the precipice of a paradigm shift, moving away from its long-standing focus on individualised symptoms. The profile of complex trauma in homelessness, and the level of unmet need, can feel very much an example of how current mental health service structures and norms are flawed. So rather than focusing energy on learning the problematic system 'as is', it's much better to have a 'dial-a-friend', or group of them, who can be your guides to move forwards. Getting in place good clinical governance, supported by experts, helps reduce risks and anxiety when trying new approaches – though I often also comfort myself with the idea that the 'do nothing' option usually has big risks too!

Integrated Commissioning

There are many ways to organise the functions of commissioning, I have been lucky to work in a team where it was integrated: our team did everything from the strategy, needs assessment, procurement, contract management, to case conferences, deaths reviews, and working on the interfaces with adjacent services like mental health or drugs and alcohol. The benefits of that holistic lens were invaluable in terms of seeing the system as an eco-system and creating a toggle between the big picture and zooming in form there to actual people and their experience. Where commissioning functions are sliced and diced, I recommend the need to create regular spaces to triangulate viewpoints on PIE work.

Never Underestimate the Small Stuff, and Build Trust through Action

When I look back at our journey I see the effectiveness of small-scale actions building up over time. The small-scale changes or marginal gains built up trust, respect, and relationships over a period of time to form a firm foundation for sustainable change. The small gains, on many fronts simultaneously, underpinned by consistent visible behaviours, show people our values and the goals for change. This was undoubtedly the bedrock that attracted partners to put time and effort into external bids with no guarantee of success but which ultimately were successful, and which significantly accelerated our PIE work.

Change Management Model

"To deliver transformational change we don't need the best people, we need the best teams. For transformational teams we need to seek 1) connection with passion 2) collaboration skills 3) high quality interaction 4) collective talent" @digitalonto (Bevan, 2022c).

Although we didn't start with one, now I always hold a change management approach in mind when approaching a new area, and I highly recommend John Kotter's (2006) "Our Iceberg is melting", which was in fact recommended to me by a psychologist.

It's a quick story to read, told as a fable about a penguin colony. One curious penguin discovers a potentially devastating problem threatening their home – and pretty much no one listens to him. The characters in this fable are people we recognise and the story unfolds on how change was created. The eight-point change management plan involves creating urgency, pulling together a guiding team, developing the vision, communicating for understanding and buy-in, empowering others to act, producing short-term wins, not letting up, and creating a new culture. They are highly useable as a change management approach for PIE.

Securing Senior Buy-in and Shared Visions across Silos

Without doubt, defining a shared purpose and vision and bringing more and more people on board across the system are the key ways to accelerate PIE, and we have made progress securing buy-in across sectors. I have a variety of 'playlists' of PIE and trauma informed chat: the 1-minute elevator pitch, the 'invest to save' economics version, the one with the stories, the 30-minute 'system lens' one. The art is matching the pitch to the audience, but my top tips are firstly to have a variety of options, from presentations and forums to online training, that are snappy and accessible. Secondly, make time to help people on their journey and especially create a space where senior people can feel free to ask questions and be vulnerable. Many senior leaders have 'armour' – it feels like their jobs require it –-and the language of attachment, relationships, and complexity can feel quite foreign, so finding a way in for them may need some thought.

Lived Experience Perspective Superpower

"Get comfortable with feeling discomfort" (Ayelet Fishbach, 2022): I often say that the people with lived experience who I regularly meet with are my superpower in commissioning: their ability to see the gaps, see the wood for the trees, and hone down on what really matters, are second to none. But it's not easy listening and as a commissioner it can be hard to hear, so my initial responses can easily feel to be to justify the arrangements in the system, explaining why it is, and how we are doing our best in the circumstances. Getting accustomed to, or even comfortable with, hearing it 'like it is' when you have no neat replies on how you'll improve things can be new territory.

While the processes and diagrams of the commissioning cycle create the illusion of order and control the day-to-day work in commissioning, the reality is often messy and not nearly as planned and considered as it should be (e.g. with last minute bids with short timelines, or too much plate-spinning when commissioning resource is stretched, etc.). So having connections 'on tap' with people with lived experience who can give you opinions on directions of bids, commissioning dilemmas, etc. is invaluable, and meeting with them regularly has drilled that perspective into my mind and I hope infuses the everyday work I do. When we do have time and space for planned project work, having the discipline of always involving people with lived experience at the ground floor always pays dividends.

Procurement Matters

Sometimes people question whether these new ways of approaching commissioning and PIE are compatible with procurement codes and regulations. My top tip is to really know your procurement stuff because knowing it really well allows you to find the flex to do things differently, applying those human, learning principles, for example when a waiver is allowed, or the brackets of low-level funding that only require one quote. The majority of our innovations originally started small with under £10k 'test and learn' pilots. I thoroughly recommend small value pilots as they can take the pressure off in so many ways when trying new things.

Without doubt, longer contracts with break clauses, where possible, are always beneficial. Longer contracts allow time to experiment, learn, and adapt, and to build effective working partnerships. Building this learning cycle into specifications is ideal, being clear from the outset that there will be iterations and that the world doesn't and won't stand still.

In relation to tendering I recommend being really clear what you mean by PIE, perhaps pointing to a key document, and think about assessment questions that allow organisations with a genuine and demonstrable 'top to toe' track record (e.g. staff retention, staff satisfaction, low eviction/abandonment or incident rates, etc.) on PIE to demonstrate this.

There are times in procurement that involve contract ends and finishing relationships. Applying a human approach to this, such as a phone call to follow up from the official letter, thanking people for their work, thinking about the endings for clients, are simple things that can help apply PIE principles to procurement, and commissioners can apply the same attention to unsuccessful endings as PIE provider do to ones in hostels. It feels like sometime commissioners can be scared to be human in case it breaches poker-faced, risk-based procurement codes, but the two can be compatible.

Holistic, person-centred services are so important, but siloed commissioning, with separate approaches from drugs and alcohol, homelessness, health, etc., creates barriers to this and is therefore problematic. Finding ways to pool budgets and jointly fund teams has to be the way forward, and we have had good success finding ways to join up funding strands from the NHS, Public Health, and the Rough Sleepers Initiative for PIE. The first step has always been about building relationships and the shared vision, and that has created the energy to secure approval to create the 'nuts and bolts' administrative vehicles to make it a reality through, e.g., a Memorandum of Understandings, etc. Once a 'template' of collaboration is created, it can be repeated.

Contract Management and KPIs

If relationships hold the primary key to sustainable change, there needs to be a change in the whole approach to contract management, impact measurement, and evidencing success, and that can feel challenging. I cringe thinking back to the rigidity of the old supporting people norms and the commissioning style it created, and it has felt good to let go of the factors that created gaming. If you turn down a lot of referrals that might be difficult and cherry-pick the compliant ones, of course positive move-on stats will be better. For people with massive histories of abandonment and evictions, just sustaining accommodation a little longer needs acknowledging and celebrating; not everyone will be able to move forwards into independent accommodation, so there needs to be flexibility with move-on tar-gets and length of stay. We let go of the need for extensive 'hard' outcomes and re-evaluated the 'soft' ones; we let go of the belief that paperwork and recording is more important than building relationships. The simple truth is that outcome measures can struggle to capture what makes life worthwhile and meaningful, or what makes a service for multiply disadvantaged people successful – which can be the same thing.

A different approach to quality and value for money was needed. Getting along-side services and spending time with them is a good way to assess quality. In my experience staff feeling good about the work is a great quick proxy for quality. Do workers enjoy working there? Are they proud of the organisation? Do jobs get filled quickly? Another key avenue in thinking about quality is whether the service in good standing with the provider community? We also started asking for PIE self-assessment audits instead of QAFs.

Measuring Impact

"Data is critical to improvement but without a meaningful context that people can connect with, it's hard to use data to motivate change. When we explain data with a compelling story that links to peoples' values and sense of shared purpose magic happens" (Bevan, 2022d).

I've played the game to win bids and committed to a range of data collection points that ultimately had a negative impact on staff morale and productivity and didn't help relationships. There are so many possibilities with data from qualitative to quantitative, from client feedback, staff feedback, outputs, case studies, take-up of services, etc. it can be hard to know where to focus.

I have a number of learnings, a key one being to think ahead and keep it pro-portionate and doable in the long term. Thinking about your audiences is crucial. The more you can think ahead and plan who you are talking to, and what change you expect to see, and hone down a mixed set that cover the needs of the various audiences, the better. A triangulated combination is likely to be the best approach: a mix of quantitative data and qualitative data, with outputs and outcomes. I rec-ommend working out the things that are easy to collect and make those easier or automated, and work out at the outset how you will aggregate them meaningfully, for example attendance figures to show take-up, baseline data from CHAIN on length of history rough sleeping, etc. Because progress can come in small steps, an annual impact report might be more feasible than quarterly reports; though it's obviously important to celebrate small steps they may not be worth attentive data capture along the way. With the areas that will take effort to gather, make sure that they are really worth it, that you have the capacity and skills for analysis, and that it's part of the overall service plan, for example that staff measures like the Maslach Burnout Inventory (1981) are going to be repeated at a frequency that is sustainable, e.g., annually. Cost-benefit analysis can be hugely powerful and have high currency with health and criminal justice partners and does not actually need to be that hard to produce: think ahead about partners to gather info from, and the arrangements for that, and establish baselines for clients who are known to be a big impact on the public purse.

With the client data side of things, once you've collaboratively honed down on small set of the most meaningful impacts, I recommend creating a two-tier process so that the initial tier is focused on a warm welcome and engagement, with the need for only the most basic info, and then, once engagement is established, collecting the more onerous data requirements.

Empathetically Challenging System Blockages – Facilitation Skills to Create Psychological Safety

At times the structural and systemic barriers can seem insurmountable around mental health, multiple disadvantage, and the siloed services that leave so many locked out. The lack of appreciation of the impact of trauma, and the wide gaps created with the focus on symptoms and diagnosis, and exclusion of people using substances, can make the need for a radical paradigm shift very clear. The critique that the PIE movement can pose to mainstream mental health services can feel like a very tricky area.

As usual, breaking things down into manageable steps is a good strategy – and in my experience so is booking a big room (although Teams can work too). Karen Treisman (2020) has a phrase about "honouring the fences", creating time and space to understand why criteria have hardened, why services no longer work with the people they used to, why the fences were built. In my experience, workers and managers in the services that may feel exclusionary welcome the opportunity to tell their story (and there are so many stories of the impact of austerity and how a new narrative had to be created). Creating a safe space for honest conversation can generate ways to move forwards, and perhaps a feeling that we can break the walls down, one brick (or fence panel!) at a time. A culture of spaces with psychological safety is crucial for enabling this change to happen. Thinking carefully about the facilitation skills needed to create spaces for the system to come together, where people feel able to speak up, offer ideas, and ask questions, has stood me in good stead. It involves being comfortable with the tensions and being able to hold different perspectives in mind while being hopeful and believing in people, being realistic and a person who "says it like it is", yet staying unreasonably optimistic. I gained a lot from the free online NHS School for Change Agents (2024) on this front.

Finding Your Tribe and Self-Care

"Find your tribe": the number one rule of being a change agent is you can't be a change agent on your own. Linking up with the movement for change across PIE, mental health, and other systems can make a huge difference, ideally finding people to work with who want to do the same as you. It's a slog through the inefficiencies and the imperfect system but creativity and problem solving can help, and working with others and building a coalition mobilising for concrete change certainly helps.

Whether it's frontline work or commissioning, staying emotionally centred and healthy is a key component to doing quality work. While it's at a much greater distance, it's still demanding and emotionally draining to bear witness to trauma and loss as a normal part of your work. It can feel hard to be stuck in the middle of a disorganised system with high needs and decreasing resources; it's easy to get 'hard' yourself, easy to get burnt out or conversely pulled into action too much. Just as social support and self-care are critical for workers in services, they also apply to commissioners who also need the protection of training and support, supervision, incident debriefs, and reflective practice. Reflective practice has been hugely beneficial for our commissioning team, especially during the most demanding times such as the pandemic.

Conclusion

"Relationships and connections are the bedrock for large scale change. Research suggests organisations with high levels of social capital – relationships with/between groups that form trust, relatedness and collective capacity - get better change outcomes" (Bevan, 2022e).

When I look back at what has been achieved, from big cross-organisational service developments to breakthroughs in understandings of need, there is no doubt in my mind that all the same principles of trusting, reliable relationships built on authenticity, connection, and competence have been at the heart of the foundation of the work and are key for the commissioning for PIEs, and are the bedrock for the large-scale change needed ahead. I hope the simplicity of that message helps others to embrace complexity in commissioning and focus on fostering connections, giving voice, and building community.

References

Bevan, H. (2022a) [Twitter] 9 December. Helen Bevan on Twitter: There's a buzz within the NHS improvement community about these "6 improvement lessons to apply as winter pressures bite". Available at https://t.co/wSHy2pbiz4"/Twitter.

Bevan, H. (2022b) [Twitter] 13 December. *Creativity is essential for improvement. It needs two things 1) time and 2) space.* Available at https://t.co/hqTm1q3v6K. By @gapingvoid https://t.co/q75XbhWVLb"/Twitter.

Bevan, H. (2022c) [Twitter] 19 December. Helen Bevan on Twitter: "To deliver transformational change we don't need the best people we need the best teams". Available at https://t.co/qXBZogpPet"/Twitter.

Bevan, H. (2022d) [Twitter] 30 May. Data is critical to improvement but without a meaningful context that people can connect with, it's hard to use data to motivate change. Available at https://t.co/bzhgKC4cHu"/Twitter.

Bevan, H. (2022e) [Twitter] 16 December. Helen Bevan on Twitter: "Relationships & connections are the bedrock for large scale change". Available at https://t.co/WSrXULL0Cx"/Twitter.

Churchard, A., Ryder, M., Greenhill, A., & Mandy, W. (2019). The prevalence of autistic traits in a homeless population. *Autism*, 23(3), 665–676. https://doi.org/10.1177/13623613187 68484.

Collaborate (2017) 12 May. Available at a Whole New World – Funding and Commissioning in Complexity – Collaborate (collaboratecic.com).

Collaborate (2019) 19 March. Available at Exploring the new world: practical insights for funding, commissioning and managing in complexity – Collaborate (collaboratecic.com).

Daskal, L. (2022) (Helen Bevan slide deck, 24 Dec 2022) [Twitter]. Available at https://t.co/ bUEgioGxsg. https://t.co/B7hUF7crdR"/Twitter.

Goodreads (2024) accessed at https://www.goodreads.com/quotes/954454-there-comes-a-point-where-we-need-to-stop-just

Fishbach, A. (2022) *Get comfortable with feeling uncomfortable.* 7 Feb 2022. Behavioural Scientist. Available at Get Comfortable with Feeling Uncomfortable – Behavioral Scientist.

Homeless Link Resources. Available at Psychologically-informed | Homeless Link Accessed at https://homeless.org.uk/areas-of-expertise/improving-homelessness-services/ psychologically-informed/

Kotter, J (2006) *Our Iceberg is melting: Changing and Succeeding Under Any Conditions.* London: Macmillan.

Levy, J. (2021) *Pre Treatment in Action: Interactive Exploration from Homelessness to Housing Stablization.* Ann Arbor, MI: Loving Healing Press.

Maslach, C. & Jackson, S. E. (1981) *Maslach Burnout Inventory–ES Form (MBI)* [Database record]. PsycTESTS.

NHS School for Change Agents (2024). The School for Change Agents – NHS Horizons (horizonsnhs.com). Accessed at https://horizonsnhs.com/school/

PIE Link Website (2024). Available at http://pielink.net/.

Rodgers, R. & Hammerstein, O. (1949) Happy Talk, *South Pacific.* Accessed at https://rodg ersandhammerstein.com/song/south-pacific/happy-talk/

Treisman, K. (2020) "Trauma Reducing, Not Trauma Inducing". Available at Dr Karen Treisman – Drop the Disorder poetry evening; July 2020 – YouTube.

Chapter 13

Some Themes and Recommendations

Peter Cockersell and Sione Marshall

This book is about leadership of and within organisations that work in the field of health and social care and support. Specifically it is about leadership in implementing psychologically informed and trauma informed approaches for organisations that work with people who have been exposed to trauma and traumatic experiences often over long periods of time, what we call compound trauma. It contains perspectives from services working with homelessness, violence against women, young people and people experiencing severe mental health problems, and from providers and commissioners of refuges, day centres, hostels, registered care and community services, and includes people working in the voluntary sector, the NHS, and with local authorities, as well as consultants who work with some or all of those. Hopefully, the many different voices come through in the emphases and styles of the different chapter authors.

Within this diversity, however, we see a number of themes that emerge and re-emerge as leaders recount their experiences. Their accounts build on and support the two ideas informing chapter one's invitation to think about how leaders and organisations can affect the shape and journey of psychologically informed environments (PIEs). Firstly, that relationships drive change for all of us, so, as in life, they are central to successful and sustainable change in health and social care services. Secondly, using the key areas of PIE as guiding principles for both leadership approach and organisational development can drive the use of psychologically and trauma informed approaches and therefore the creation of effective PIEs.

We use this chapter to draw out these themes and create recommendations from which influencers, middle and senior managers, board members and commissioners can grow their own ideas for developing their own PIE and trauma informed care (TIC) approaches in their own fields of influence.

Managing Relationships

For us probably the strongest of all the themes in the book is the crucial importance, indeed the complete centrality, of relationships. Attachment is perhaps the most basic of all human instincts that make humans human and is also probably

DOI: 10.4324/9781003415053-16

the most researched and most evidenced of all the psychological processes (e.g. Cassidy and Shaver, 2018), so it's perhaps rather bizarre that it isn't specifically highlighted in the majority of either PIE or TIC literature. Perhaps because attachment is so natural to humans it has been easy to overlook its central importance in designing services that are intended to care for and support humans who have been or are experiencing severe stress, but it is extraordinary nonetheless that attachment theory is not central and forefront in PIE or any other caring system. You don't need to be a clinical psychologist or psychoanalytic psychotherapist to know that when life becomes challenging you seek attachment figures to restore your sense of safety and security and that it is only when you have done this that you can comfortably explore your new surroundings. The importance of attachment in creating a sense of emotional and psychological safety underpins PIE and TIC, and all the stories and examples in this book.

What everybody *does* talk about is the importance of relationships. Relationships drive effective interactions between frontline staff and clients, between staff and managers, between leaders and their organisations, between organisations and the systems they operate in. We form and develop relationships over time and through interaction with people who then become important to us and with whom we then feel in some way connected: relationships are attachment theory in action.

So our first recommendation would be to consider the importance of attachments, and to train staff in understanding how attachment works, both in the comforting nature of forming reliable attachments and in the traumatising nature of ruptured and lost attachments. If we do not frame our services with mindfulness of the dynamics of attachment theory, they will inevitably fail to support people whose attachments have been put under intolerable stress. Where social collaboration has broken down, where there is so-called siloed thinking and working, there cannot be effective services for people who have experienced trauma because it is the very breakdown of social collaboration and collective caregiving – a kind of collective splitting and denial – that lies behind the marginalisation and exclusion of those most in need of other people's emotional and psychological support.

The experience and wisdom of the authors represented in this book (and attachment theory!) show that it isn't enough to just have transactional, contractual type relationships: to be effective, relationships need to be meaningful, sustained and dialogical. The meaning in these relationships is created by a shared value system. This social fabric acts as an invisible driving force for the collective action realised by these relationships/connections (Beck and Cowan, 2006) and needs to really involve people at an emotional level because otherwise those emotions will be left to be enacted through unconscious conflict mechanisms. These in turn need to be supported by physical environments that also enable these connections.

And there need to be sets of relationships: there need to be relationships of different kinds and at different levels with all the 'stakeholders', which means with and between commissioners, other agencies, boards, senior staff, managers, front-line workers and whatever group of beneficiaries the service is hoping to work with. All of these people need to be in sustained, meaningful and dialogical relationships with each other for the system to work effectively to relieve trauma and enable individual and collective growth, and for everybody to feel meaningfully involved and valued.

To reverse this we need to work towards creating meaningful dialogic and egalitarian relationships across our areas of influence, within organisations and between them, within disciplines and between them, within ourselves as individual leaders and between us as individuals working within a collective, a team, a system, towards a particular goal. The preceding chapters provide fantastic examples of people doing just this.

So the first recommendation for any leaders working to implement PIE or TIC in their organisation or their system, whatever that implementation looks like on the ground, is to remember the central importance of *managing relationships*. It all stems from this.

Client Involvement

For us, the second theme that really comes out in chapter after chapter is the importance of client involvement, which wasn't specifically highlighted as one of the five principles in the original 2012 PIE guidance (Keats et al, 2012), though it was in Cockersell's revision of them to seven (Cockersell, 2018), but which does appear as 'peer support' and 'collaboration' in SAMSHA's TIC principles (2014). Collaboration is a good word: it comes from the Latin roots 'cum', meaning 'with', and 'laborare', meaning 'to work', so 'working with' or 'working together'. There is an implied equality in people working together for a purpose, and 'a group of people coming together to resolve a shared problem' was the definition of a therapeutic community proposed by Craig Fees, an archivist and historian of therapeutic communities (personal communication). The power of a group of people coming together to resolve a shared problem shines out as a motif throughout this book and demonstrates the power of collective thinking and action in making possible, even in times of austerity, what is otherwise not. It is a message of hope, and optimism for the future, qualities that are essential in the process of recovery from trauma and distress.

But crucially, we are not talking about a group of professionals coming together to exercise their expertise doing something to someone who in some way is seen as not able to participate in doing it for themselves, the 'deficit model'. This is not about prescribed treatment or the imposition of a model (see further on in this chapter where we think about the 'psychological framework' and the concept of 'trauma'); the different chapter authors describe various kinds of journey that they and their organisations, and in some cases the wider system around them, went on together. They very literally describe a process of co-production, co-creation, the collective action of working with each other to create something greater than the parts and which works for everybody. Seen like this, client involvement is not something you 'do' as part of the delivery of your service, rather it is part of learning what it is that you need to do, both strategically and on a day-to-day basis.

So the integration of client involvement as part of the collaborative process of service design, creation and delivery is the second recommendation that we feel comes out of these chapters. It is not a separate thing to be done 'as well as' commissioning or delivering a service, or being psychologically or trauma informed. You can't do the other things properly without client involvement: it's what keeps the whole process real.

Keeping the process real is another piece of learning that comes out of these chapters (as does learning itself, but more of that too later). Peter Cockersell remembers Duncan Selbie, shortly after he had been made CEO of Public Health England in 2012, saying something like: 'The further you are from the front line, the more you believe that what you say happens actually happens' (from memory). There is an inevitable remove for most leaders of organisations, especially large ones, and leaders of whole systems from the realities of day-to-day frontline work. Their minds are also full of different priorities – finance, funding deadlines, governance issues, market positioning and of course politics, with a big or a small 'p' – and they often feel they have to go along with powerful external influences such as Government policy, statutory directives, national guidance or simply fashion, the latest 'magic bullet' solution to whatever social problem their agency is supposed to be helping resolve.

This makes client involvement even more important: the leaders need to know what the clients are experiencing in their lives and from the services that are supposed to be supporting them. It means talking to the staff is vitally important: again the leaders need to know what the staff are experiencing in their working lives and from the managers and procedures that are supposed to be supporting them. However, keeping the staff on board with what is actually possible, given the political, systemic and financial conditions within which the organisation or system operates, and keeping the clients in the loop about what can and can't be achieved by and with the staff and the support services available are equally crucial. To successfully implement a group of people coming together to resolve a shared problem there has to be at least approximately common perception of reality: there have to be the honest, open and sometimes difficult conversations that again so many of the chapter authors mention.

Many of the authors emphasise that the journey of developing PIE or TIC, or whatever variation of those they are implementing, is a process of learning – learning by everyone, and from everyone. It is not a simple teacher-student relationship: each part of the organisation or system has something to learn and something to model as learning for the other parts. In this sense, understanding that every individual in the system has a part to play in leading change, has the ability to be a 'change agent' (Budak, 2022), is the very essence of collective action. We are all teachers and we are all learners, and it is our collective and collaborative learning from our myriad experiences and from our multiple expertises that enables the group to find the most effective response(s) to the shared problem, responses that no individual person, organisation or aspect of the system could achieve alone.

Reflective Practice

This concept of an environment of continuous shared and mutual learning is at the centre of reflective practice, from its origins in the work of Donald Schon (1983) to its various guises in the practice described by the authors in this book. Ali Curran, from her experience facilitating reflective practice, and managing a team of facilitators, across a multi-sited organisation with groups comprising senior managers to frontline staff goes into this in some depth in her chapter, but all the authors refer to their own experiences of reflective practice in their chapters and there is a unanimity in agreeing its importance. This is then the third recommendation that we would like to draw from the experiences of the authors: it is crucial to establish processes of reflective practice, both formal and informal, throughout your team, organisation or system, wherever it is that you are trying to implement PIE or TIC. Reflection enriches everyone's experience.

At the very basic level, reflection is simply thinking about what you do and how you feel about it, or what you've done and how you felt, and including what other people or environmental factors do or did and how they make or made you feel. It's a basic but very human function: in any moment, we instinctively interact with our environments. However, as humans we don't have to just interact with our environments instinctively or reactively because we also have the capacity to experience ourselves in these interactions, and at the same time to think about and choose alternative interactions from our stored memories of possible interactions, and from our imaginations of the potential interactions we've never had yet. Our brains have around 100 million million neuronal connections and that's only a part of our minds, which include our bodily neurology and all our senses as well. It's an amazing thing, the human mind! It gives us so much potential for adaptation and resolution of problems or distress. And when we do this in a group, if we are prepared to be open, we have lots of minds to share our minds with, and the power to create new solutions increases exponentially. Indeed, from the perspective of interpersonal neurobiology, and neuropsychoanalysis (Solms, 2018), it is only in social relations that we truly experience our minds: they are our experience of our extended nervous system in relation (relationships again!) with our physical and social environment (Siegel, 2020).

This is straying into the territory of psychology. Several of the authors in this book are psychologists, a few are psychoanalytic psychotherapists or group analysts, and the majority are neither. However, there is a very strong consensus that the aim is precisely *not* to turn all your staff into psychologists. This was explicit in the original PIE guidance and is implied in the principles of TIC. Many of the authors in this book specifically mention the risk of pathologisation of the clients from the focus on psychology or trauma, and how important it is for the clients for this not to happen. It is again a strong emergent theme of great importance that the different distressed populations that the organisations and systems in this book work to help are all impacted by social problems, and their personal distress and complex needs arise from social situations. Compound trauma is a social problem.

But its impact is felt by the individual, and becomes internalised by the individual, and then manifests itself in presentations such as mental illness, self-harm, suicide, substance dependency, etc. This is the realm of psychology. Because the problems were created socially, they can be resolved socially if the social circumstances permit (e.g. through positive relationships, client involvement and collaboration, and reflective processes, as we've already mentioned); but the internalisation can feel difficult for the person experiencing it, and difficult for the staff they are interacting with to understand. This is where psychology can help. It can help and support staff and clients, and the whole organisation, in understanding why people feel and behave the way they do and what might be helpful, and what harmful, when working with them. It can help achieve the PIE goal, that the staff can explain their interactions in terms of the psychological and emotional needs of their clients. It is only when our psychological and emotional needs are met that we can truly get on with our lives and achieve more of our potential, or just do our job well: this is as true for the chief executive as the client, for the commissioner as the cleaner.

A Psychological Framework

So our next recommendation relates to the psychological framework. There are lots of different frameworks integrated into the work described in this book: some are overtly psychodynamic or psychoanalytic; some are strengths-based and use positive psychology; some are attachment-based; all could be described as person-centred. The important thing is that there is some kind of shared understanding of the impact of trauma, particularly compound trauma, and damaging/ruptured attachments on development and on how people interact with others. It is not necessarily the trauma per se that is damaging but its existence within at the very least an unsupportive network but more usually a dark web of secrecy, relational abuse and broken trust. Psychology can help staff and clients make sense of the impact of their life experiences; this is, after all, why people go to psychotherapy. However, what we're talking about here may or may not be overtly designed as therapeutic in the narrow sense, but in a wider sense, is about providing an environment, a PIE, that is most likely to enable someone to recover from whatever damaging life experiences they have been through and to move forward into a happier and more fulfilling phase of their lives. For that there seems to be a strong consensus from all the authors that you don't need to be a psychologist to implement and enable these environments.

The truth is, we would say, and this would be our recommendation, that to implement PIEs or TIC, you absolutely don't need to be a psychologist – but it is definitely useful to know some, and if possible to have some psychologists or psychotherapists 'on tap'.

Leadership Perspectives

The evidence of the chapters in this book from a diverse range of services meeting different client groups' needs and from statutory, voluntary, health, and social support perspectives suggests that PIEs and/or services using a trauma informed, strengths-based or person-centred approaches, or all of these together, become effective as they work collaboratively and collectively within themselves and within their systems, with serving their clients at the heart of what everyone does, whether that's the chief executive or the frontline volunteer. The chapters reflect both a wonderful diversity of people, approaches and organisations and a group of common characteristics that shine through all of them; we have suggested in this chapter that these common characteristics are, at least most significantly, managing relationships, client involvement, collaborative approaches, reflective spaces, and a psychological framework and that these are the cornerstones for implementing PIE and TIC.

But this book is not just about implementing PIEs and TIC in organisations, it is about leadership: the diverse writers, who range from frontline managers to chief executives, psychologists to senior managers and commissioners to advising consultants, highlight different aspects of leadership and illustrate them with their different experiences. There are themes here too which emerge consistently or frequently from within this diverse range of authors and the different types of organisation represented in this book.

We're not thinking so much of formally described leadership styles, though enabling leadership, servant leadership and situational leadership would all get a mention if we were. Rather, we're thinking of values and attitudes that permeate the approaches the different authors describe: things like being unafraid of having difficult conversations, facing up to the realities of service delivery in challenging environments rather than believing their own or their funders' hype, genuinely listening, engaging with the clients who use the service and seeking out their opinions, support and participation in service design and delivery, holding firm to principles and values yet accepting uncertainty and that even leaders don't have all the answers.

We think the logic that comes through from within these chapters is that it is not so much that it is useful to recommend a particular *way* of leading the implementation of PIEs or TIC – all the organisations and systems in the book have done it slightly or very differently; it seems more useful to suggest that certain attitudes need to permeate the leadership to make PIE or TIC really take hold in an organisation. As well as the ones listed in the paragraph above, one that really seems to stand out is passion.

All the leaders in this book share this one thing: they really care about implementing a psychologically informed approach, including TIC or a strengths-based approach, because they really care about their services' clients and that the service is doing the very best it can to meet their clients' needs. All the leaders in this book passionately and sincerely, practically and systemically, have their clients as the primary focus of what they do. They are not there primarily to meet their funders' needs, or the needs of some management system or political dogma: they are there to meet the needs of the clients they are supposed to be helping, and they work with their clients to refine how they do that. They all recognise that this is a process which takes time and represents a continuous cycle of learning in the form of assessment, implementation, reflection and evaluation: there are no magic bullets or wands in this process or book.

We would say then that the recommendation for leaders is simply this: lead with passion, pragmatism and patience, and inclusivity.

Concluding Thoughts

This brings us back to diversity, which is where we would like to end this chapter and the book. Several authors talked about trying to increase the diversity of their offer and to ensure that their PIE or TIC approach meets the needs of diverse people within their client groups, people with different ages, ethnic or cultural backgrounds, sexualities, genders and belief systems. The same of course is true for the workforce: there is much for leaders to think about in terms of the diversity of the workforce, both in ensuring egalitarianism and in drawing in the benefit of diverse perspectives on the work the organisation does. To be effective, the work of caring organisations has to be individualised and person-centred: how much easier is this to do with a diverse population of clients when you have a diverse workforce and their diverse voices are heard throughout, whether that be in 1-1s, teams, groups, organisations and/or systems.

We live in polarised times politically, and there is a polarisation in the work we do with marginalised groups who are at the sharp end of 'us and them' social splitting. So let us, in implementing PIEs and trauma informed approaches in our teams, in our organisations, in our systems, and gloriously in whole areas, stand up for polyphony and plurality and, in doing so, move from a position of 'us and them' to one of 'we'.

The final recommendation then that we have for leaders in PIE and TIC is: be the champions of what you believe in!

References

Beck, D. E., & Cowan, C. C. (2006). *Spiral Dynamics: Mastering Values, Leadership and Change*. Malden, MA: Blackwell Publishing.

Budak, A (2022) *Becoming a Changemaker. An Actionable, Inclusive Guide to Leading Change at Any Level*. New York: Balance.

Cassidy, J. and Shaver, P. (2018). *Handbook of Attachment: Theory, Research, and Clinical Applications*, Third Edition. New York: Guilford Press.

Cockersell P. (2018) Applying Psychology as a Response to the Impact of Social Exclusion: PIE and Psychotherapy in Homelessness Services. In Cockersell, P. (Ed) *Social*

Exclusion, Compound Trauma and Recovery. The Process of Social Exclusion. London: Jessica Kingsley Publishers.

Keats, H., Maguire, N., Johnson, R. and Cockersell, P. (2012) *Psychologically informed services for homeless people* (Good Practice Guide). Southampton: GB. Communities and Local Government.

SAMSHA (2014) *SAMHSA's Working Concept of Trauma and Framework for a Trauma-Informed Approach, National Centre for Trauma-Informed Care* (NCTIC). Rockville, MD: SAMHSA.

Schon, D.A. (1983) The Reflective Practitioner: How Professionals Think in Action. Basic Books, New York.

Siegel, D. (2020). *The Developing Mind*, Third Edition. New York: Guilford Press.

Solms, M. (2018). *The Feeling Brain: Selected Papers on Neuropsychoanalysis.* London: Routledge.

Index

For Product Safety Concerns and Information please contact our EU
representative GPSR@taylorandfrancis.com Taylor & Francis Verlag GmbH,
Kaufingerstraße 24, 80331 München, Germany

Printed and bound by CPI Group (UK) Ltd, Croydon, CR0 4YY

08/06/2025

01897002-0011